TEEN

WICCA FOR A NEW GENERATION

WITCH

About the Author

Born in the heart of Pennsylvania, Silver has been interested in the magickal arts since childhood. "York, Cumberland, and Lancaster counties are alive with magick," she says.

"The best way for a magickal person to be accepted is to let people know you firsthand," explains Silver. "Once they get to know you and understand your personal values and principles, their attitudes on your alternative religious interests take a back seat. Let them know you—for you inside and the works that you do. It should be that way for everybody."

Born on September 11, 1956, Silver is a true Virgo: she adores making lists and arranging things. She is currently working toward her clinical hypnotherapy certification. Definitely a lady of the 90s, she's hard to pin down. "I spend a great deal of my time with my four children," she says. "They come first in my life—everybody else, take a number!"

Silver teaches several magickal sciences as she tours the United States. She has attained Wiccan Priesthood, and is the Tradition Head of the Black Forest Clan, covering eight states, and an Elder of Family of Serphant Stone. She is the Director of the International Wiccan/Pagan Press Alliance, and also runs a healing circle for individuals of all religions.

To Write to the Author

If you wish to contact the author or would like more information about this book, please write to the author in care of Llewellyn Worldwide and we will forward your request. Both the author and publisher appreciate hearing from you and learning of your enjoyment of this book and how it has helped you. Llewellyn Worldwide cannot guarantee that every letter written to the author can be answered, but all will be forwarded. Please write to:

Silver RavenWolf

℅ Llewellyn Worldwide

2143 Wooddale Drive, Dept. 978-1-56718-725-0

Woodbury, MN 55125-2989, U.S.A.

Please enclose a self-addressed, stamped envelope for reply, or $1.00 to cover costs. *Silver cannot get back to you if you don't, so always include a SASE!* If outside U.S.A., enclose international postal reply coupon.

TEEN WITCH

WICCA FOR A NEW GENERATION

SILVER RAVENWOLF

Llewellyn Publications
Woodbury, Minnesota

FIRST EDITION
Twenty-ninth Printing, 2020

Book design and editing by Rebecca Zins
Cover design by Ellen Lawson
Cover image © iStockphoto.com/164882104/©kevinhillillustration
iStockphoto.com/481659122/©PaulStelz
iStockphoto.com/523761968/©itskatjas

Library of Congress Cataloging-in-Publication Data
RavenWolf, Silver, author
Teen witch: Wicca for a new generation / Silver RavenWolf.
p.   cm.
Includes bibliographical references and index.
ISBN 13: 978-1-56718-725-0
ISBN 10: 1-56718-725-0 (trade paper)
1. Witchcraft.   2. Neopaganism.   3. Magic.   I. Title.
BF1571.R38   1998
133.4'3—dc21   98-26071
CIP

Llewellyn Publications
A Division of Llewellyn Worldwide Inc.
2143 Wooddale Drive
Woodbury, MN 55125-2989
www.llewellyn.com
Llewellyn is a registered trademark of Llewellyn Worldwide Ltd.
Printed in the United States of America

This book
is dedicated to
Lady Breid FoxSong

Contents

Introduction: Just for Parents

Okay—you've picked up this book, and you're going through minor coronary arrest. How could this be? Your child has a book on WitchCraft! Shudder. Before you rush into their room and put them on a plane to the nearest church camp, or bus them to a convent, or throw holy water on them in the presence of your favorite ministerial counselor, or carry all of their books and magazines to the attic until you can sort them out in heart-thumping silence, or melt into a sobbing puddle at their sneakered feet, relax and spend a few minutes with me— a mother of four healthy, happy children, a parent who has been married for nineteen years—one of the most famous Witches in the United States today.

This is an okay book for your children to read. There's nothing bad in here, and maybe the book will help you understand why WitchCraft is one of the fastest growing religions in America. You can stop worrying that the child you've battled the odds of peer pressure to maintain and worked so hard to support will attack you in the dark with a butcher knife and try to sacrifice Fluffy when your back is turned. It ain't gonna happen.

Through statistical analysis we've discovered that one in every five people in the United States has dabbled in the world of the "unknown," whether we're talking about ESP (extrasensory perception), tarot cards, angels, creative visualization, Paganism, metaphysics, WitchCraft, New Age beliefs, et cetera. Let's face the truth. I'm a parent, too, and I worry about the same things *you* do. I figure I worked hard to birth my kids and take care of them, and I don't want some nut coming in at the last minute and blowing all my efforts into the toilet of drugs, alcohol, teen prostitution, and whatever other muck teens occasionally manage to wade into. The dangers are there and, hopefully, this book will help them avoid some of those bad places. Yes, I said "avoid."

If your child has handed you this book, please take the time to read the text rather than going into a tizzy, screaming at your kid, and whisking the material out from under them. If your child has the curiosity itch, let them talk to you about what they are feeling and how they wish to relate religion to themselves— and for pity's sake, don't "tell" them what religion is and is not. Let them discover spirituality for themselves. If your child has this book it means that they wish to search the universe for answers they've not received from traditional teachings. No, you didn't let them down. All kids seek to experience new things, even religion. Let them search. You can help a child navigate, but you cannot steer the ship forever. Someday, they will do that on their own, with or without you. Let it be *with* you.

I'm in the process of raising four kids. They are all Witches, just like me. WitchCraft is an earth-centered religion focused on raising an individual's spirituality. WitchCraft is not, nor was it ever, a vehicle for Satanic worship. If you believe this, then you've fallen into a misinformation trap that we quickly need to get you out of so that you can relate to the interest of your child. I suggest that you take the time to read this book all the way through; then, if you don't agree with the information, at least you are making an informed choice. If you allow your child to read this book, be open and free with unbiased input for them. Gently say, "Well, your father and I believe this or that because . . ." and give them a good answer—a thoughtful answer. This gives your child the opportunity to respect what you believe. You cannot force any human being to believe in God; they must come to God on their own terms.

Teen years are tough times. As a parent of four teens (my youngest is in middle school) I can relate to all your fears and all the dreams you have for your child. You worry about drugs, strange ideas they seem to have floating around them from peers you wish the good Lord would ship to Siberia (or even off the face of the planet if this was possible), sexual desire (personally, I think that the Goddess should have installed an on/off switch where sexuality is concerned, allowing parents to glue that "off" button in place until the kid reaches the age of twenty-five), fast cars, raging hormones, and a steady non-pluggable hole in your checking account. As you will understand when you read this book, Witch-Craft isn't something you need to worry about. Celebrate that your child seeks empowerment. If you feel that the Craft is still against your belief system after you've read the book, don't panic. I've written this book so that your teen (or you) can take any of the techniques herein and use them in your own religious background.

You may just find yourself interested in the topic.

You never know.

It can happen.

★

Introduction: Just for Teens

Of all the books I've written on the subjects of magick and WitchCraft, this book did everything it possibly could to convince me to write the words for you. Like a little person demanding a cookie (NOW!) the idea tugged at my mind, tickled my fingers, and threw tantrums to get me to sit in front of my computer and begin banging out the pages. I've received thousands of letters from young people aged eleven through eighteen asking me what WitchCraft entails. At every seminar I give, teens ask me questions not normally discussed in other Craft books—you know, subjects like lockers, peer pressure, homework, crabby teachers . . . I guess the list could be endless. Teens also want to know what WitchCraft *really* involves, and how the religion of the Craft can help them attain their dreams. After much thought, and a lot of prodding, I decided to write this book just for you, the teenage Witch.

The magickal community calls me Silver RavenWolf. Some people call me Mama Silver (and no, I'm not big, fat, old, and gray just yet). They call me Mama because of the way I write. I care about those who read my books, and I write to them like people talk. I'm a lineaged Witch and author. Lineaged means I've gone through years of private training, made mistakes, rolled with the punches of life, and elevated through ceremony to the position of elder in my group. Currently, I am responsible for eleven covens in eight states. I've written several books on WitchCraft for adults (the people who, just because they grew up, aren't necessarily super intelligent). I have four children of my own, ranging from twelve years old to nineteen years old, so I have a pretty good idea of what happens in the exciting voyage through the teen years. I am happy to tell you that, so far in my journey of parenting, I am still breathing. Besides, I believe I managed to survive that cycle of life myself, once upon a time, and my kids live normally (barring the fact, of course, that they are all Witches too). I don't think this constitutes abnormal behavior, but some stick-in-the-mud unenlightened people do. Their loss.

You picked up this book because you're curious about WitchCraft (or Wicca). Pretty obvious, since that's the subject of the book. You want to know what is true, and what isn't. You've heard good stories and bad stories about the Craft. You may have seen movies where the Craft appears as a sinister practice, filled with blood and guts and scary things, and you may worry that either yourself or a friend may have jumped in over his or her head by getting involved in Witch-Craft. That's okay. We need more compassion and caring in the world. If something frightens you, you need to investigate all the facts so that you can make a rational opinion. In these pages I'll separate the truth from the fibs.

Teen Witch represents a book of beginnings, a way to look at the universe in a different way. Consider this book as your first step into the world of "what could be." WitchCraft *depends* on your positive self-growth. The religion concentrates on making you a better person so that you, in turn, can help others. You can find lots of books in stores about WitchCraft. Many of these books have good things to say, but some books aren't worth the paper they are printed on. Throughout the book, and in the back, you'll find a suggested reading list, with age level indicators and a brief description of what the book talks about. This will make your choices easier if you want to learn more about the Craft.

Most teens don't have a lot of money, so I know you want to spend that birthday check from Grandma or the cash you earned from mowing the lawn wisely. Even if you have a job, teens historically don't pull in tons of money, so I've tried to keep your financial needs in mind. If you like this book, you'll want to read more, because none of us (myself included) knows everything about the Craft, or about God. You never stop learning. This book covers only the basics of the Craft, and how those basics relate to young people.

How I Got Here

I was thirteen years old when I entered the fantastic world of Wicca. My dad practiced the Lutheran religion and my mother, rest her soul, participated in an offshoot of the Baptist religion—First Christian Church Disciples of Christ. From my very young years to age seventeen, we regularly went to a little red brick Baptist church nestled in the center of town. Neither of my parents were Bible-thumpers, but each held religion sacred in their own way. When I turned thirteen, my cousin, Tess, gave me a pack of tarot cards. Now, tarot cards have nothing to do with the religion of Wicca. The cards are a divination tool that can help you make good choices in life, but they don't represent a single religious dogma and you aren't supposed to live your life by them. Like the Fool (the first card in a tarot deck), I began my journey into religion, science, and magick[1] when my cousin gave me that deck of cards.

---

1. Throughout this text you will see the word magick spelled with a "k" to show the difference between real magick and illusionary magic (i.e., rabbits out of hats).

I had always loved Tess very much, though I don't get to see her anymore because of the nasty things that families manage to work themselves into over time. (You know the turmoil that springs up and somehow never quite bubbles away?) I looked up to Tess. Seven years older than me, blonde, blue-eyed, athletic, and incredibly smart, the blood of an artist coursing through her veins. Tess was everything I wanted to be.

One summer afternoon she came to visit me. We walked into the fields behind my house, just enjoying the warm sun and laziness of the day. After thirty years, I can't recall all of the conversation, but what I do remember changed my life forever.

"What they tell you in church isn't the whole truth," Tess said quietly.

I looked at her uncertainly for a moment. Tess wasn't the sort to talk about religion. "What do you mean?"

"There's more."

"More? How so?"

We stopped and stood in the middle of the field. Tess glanced back at the house, and a soft, fragrant breeze picked up her blonde hair and tossed the golden strands. My dingy brown ponytail stayed cemented to my head.

Tess looked at me closely, then said, "Hell isn't a place you go after you die. Hell is here."

Nothing in my slim thirteen years of life had prepared me for that statement. I was a young Baptist kid with two average American parents. We had a house, a car, food, clothing, and a pet cat named Tigi—we were the epitome of middle America, including homemade apple pies and Fords. My Dad went to work promptly every day for the federal government, from 3:30 P.M. to 12:30 A.M. on the dot. My mother did the chores around the house and socialized with the neighbors. My grandma, until her death a year before, treated me like grandmas were supposed to. I thought *all* grandmas were loving, caring, transplanted from West Virginia, and fat.

We had a little garden out back and each summer my Dad battled the recreational adult baseball players who socked hard balls into the tomatoes and broke the plant's stems. One time the circus came to town and camped in the field. That year my mother woke up one morning and looked out the kitchen window to face four elephant backsides, standing primly in Dad's garden. Her shriek still rings in my head. My Dad was a nice guy, though. It was a drought year, and he gave the circus owner water for all the animals.

I had been in the same school system all my life. I wasn't in the "best" clique because my parents weren't rich enough, but I was in the "second best" one. My parents didn't take drugs and they didn't drink more than mere socialization on Saturday nights, when they went to the "best" restaurants in town with their friends. Mom and Dad didn't fight much, and when they did, I wasn't around. No affairs, no broken marriages, no sexual malfunctions. What was Tess talking about? From what I understood about the Christian Hell, my life was as far away from that boiling place as you could get. Desperately trying to relate to her (because somehow, I knew she needed me to), I decided to let her explain, rather than question. Evidently her life had grown into a living nightmare while mine had plodded pleasantly by. My biggest challenge lay in being skinny as a lamp post and having a face duller than Mom's battered muffin pans. The largest recent battle I'd fought with my parents consisted of my wheedling to buy a real stereo system. Telephones were those horrible, black, rotary clunky things, and you could only get three channels on our black-and-white television. I dreamed of phones where you could see the person you were talking to, and of a hundred channels on a color television. (The least my parents could do, I thought, was buy a stereo.) What terrible thing happened to beautiful, blue-eyed Tess that I managed to escape?

"A long time ago," she said, as she stared up at a fleecy white cloud scuttling across the sky, "religion was different. Did you know, for instance, that everyone on the planet thought God was a woman?"

My eyes popped at that one. A woman? No one at the Baptist church had ever said anything about God being a woman. This was news.

She nodded at my shocked expression. "And did you know that in the medieval times men were so afraid of women that the Christian men of the day killed two million people, mostly women and children? The historians call that era The Burning Times. The Christian men claimed the women were Witches."

My mind reeled but my mouth remained shut. Killed two million people? I'd never heard that. I'd heard about the Romans killing the Christians in the arena with lions, but this was a switch. The other way around? What was she telling me? Witches? I thought Witches were evil and worshiped the Devil. Something was *very* wrong here. I knew my cousin appeared distressed, but nothing coming out of her pretty face made any sense at all. She was an honor student. An only child. A saint! Still, I let her go on. When we were younger, she used to tell me great ghost stories in the back of her parents' car while all the adults jabbered about boring stuff at the family reunions. Like her ghost stories, I thought this story was going to be a whopper.

"That's right," she said. "They murdered two million women and children. Men did. Christian men. What do you think of that?"

I said nothing because had I opened my mouth, nothing would have come out.

"You don't believe me, do you?"

Actually, she'd thrown me for such a loop, I didn't know what to believe. "Go on," I said quietly.

She sighed a big breath that seemed to come from a well of pain. "I've learned a lot lately," she said, avoiding my eyes and stepping away from me. I followed her, watching the sun glint on her blonde hair. How envious I had always been of her, but now I wasn't so sure I should be. Something wasn't right here. I could feel it even then. "You can check it all out in history books," she continued. "The real ones, I mean. Not the junk they spoon you in school. Go to the library. You'll see."

"I'll do that," I murmured, and I knew I would. Tess was smart, she always got straight As. Her mind would reach out to learn things I couldn't comprehend. I was only an average, skinny kid, after all. Not the stuff of Tess, whom my aunt and uncle always bragged about. The lovely Tess. The shapely Tess. The beautiful, intelligent Tess. "But why do you think this place is the Christian Hell?" I asked.

"Well, not Hell, really," she said. "There's no such place as Hell."

Again my eyes wanted to bounce off my head. Everybody knew that Hell was real. It's the bad place where bad people go. I mean, the ministers always talked about Hell, not that they'd seen it, mind you, but . . . .

She shrugged. "There's a belief that over half the planet has. HALF THE PLANET," she repeated, boring her blue eyes into my chocolate brown ones. "They call this belief reincarnation. You keep getting born over and over again. The early Christians believed in reincarnation too, but somebody wrote it out of their books. I think reincarnation is logical. The idea makes everyone equal. Life on earth is like a school room. We keep coming back to learn lessons. Everything we do, we must be responsible for. We can't just do bad things and ask for forgiveness, we have to *accept* the reaction of what we do will bring. For every cause, there is an effect. We can't blame anyone else if we do wrong. No one *makes* us do bad things. If we do wrong, we have to pay for what we've done. And we have to pay here, not some mythical place with monsters for pals."

"And the Witches . . ." I breathed.

"Well, to begin with, they don't believe in the Devil. The Devil belongs to the Christian religion, not to the Old Ways. Witches believe that if you give something evil a name, then you give it power, so they stay away from things that are evil, including the Christian Devil."

I scrambled to catch up with her because she had picked up her pace. "You mean Witches aren't bad?"

"No. Some people want you to think the Witches are bad, but they aren't. Real Witches don't believe in hurting people. In fact, they take an oath of service to help people the best way they can."

"Wow!" My mind reeled. Why hadn't my own parents told me the truth about the Witches? I would have to talk to them about this stuff later. I also realized that Tess hadn't answered my question. What was going on in her life that she thought this place was something like the Christian Hell? I had so many questions dancing in my mind. "But what about all the movies that show Witches as demented, evil people? What about those?" I asked.

Tess laughed. "They're just movies, silly. Stories that need a plot. None of those people who wrote that junk really investigate anything. They want money and thrills. They aren't interested in the truth."

"The truth?" I echoed.

"The truth," she said firmly. "Here . . ." she rummaged in her purse. "I brought something for you." She stopped walking and dug to the bottom of the leather bag. I liked that purse. Its leather fringes danced and spun as she moved the things around inside. Curious, I inched closer, trying to peer around her scrabbling hand. In a flourish she produced a pocket book, and handed it to me.

"*Diary of A Witch*," I read aloud, "by Sybil Leek. Who's she?"

"Read it and find out," said Tess with a mysterious look in her eye. She looked over her shoulder as if, way back at the house, someone would hear us. "Don't ask me how I know, but I'm supposed to give this book to *you*. That's why I came over here. Things are bad for me at home. I don't think I'm going to see you for a while."

"Bad? Bad how?"

She smiled sadly. "You're too young to explain it to. Besides, you'd tell Uncle Bernie, and there's nothing he can do about it."

Uncle Bernie was my dad, and although Tess and I hadn't seen each other much over the years, I guess she instinctively knew that I told my dad a lot of things because he listened to me. I have always been the type of person who would back off if someone didn't want to tell me something, even though they mentioned it. I kept quiet now.

Tess tapped the book, and said, "You must read this book. It is supposed to change your life."

I folded my lower lip under my upper one for a moment. "Says who?"

"Just trust me, okay?"

I nodded solemnly. After all, Tess was seven years older than I—a lot of track time to a thirteen-year-old. Had I known then what I know now, I could have told Tess that you have to be an active participant to make your life better. The future isn't a fixed or fated thing.

My mother interrupted our conversation, calling us back to the house. Due to extended family difficulties, miscommunication, and general activity, I lost contact with Tess. I saw her briefly during a rocky time in my life but, as things smoothed out and I began to make wise choices, I lost touch with her again. At the time, we didn't speak of the book she'd given me, or of my religious preference.

At age forty, I found out why she thought her life, all those years ago, was a living hell. I wish she'd have told me then, but there's nothing I can do about it now. If she had talked to a responsible adult, like my father, about what was happening to her, she could have avoided a lot of pain and suffering both for herself and for the many people around her. If you are in trouble or you see things that you know are bad, you have got to tell an adult that you trust, because often they can help you even though you think they can't. I know it's a lot to ask, since we just met and all, but trust me on this one.

In the coming years I would investigate all that Tess told me. I would have many good conversations with my father on topics like reincarnation, God, magick, the divine female and lots of other things. In the end, whether by accident or design, I would become one of the most well-known Wiccan authors of my time. Now don't that beat all? And all from the gift of one three-dollar paperback.

Every book has an underlying reason why the author picked up the pen or pencil and started jotting down ideas. Often, the reader doesn't know why the author wrote the book, especially if the book is a good one and they learn a lot from the text. Sometimes, readers feel comfortable with the presence of the book, and don't care about why or how the text got from the author's mind to their hands. Lots of times, after an author dies, people will go on and on about why this author wrote that book, and they come up with all sorts of silly reasons. We'll save them the trouble, you and I. I wrote this book for you, and for the Tess that once was.

★

The Craft: What It Is and What It Isn't

Ten thousand years we've struck the fire,
Creation's music freely sung
With Magick joined we've praised the stars
Since first the world begun.
Our spirit lives in timeless dance,
The Tarot and the Rune,
And nights united in the power
Of Drawing Down the Moon!
—DAVID O. NORRIS, 1994

·⋆*The years between puberty and adulthood can be exciting and difficult. I remember my teen years as one upheaval after another, from high to low and back to high again. I watch as my own four children experience these same fluctuations in emotions and experiences. It's tough. Don't let anyone fool you.

Sometimes you feel that all you've got are your friends. If your parents don't approve of those friends, then your whole world seems like milk dribbling off a chocolate chip cookie, leaving mushy brown crumbs on the floor of your life. Things get worse if your friends treat you badly, but you hang onto them anyway, because they're all you think you have. Who cares if Emily has a ring the size of a pancake hanging off her nose? She's just expressing herself! There are times when we look up to people, both big and small, and suddenly realize these people are really not who we thought they were. Getting to that realization can sometimes be traumatic and difficult.

You go through a time when you positively, without a doubt, know that you are always right and everyone else is wrong. You convince yourself that your parents came from another planet and that they couldn't possibly have been young—indeed, they vaulted full-grown from the cabbage patch on Mars to your home, marriage vows included (or not). You begin to wonder how you got into this family in the first place. Visions of baby switching at the hospital to your parents finding you at the Laundromat and taking you home, without telling anyone, of course, make you wonder if your *real* parents aren't some-where else, living in a mansion complete with pool, servants, and all the McDonald's hamburgers in the world. Naturally, these mythical parents swoon and weep for their lost prince or princess—which would be you, obviously.

You may think life isn't worth living when you bring home your report card and your parents ground you until the end of the next semester. Fantasies of jamming stuff in a duffel bag and hiding in your friend's basement surrounded by candy bars, pizza, and diet cola hit you full force. In retaliation you lop off your long hair. You cry for hours because now you look like you stuck your head in a blender, and then you stay up all night writing poetry that begins with the line: "I sit and stare at these four walls," with the lament repeating every other line.

Then there comes the time when you hide in your room every second you can, blasting your brain cells with the latest CD, thinking that if you become deaf, the world will finally understand you. You've holed up because the girls you look at won't look back, or the boys you favor really only want one thing, and if you gave that up your parents would immediately put you in a convent complete with a torture chamber equipped with Red Riding Hood and Three Little Pig videos for your painful entertainment.

Or how about the time that your best friend snuck out with your boyfriend (on several occasions) because your parents won't let you go to those hot teen spots? Or when you sat by your phone and cried for four days because your boyfriend didn't call you like he promised? Or when your date ditched you at the homecoming dance and waltzed off with that girl-who-has-all-the-money or the boy-who-has-the-spanking-new-cherry-red-pick-up-truck? How about the time everyone got drunk at that party, and you had to walk home because you knew it wasn't right and you were afraid to call your parents to come and get you? Then there was the time when you started your first job, and suddenly everyone—from adults to kids who had been there longer than you—started bossing you around and making fun of you. That was a real kicker.

Rules at home, rules in school, rules on the job—ah, yes, those were the days. And these are the days you search for the "reason why." Why is this happening to me? Why can't things be better? Why doesn't anyone understand me? Why won't anyone listen to me? What have I done to deserve this? Somehow, some way—you picked up this book, and you wonder—can WitchCraft help me?

My answer would be yes, indeed, but don't forget that any positive religion (Christianity, Judaism, Islam, Hinduism, Buddhism, et cetera) can give you the necessary support you need at this time in your life. Teens often look to the Craft because the religion appears powerful, glamorous and foreign; and their parents don't like it. The practices of the Craft appear to be different from other religions, which makes this belief system alluring. As you learn about Witch-Craft, you'll find that the religion of Wicca isn't so different from the spiritual structures that you may have already experienced.

In this first chapter I'm going to work through a lot of the misconceptions that teens (and grownups) have about the Craft. Once we have that out of the way, we can have some major fun.

I'm in Michigan, in the Lansing Conference Center, walking slowly down the long, red carpeted hall toward the Governor's room, where in a few moments I'll be giving a lecture titled *Living a Magickal Life*. I realize that twenty years ago this would never be happening, this acceptance of a woman coming into a large, modern conference center that literally faces the capitol of the state of Michigan and talking about WitchCraft to a big audience. I also realize, as I enter the room and grin at the smiling faces of my audience, that we've still got a long way to go, we Witches. We can talk about our religion in Lansing, Michigan, but there are still many places in the United States where uneducated, unenlightened people believe that Witches are bad, and therefore these poor, unfortunate souls will do anything in their power to discriminate against us. Over centuries, people who knew nothing about the Craft have tried to turn Witches into all sorts of mythical beasts, fibbing like crazy to the public. Well, I'm a Witch, and I've had enough. I'm going to use my magickal power (the gift of the written word) to turn those myths back into truth.

This book, designed for you teens, adds to the cauldron of my continuing efforts to fight against discrimination and to teach people that WitchCraft can help them in improving their lives and making them better people, if they so desire. Some day, I want to be able to walk down any hall of any building in the United States and know that people don't misunderstand Witches anymore.

The Basic Theology of Wicca

When someone asks me, "What is Wicca?" a thousand wonderful things come to mind, but the person who asks the question usually expects a limited answer. Although I could talk for hours on what the Craft is or is not, the basic answer would be: *WitchCraft is a nature based, life-affirming religion that follows a moral code and seeks to build harmony among people, and empower the self and others.* If you think about it, we could use that statement for almost any positive religion, couldn't we? Witches usually follow their own path, and don't meander along with a crowd just because somebody says so. Witches practice individualism, freedom of thought, and have a close connection with the world around them, including plants, animals, and people. We commune with streams, sky, fire, trees, animals, and rocks, much like the indigenous ancestors of America. We see everything on our planet as a manifestation of the Divine.

The Principles of Wiccan Belief

At the Spring Witchmeet of 1974, held in Minneapolis, Minnesota, the Council of American Witches adopted a document titled "Principles of Wiccan Belief" to inform, educate, and define for the public, and the new Craft practitioners, the central belief system of Wicca (WitchCraft). This document represents an overview of Craft Law and theology but does not contain the many nuances of the religious structure that most Witches may follow. As with any religious belief that has had time to grow and change, no single set of thirteen statements could completely define the faith. The Principles of Belief serve well as a simplified explanation of the system.

Unfortunately, the Council of American Witches disbanded in that same year, but this does not mean the efforts they made were inconsequential; quite the contrary! Twenty years later, in 1994, the religion known as WitchCraft (Wicca) made history when members of its belief system answered an invitation to attend the World Parliament of Religions Conference in Chicago. Those attending included Selena Fox (of Circle Sanctuary) and members of the Covenant of the Goddess (COG). Through their fine efforts, Wicca moved from what many thought of as a fad to find a definite place among the various religions of the world.

The Principles of Belief, as set forth by the American Council of Witches, are:

The Principles of Belief

1. We practice rites to attune ourselves with the natural rhythm of life forces marked by the phases of the moon and the seasonal quarters and cross-quarters.

   Teen Speak: Witches celebrate God through religious services, commonly called rituals. A rite is a segment within a ritual. Most of our church services correspond to set days throughout the year. Some celebrations follow the phases of the moon, where other services match the seasons of the planet. Rather than wasting space and building a place to hold church services that will remain vacant for most of the week, Witches often meet in their homes and have their church services there.

2. We recognize that our intelligence gives us a unique responsibility toward our environment. We seek to live in harmony with nature, in ecological balance offering fulfillment to life and consciousness within an evolutionary concept.

   Teen Speak: God has given us the ability to know right from wrong. Since we stand at the top of the food chain (well, at least most of us) we have the responsibility to make sure that the planet doesn't get gummed up because we are so darned "smart." The best way to protect the planet and all the creatures on it is by living in harmony with all our bird, bee, and animal buddies. In essence, we need to be ecologically conscious of our actions at all times.

3. We acknowledge a depth of power far greater than is apparent to the average person. Because this power is far greater than ordinary, we sometimes call this force "supernatural," but we see this power as lying within that which is naturally potential to all.

   Teen Speak: Over the centuries, humans have managed to suppress many of their innate talents. The power of the mind truly is an incredible thing. Did you know that we don't bother to use a huge portion of our mind power? We've become lazy, and access only what we think we need. It is from this unused mind that wondrous abilities unfold, such as clairvoyance, telekinesis, clairaudience, extrasensory perception (ESP), remote viewing—call it what you will. Everyone has these abilities, but most don't use them, and some people fear these powers. Witches, and other enlightened souls, strive to strengthen these natural gifts. In the eyes of the Witch, everyone and everything stands equal.

4. We conceive of the Creative Power in the Universe as manifesting through polarity—as masculine and feminine—and that this Creative Power lives in all people, and functions through the interaction of the masculine and feminine. We value neither above the other, knowing each to be supportive of the other. We value sexuality as pleasure, as the symbol and embodiment of Life.

Teen Speak: Just like any other religion, Witches believe in God. We see God as having two sides—masculine and feminine. Together, these two sides mix to create the whole of God. Witches respect both men and women, and the male and female properties of everything. We agree that men aren't better than women, and that women aren't better than men. Witches believe that having sex with another person is not a "bad thing," though we do feel that sexual acts and interests carry a heavy responsibility.

5. We recognize both outer worlds and inner, or psychological, worlds— sometimes known as the Spiritual World, the Collective Unconscious, the Inner Planes, et cetera—and we see in the interaction of these two dimensions the basis for paranormal phenomena and magickal exercises. We neglect neither dimension for the other, seeing both as necessary for our fulfillment.

Teen Speak: We know that energies exist in the world, seen and unseen. We value the world of the mind as much as we value the world around us. The Collective Unconscious means the psychic connections between people, plants, animals, insects, and Spirit. We call the powers of the mind the Inner Planes. Witches realize that the techniques known as paranormal phenomena and magickal application begin in the mind and manifest in the universe. We pay attention to what we think and what we do. We believe that to think a thing is to create a thing.

6. We do not recognize any authoritarian hierarchy, but do honor those who teach, respect those who share their greater knowledge and wisdom, and acknowledge those who have courageously given of themselves in leadership.

Teen Speak: Unlike other churches that feel the need to have a central government that dictates the rules and activities of its followers, the Wiccan religion does not have a central government. We do have teachers and leaders that we honor for their wisdom and the time they have donated to the Wiccan way. Each Wiccan organization, church, coven, group, or open circle governs itself.

7. We see religion, magick, and wisdom-in-living as united in the way one views the world and lives within it—a world view and philosophy of life, which we identify as WitchCraft or the Wiccan Way.

   Teen Speak: Wiccans believe that religion, the power of the mind, magickal applications, wisdom, and faith in Spirit do not function separately, but together. We try not to wear blinders to what goes on in the world, and to keep an open mind as much as possible.

8. Calling oneself "Witch" does not make a Witch—but neither does heredity itself, nor the collecting of titles, degrees, and initiations. A Witch seeks to control the forces within him/herself that make life possible to live wisely and well, without harm to others, and in harmony with nature.

   Teen Speak: Putting down this book, going to school, and proclaiming to one and all does not make you a Witch. Wearing black clothing and lots of gaudy jewelry and threatening people with the silly nonsense of cursing them puts you far away from the path of the real Wiccan. Joining a coven and taking an initiation and collecting status within that group also doesn't make you a Witch. How you live, how you deal with others, how you incorporate Wiccan laws into your life—these all determine whether you are, or are not, a Witch.

9. We acknowledge that it is the affirmation and fulfillment of life, in a continuation of evolution and development of consciousness, that gives meaning to the Universe we know, and to our personal role within that Universe.

   Teen Speak: Witches respect all life, whether that life belongs to a bug, a weed, a beautiful tree, a tiger, or the rude man who lives down the street from you. All must survive to evolve.

10. Our only animosity toward Christianity, or toward any other religion or philosophy of life, is to the extent that these institutions have claimed to be "the one true right and only way" and have sought to deny freedom to others and to suppress other ways of religious practices and belief.

    Teen Speak: Witches are sick and tired of people in other religions passing judgment and spreading lies about our belief system just because they are either insecure in their own faith or don't realize that many paths to God exist in our universe. These unenlightened people think that hurting us is better than admitting that people should be free to believe as they want to believe. Witches do not hate Christians, or Jews, or followers of Islam; however, when people from these structured groups try to hurt us with lies, gossip, or physical force, they can expect the Witches to be upset and to fight back.

11. As American Witches, we do not feel threatened by debates on the history of the Craft, the origins of various terms, the legitimacy of various aspects of different traditions. We concern ourselves with our present, and our future.

    Teen Speak: There is no one right way to practice the Craft. The religion is what you make of it.

12. We do not accept the concept of "absolute evil," nor do we worship any entity known as "Satan" or "the Devil" as defined by Christian Tradition. We do not seek power through the suffering of others, nor do we accept the concept that personal benefits can only be derived by denial to another.

    Teen Speak: We do not worship the Devil nor do we believe in the Christian Satan. We believe that to give evil a name is to give evil power. Witches do not find an interest in working with, in, or through evil. We do not believe that a person gains power by hurting, threatening, or killing someone—that would be evil.

13. We work within nature for that which is contributory to our health and well-being. Not bound by traditions from other times and other cultures, we owe no allegiance to any person or power greater than the Divinity manifest through our own being. As American Witches, we welcome and respect all life-affirming teachings and traditions. We seek to learn from all and to share our learning. We do not wish to open ourselves to the destruction of Wicca by those on self-serving power trips, or to philosophies and practices contradictory to these principles. In seeking to exclude those whose ways are contradictory to ours, we do not want to deny participation with any person who carries a sincere interest in our knowledge and beliefs, regardless of race, color, sex, age, national or cultural origins, or sexual preference.

Teen Speak: Witches work with nature rather than against nature. We believe that God is the supreme power and that no human or group of people is more powerful than God. Witches respect all religions on the face of the planet, and respect an individual's right to practice a positive faith. We do not teach our mysteries to fools, and we will exclude those people whom we feel are either self-destructive or whom we feel have the potential, or the history, of hurting others. Most Wiccan organizations screen prospective members.

✦ ✦ ✦

Those of the Wicca follow an intricate set of laws in their personal and group practice. Collectively, Witches call these laws **The Ordains**. The Ordains fall into three basic categories: Spiritual Laws, Practical Laws, and Coven Laws. The Spiritual Laws represent a code of ethics or morals giving the Crafter a guideline for spiritual living, whether you choose to practice as a Solitary (a Witch alone) or within a group structure. These Spiritual Laws apply to all magickal people, and most magickal individuals incorporate these laws into their group workings and their solitary practices.

> **The Ordains** n. A set of spiritual, practical, and coven laws that govern those of the Wicca.

Witches think of the Practical Laws as the blossoms of experience from those who have practiced the religion before you. Therefore, not all of the Practical Laws will apply to every person. Think of these laws as guidelines.

The third type of Craft Law (Coven Law) belongs to group hierarchy, and most of these laws do not apply to the Witch practicing alone. This doesn't mean that solitary Witches should ignore these laws entirely, as many in their community may follow some sort of coven or group government and they practice Witch-Craft within the confines of these laws. Coven Laws fall into two categories: Those Laws created for general Wiccan government, and those Laws created by the current organization, group, or coven. The laws created by each group may not contradict the general Coven Laws but seek to enhance the organization and assist in creating a harmonious balance among the group's members.

Through the Principles of Belief and the more intricate Ordains, New Generation Witches (Witches of the 90s) can practice a structured religion that doesn't appear structured. That's the enchantment, and the mystery, of the Craft.

Where Witches Get Their Power

When you look at a Witch's hat straight on, you see three sides, don't you? Indeed, a Witch's hat looks like a triangle and represents what we call the **cone of power**. WitchCraft encompasses three angles or sides of belief: Love, Positive Creativity, and Spirit. Love conquers all things. Love opens doors, soothes the soul, and makes us all one. This love includes the good emotions you may feel toward your parents, the planet, your siblings, a pet, your friends, or that special person in your life. The Witch does his or her best to love all creatures, big or little. That's the foundation of the Craft, or the bottom of the hat—Love.

The main purpose of being human falls under the art of creation, whether you make jewelry, invest your time in the science of numbers, write poetry, practice positive magick, or give sincere advice—it doesn't matter, if you create in a positive way. We can create good things, or we can create negative things. This is the gift of free will. The Witch strives to create in a positive manner. That's the second side of the hat—Positive Creativity.

cone of power n. Energy. A combination of Love, Creativity, and Spirit that forms the basis of a Witch's power, which he or she raises to accomplish a desire.

Spirit (or the Lord and the Lady) comprises the third side of the hat. This is the belief in divinity, the knowing that God, in whatever form, exists and the understanding that God is within us and around us, willing to help us if we only ask. Witches see God as both masculine and feminine, so often we call God the Lord and the Lady. Sometimes we say Spirit. We realize that Allah, Jesus, and Buddha are all faces of the masculine side of God; however, we also give equal importance to the feminine side of God. We call this side of God the Lady. In the Christian religion, the female part of God manifests through Mary, but Mary doesn't have equal status with God. Usually, the Christians see God as only masculine. We feel that the masculine and feminine sides of God are extremely important. No religion is wrong in the way they see God. There are only differences in ideology and theology. The Lord and the Lady (or Spirit) is the third side of our Witch's hat.

If we put the three sides together—Love, Positive Creativity, and Spirit—Wiccans make a cone of power from which their magick springs. That power incorporates our love, our creative abilities, and the strength of God as we see him or her. Witches can, and do, make miracles happen for themselves and others through Love, Positive Creativity, and Spirit.

Right about now you are saying, "But, but, but . . . that's not what my friends, or maybe my parents, or perhaps my minister says about Witches. They tell me something different. How can what you are saying be true?" I think the thing that irritates me most about human beings is that they are willing to believe anything evil, morbid, or gross without question. Try to tell them something different and bingo! They demand "truth." "Show me," these unenlightened people say. "Show me that what I've heard all these years isn't true. I will believe bad things because this belief makes life more interesting. If you tell me good things, then I will be bored." People amaze me. Most people will buy rumor over truth any day. Just look at the sales of the trash papers in the grocery stores if you don't believe me.

The Persecution of the Witches

I wasn't going to cover the persecution of the Witches, but then, I promised you the truth, didn't I? Whether you believe it or not, since humans sought to join the other creatures on this earth there has always been magick and individuals chosen by Spirit to work that magick. Indeed, anyone can study and employ magickal practices if they work long and hard enough. Our gift of free will makes us unique but, in that thrust for individuality, humans may use this free will in a bad way. Take, for example, war, crime, hatred—the list of negative things born by humans running under their own steam looks embarrassingly long.

Evil, as much as we'd like to lay the blame elsewhere, does not belong to some strange entity floating around, rubbing its clawed hands in delight, salivating about what it can force us to do. It is my firm belief that we humans create the evil in the world and are too chicken to take responsibility for what our minds, hearts, and hands have wrought in negative circumstances. Humans find great joy in laying the responsibility on some mythical being rather than owning up to what we have, in error, created ourselves.

During the **Dark Ages**, the Church sought to get rid of the Pagans and Witches from the countryside so that the Church could amass both power and property. In essence, the Church developed a marketing plan to sell Christianity and, much like the political marketing plans today, used various methods to push their product, including fear, torture, and misinformation. During this process the Church incorporated

Dark Ages n. An era from about A.D. 476 to about the year 1000 characterized by repression and unelightenment.

many entrenched beliefs of the country folk (the Yule log, Christmas trees, gargoyles to guard churches, the Easter bunny, et cetera) into Church custom and policy to keep the people they were trying to brainwash happy. The church even took the Pagan Gods and Goddesses and turned them into Saints—St. Brigit as case in point. When the Church could not convince the people to give up their Pagan ways, they moved to stronger methods. During the Dark Ages, historians believe that over two million people were murdered by the Witch Finders.

In the eighth century, a document written by the church titled the *Canon Episcopi* declared that Witches were illusions but, at the same time, the Church created a very deadly weapon—the Inquisition. The leaders of the Inquisition overturned this document and thus began their wicked persecution of innocent people all across Europe. These men of blood had the full sanction of the Church. Most persecutions took place between the fifteenth, sixteenth, and seventeenth centuries. By the time these fanatics of the Church were through, the female population had dipped to an alarming rate, and almost no wise women, midwives, or local healers remained alive. During that time, religious leaders changed the Bible, particularly in one passage, where it still says "Thou shalt not suffer a witch to live." In the original language of the Bible the wording was "Thou shalt not suffer a poisoner to live." As you can see, the men of the Inquisition ruled with an iron hand, even changing many of the passages in the Bible to suit their own purposes and free themselves of the responsibility of their own evil.

During the eighteenth century, the wickedness that sucked the life out of the population of Europe began to dwindle. Many historians call the beginning of this time the Age of Reason—meaning people actually began to think about what was happening around them rather than going along just to keep peace. In 1736, WitchCraft ceased to be an offense punishable by death in England and Scotland. In 1722, the last documented Witch Burning in the British Isles took place in Scotland, when a woman by the name of Janet Horne suffered execution. A look at history, even into the early twentieth century, shows occasional burnings and hangings involving suspected Witches.

In England in 1952, the government repealed the last of the WitchCraft laws, meaning it was no longer a crime to practice the religion of WitchCraft in that country. We in the United States are fortunate, because the laws here protect our faith . . . supposedly.

Does this mean that the persecution of Witches has drifted into the dark and dusty corners of history? Obviously not. Even though most sane people realize that Witches don't hurt anyone, the rumors and misinformation persist. Some church officials still can't get it through their heads that we don't participate in negative activity, and many individuals in the media persist in yellow journalism, using us to boost their ratings with sensationalism.

This Little Lamp of Mine—I'm Going to Let it Shine

Let's light the lamp of truth and shine some rays of clarity on those nasty rumors you've probably heard. Once we correct the misinformation, we can get on with helping you to be a better person. You don't have to practice WitchCraft to make yourself a better person. We have lots of religions on this planet, and each religion serves the needs of the believers of that religion. I see God as a big, beautiful diamond with many facets. Each facet of God manifests as a positive religious belief. Witches see themselves as one of those facets on that diamond. Christianity, Judaism, Islam, and hundreds of other positive religions make up that big diamond too. Together, we are all one. I've written this book for you so that you can understand what Witches think, what they believe, and how they try to act. So let's begin by giving you a handy-dandy list so that you can chuck those dumb rumors about WitchCraft in the garbage can where they belong.

Real Witches do not . . .

... hurt people physically, mentally, spiritually, or magickally. Witches have taken an oath to help people, not hurt people. You are not a real Witch if you hurt anybody.

... take illegal drugs. The laws of our country forbid illegal drug use; besides, illegal drugs mess up your body. Why bother? Witches do go to the doctor when they are sick and follow the directions of the doctor for good health care. Witches do work magick to help people who are sick, but they never, ever use magick instead of good medical care. They use magick with appropriate medical care.

... work black magick—that's those *other* guys. Real Witches know that whatever you do, whether in this world or in the magickal world, comes back to you three times. If you do good stuff, then you get rewarded. If you do bad stuff, you pay the price—and, let me add, you will pay dearly. Wiccans have a poem that goes: Ever mind the rule of three, what you give out comes back to thee.

. . . fly in the sky on brooms. We buy cars and trucks and stay on the road like everyone else. If we feel the need to take to the skies we choose Delta, Northwestern, or American Airlines.

. . . eat babies. (Yuckie!) We *love* babies. We want them to grow up big and strong and do good things for people, like hopefully find a cure for AIDS, cancer, and the common cold.

. . . kill animals (or anything else for that matter). Real Witches love and honor animals. Animals are a part of Spirit, just like people. Witches are big pet-people. We have dogs, cats, gerbils, bunnies, et cetera, and they all live long, happy lives and see the vet regularly.

. . . tell fibs or big whopper lies. We walk our talk, and we know that a Witch is as good as his or her word.

. . . call themselves warlocks. The word warlock means "truth twister." Whether you are a boy or a girl, man or woman, the name remains the same: Witch or Wiccan.

. . . get into sexual perversions. Enough said on that strange arena. We don't want to go there!

. . . drink or use blood in any way from animals, themselves, or any person (alive or dead). How you like your steak has nothing to do with the Craft.

. . . change their hair color in the blink of an eye. We go to the grocery store and buy hair dye to cover the gray just like your mother.

. . . steal or take part in any type of criminal behavior. We believe that if we take from someone else, we are really taking from ourselves. Stealing from ourselves would be stupid.

. . . pervert the symbols of any other religion, such as the cross or the Star of David, or desecrate graves or statues of saints. We honor the dead as well as the living.

. . . summon demons. We simply are not that dumb.

. . . worship the Christian Devil. We don't believe in Satan. We don't give power to bad things, like Satan or the Devil, because to name something rotten is to give it power.

. . . believe in the Christian Hell. Real Witches believe that we are responsible for our own actions, and that we will pay either in this life, or in the next, for bad things that we do—so, we try very hard not to do bad things. This leads us to a universal Wiccan belief—that of reincarnation.

. . . coerce or brainwash people to join us. WitchCraft or Wicca is *not* a cult. WitchCraft or Wicca is a *legitimate* religion. Our clergy can legally marry people. We also have christenings (Wiccanings or Sainings) for our babies, just like other religions. We do the sprinkle-water-thing, too. In 1994, at the World Parliament of Religions in Chicago, Illinois, Wicca or Witch-Craft was acknowledged as a legitimate religion by the other religions of the world, including Catholics, Jews, Buddhists, and many Protestant Christians. Witches can legally have churches in this country.

. . . use Satanic symbols. The Witches' pentacle, or five-pointed star point-up within a circle, represents the four elements and the human, encom-passed by Spirit. The pentacle has nothing to do with Satanism, and Witches get very, very upset with people who match the point-up penta-cle with Satanism. Just as Witches do not invert the Christian cross, they don't appreciate it when someone inverts their symbol, either.

. . . have to go through an initiation ceremony to practice the religion of WitchCraft; however, Witches who practice in a group environment that has some sort of self-government for its members do perform initiations. You can't initiate yourself but you can dedicate yourself to the Lord and Lady. Initiations represent levels of training or spiritual progression within a *group* environment. Elders of the Craft pass **power/lineage** during certain initiation ceremonies. You can't pass power/lineage that wasn't passed to you—that's why the Elders perform this function. Initiations are celebrations designed to honor your spiritual progression. Bad things do not happen to anyone in a Wiccan initiation.

> **power/lineage** n. Energy and history passed from one person to another.

. . . become Witches overnight. Today a Baptist, tomorrow a Wiccan? Nope. Doesn't work. WitchCraft requires a lot of dedication, study, and perse-verance. The religion of the Craft becomes a process of self-growth and joy. You don't slap on a pentacle, wiggle into a black dress or dark pants and shirt, paint your fingernails a disgusting color, wear wild makeup and call yourself a Witch. Nothing doing—to be a Witch isn't a fashion state-ment, or the trendy thing to do. The religion does not require you to wear black. If you go around dressed up like that, real Witches will laugh at you. The religion doesn't even require you to wear a pentacle. Real WitchCraft takes a lot of work. A Witch "is" by means of study and belief, not by what he or she wears.

. . . attack people, but they do defend themselves when attacked by others.

. . . blab to everyone that they are Witches. We practice the **Witches' Pyramid**—To Know, To Dare, To Will, and To Be Silent. To Know means that we constantly search for the truth and are strong in our beliefs. To Dare means that we are not afraid of the unknown, and that we dare to be different and to learn as much as we can. To Will means that we concentrate on being the best that we can be. To Be Silent means that we know pure thought has great power. If we tell others about our magicks, especially those who do not believe as we do, then much of the strength can seep away from our work. Therefore, we share only with those of like mind and leave other people to their own devices.

Witches' Pyramid n. A creed and a structure of learning that Witches follow: To Know, To Dare, To Will, and To Be Silent.

. . . always work magick. Most Witches practice the magickal arts but not all Witches work magick. Some of the nicest Witches I know don't work magick; they do, however, pray.

. . . gossip, tell lies, or hurt anyone's feelings on purpose.

. . . ever practice a magickal application that they do not completely understand.

. . . charge money to work magick or to pray for people, though they can ask reimbursement for the supplies they use.

. . . use their magick or other skills to show off.

. . . cast love spells to entice another person, break two people up just so the Witch can go out with one of them, or in any way seek to interfere with another person's free will. We do work to bring harmony and love into our lives, but we never, ever target anyone!

. . . abuse animals. Real Witches *do* work magick with animals. Witches respect animals very much; however, we don't have toads, or cats, or spiders that perch on our fingers while we do a little hocus-pocus dance, nor do we put animal or insect parts in bubbling cauldrons with appropriate mumbo-jumbo. Things like Eye of Newt and Tongue of Adder are really folk names for herbs, handed down from generation to generation.

If Witches do not believe in or do bad things, you say, then why are people so afraid of them? A very good question that deserves a solid answer. People fear what they don't understand, and some people obviously *don't* understand the Witches. Witches stand for improving themselves and improving life for other people. This can be a scary thing for people who don't want to change. Witches, then, honor and seek change that will bring harmony into their lives and into the lives of others. Sometimes, people don't *want* to understand the Witches, because either they don't want to admit that they have been wrong all along (because that will make them look silly or stupid) or because they fear change. Some people like doing things the way they have always done them, even if those things are bad or inappropriate.

Another reason people are afraid of Witches is because most of us have an aura of power. That means that you can just tell by looking at us that we are "different." We didn't cast a spell, or twist anyone's mind—rather, we study and try to live right. This shows. I received a letter last month from a sixteen-year-old girl named Judy. Judy told me that, after several months, her best friend accused her of taking drugs. "What would ever make you think that?" asked Judy. Her friend replied, "Because you've changed. You're more laid back. You don't get as angry anymore. Everyone has noticed." Judy laughed, and said, "No, silly, I've been studying Wicca." Judy gave her friend my book *To Ride A Silver Broomstick: New Generation WitchCraft*. Now Judy's friend is learning how to be a better person, too.

Let's talk about what real Witches *do* believe.

Real Witches do . . .

. . . believe in God as a universal force of positive energy. We see the Lord and the Lady as aspects of this universal force. This gets confusing for new Wiccans, so let's explain divinity this way. I'll use Christianity as an example, only because I converted from that religion, so I know the belief system very well. There are many sects in Christianity, right? There are Lutherans, Methodists, Catholics, Baptists, River Brethren, Episcopalians, et cetera. Some believe the Christian doctrine reads one way (and only one way) and others believe something different. Nevertheless, they all call themselves Christians. For example, Protestants don't have much use for saints or guardian angels, but Catholics believe and work with those two aspects of divinity all the time. Neither type of Christianity is wrong (even though some in each camp would argue differently—but we know that all spirituality is sacred, don't we?). Witches have the same thing in Wicca. Since I don't want to confuse you because you are just learning, I'm not going to go into those different sects in this book. You can find this information in my book *To Ride A Silver Broomstick* (you know, the one I mentioned earlier, but let's not go there just yet). No one sect of the Craft is better than the others. In this book, we're going to stick with the universal force of positive energy as these forces manifest within the aspects of the Lord and Lady.

. . . honor all positive religious paths. We understand that God is like that big, perfect diamond I mentioned earlier. These facets are all the religions on earth. Witches do not make fun of other religions, and we feel that other religions should not make fun of us.

. . . believe that we are all one. We are one with Spirit, with people, with plants, with animals, with the elements, et cetera.

. . . believe in prayer. We pray all the time. Prayer helps people. We know that focused prayer represents great power.

. . . follow certain laws. We sometimes call these laws the Ordains. Witches follow three kinds of laws: Spiritual, Practical, and Coven Laws.

. . . believe in Karma—that for every action there is an equal reaction. Remember that little poem I told you about earlier? That's right! "Ever mind the rule of three, what you give out comes back to thee."

. . . realize that to make the planet a good place to live, we have to live in harmony with others, and to do this, we work with positive energy.

. . . believe that there are three parts to a person: The physical, the mental, and the spiritual. We try to train ourselves to work all three parts of ourselves in harmony as best we can.

. . . use common sense. We do not do dumb things like drink alcohol and drive.

. . . know that thoughts are things. We are always very careful about what we think, whether we are considering ourselves or someone else.

. . . know that *power grows in direct proportion to wisdom.* We know that scaring people is not a wise way to behave, and that Witches will lose, rather than gain, power if they frighten someone. Boasting to people that you can hurt them through magick is one of the most despicable things a person can do. The boaster has no real power. We also believe that using religious doctrine to frighten someone constitutes a big fat no-no.

. . . know that the art of magick is our greatest gift. If we work bad magick, Spirit will take our gift(s) from us. If we work positive magick, then that good energy will return to us threefold.

. . . work alone, or with others, in a magick circle. The magick circle represents our temple or church. We never bring jealousy, hatred, or anger into the magick circle, as that would be disrespectful to Spirit.

. . . believe in reincarnation. We know that we live many lives in order to grow spiritually.

. . . believe that there is *no one right way* to worship divinity. We feel that each person must cultivate their own belief in God so that they can be comfortable with Spirit. We have no central government, no single spokesperson, no main organization. Each person equally manifests the power of our religion in the world today. Just because I write a lot of books on the subject and lots of people know me does not mean I am better than the other Witches in the world. My gifts are not stronger or better than yours or theirs. Because each Witch utilizes the Craft in his or her own way, you will find differences in our practices. The information I've given you here represents the generalities of the Craft as I understand them. I based these generalities on my own practice, the practices of my teachers, and on the practices of thousands of Wiccans that I have met in my travels.

Wow! Pretty amazing stuff, huh? There's nothing scary in the Craft. I ought to know. I've studied the Craft for over twenty-nine years. If I thought bad things lurked here, I'd find myself a bandwagon to another religion. Whether you are this year's prom queen, the wallflower majoring in agricultural science, the kid with the battered truck into Goth or minus four rubber tires and the appropriate metal body—from the country, the city, the trailer park, or the apartment—the religion of the Craft can speak to you . . . if you let it.

I like the Wiccan religion for one major reason: *No matter what happens, I am never at the mercy of anyone or anything. I always have something to do to help make things better.* That's the beauty of the Craft.

★

2

Secrets That Aren't Secrets Anymore: The Basics of WitchCraft

Secrets. Doesn't the word "secret" make you think of something quiet, personal, secluded, special? We all love secrets, but we hate mysteries—when someone tells us we can't have access to those secrets. Many Witches have experienced persecution because the religion of Wicca has lots of secrets. In the past, Witches haven't readily shared these secrets, which resulted in lots of accusations that simply weren't true. Some pretty rotten things have happened to the Witches, all because we hold our secrets so dear. To stop people from hurting us, we decided to tell our secrets.

Today, thanks to many magickal people—some famous, others not—the religion of WitchCraft has moved out of the closet of secrecy and into the general community. To do this, Witches discussed their secrets. Funny—once people heard the secrets, they thought the information wasn't so special at all, and didn't believe that those secrets represented the real mysteries. Silly them. Anything can be a secret if you don't talk about it. The special part comes when you don't tell.

One of the biggest secrets in the Craft is: We are all one. That's the Great Mystery. We all connect—people, plants, and animals.

All these things, including the planet we live on, become sacred to us. Witches believe that if you hurt someone, you really hurt yourself; therefore, we don't try to harm anyone or anything. All the Wiccan secrets are just like this one, simple ideas that you could have come up with yourself, or you have heard from someone before. Each secret contains its own kind of empowerment. For example, by knowing that we are all one, then we seek to do the best that we can for everyone, not just ourselves. That's real power.

While you are reading the remainder of this book, you may feel that some of the terms I use are not explained in depth. I want to make sure that you are familiar with these terms without bogging your brain with details at this time, especially since most teens reading this book plan to work alone. Let me assure you that everything you need to begin studying the Craft is here.

Who Are the Witches?

Recent statistics tell us that WitchCraft is the fastest growing religion in the United States today. To give you an idea of the Witch population, the Wiccan Pagan Press Alliance has concluded that we have as many Witches in the United States as published writers. You'll find people who practice the Wiccan faith in every type of job and in every social structure in the country. One person in every five either knows a Witch or has practiced some sort of magickal theory in their lifetime. Several parents in your school system right now practice the Craft.

If Witches are so prevalent, you say, how come I don't know any? Well, you probably do, but because of the various forms of persecution that Witches have experienced in the past, most of them aren't walking up and down the street proclaiming their faith. The most powerful Witches in the United States today look just like everyone else, have families, and hold stable jobs. You'll find Witches in medicine, engineering, aeronautics, insurance, sales, food service, journalism, the police force, science, and any other career you could imagine. Some very famous actors and actresses are Witches too. You'll find Witches everywhere, quietly going about their business and practicing their faith in private.

Can You Be a Witch?

Of course you can. Today, anyone can practice the art and science of the Craft. Anyone can practice the religion of WitchCraft. The only requirements for entering the faith of the Craft revolve around your willingness to work hard to learn the many facets of the system, and your dedication to **Spirit**. Many young people ask me if they can mix the religion of Witch-Craft with other religious practices. Yes, you can, but only after you fully understand the concept of the Wic-can religion and can move comfortably between the differences in both religious structures. You do not have to give up your current religion to investigate WitchCraft.

Spirit n. The overall energy that runs the universe in a harmonious way.

No ceremony exists where you must lay down your previous beliefs to begin a life in the Craft. It is true that, as most individuals learn and grow within the structure of the Craft, they leave their previous belief systems behind, but this comes from choice, not by demand of any person or any law in the Craft.

Wiccan Traditions

Scott Cunningham, a celebrated author and one of the most famous American Witches of our times, described Wiccan Traditions in this manner: "An organized, structured, specific subgroup, which is usually initiatory, often with unique ritual practices. Many traditions have their own Books of Shadows, and usually recognize members of other traditions as Wiccan. Most traditions are composed of many covens and solitary practitioners."

Just as Christianity has several factions, so does Wicca have its own subgroupings. Some sects take the names of specific cultures such as Strega (Italian) and Norse/Germanic. Feminist WitchCraft falls under the auspices of the Dianic Witches (female oriented and begun by the well-known and much loved Z. Budapest). Then, various sects take the names of those individuals that started them: Gardnerian (formed by Gerald Gardner in the 50s); Alexandrian (begun by Alex Saunders around the same time); the Cabot Witches (begun by Laurie Cabot, Official Witch of Salem); Starhawkians (named after popular author Starhawk); and finally, we have family clans, those groups composed of several types of sects under one umbrella—The Family of Serpent Stone (begun by the late, beloved Wil Martin); The Black Forest Clan (which is my group); and Covenant of the Goddess (COG).

I know all of this can get confusing, but don't worry. These Witches started studying somewhere, just like you. As you learn and grow in the Craft, you may wish to join one of these groups; then again, you may prefer to continue working as a solitary. The nice thing about all of the sects listed is that although they may practice their ceremonies differently, or have different requirements for entrance into their groups, each practices the same intent and follows the Principles of Wiccan Belief. Truly, it is our differences and our individualism that make us strong.

A Craft Creation Myth—The Lord and Lady

Long, long ago, the world slept in the arms of the dark void. From this place of nothingness, Spirit drew together and created Our Lady of infinite love. The Lady danced among the heavens, her feet beating out the rhythm of all creation. Sparks of light catapulted from her hair, giving birth to the stars and planets. As she twirled, these heavenly bodies began to move with her in the divine symphony of the universe. When her dancing quickened she formed the seas and the mountains of earth. She chanted words of love and joy, and as these sounds fell to the earth, the trees and flowers were born. From the pure, white light of her breath came the colors of the universe, turning all things to vibrant beauty. From the bubbling laughter in her throat sprang the sounds of the pristine running water of the streams, the gentle lapping vibrations of the lake, and the roaring screams of the oceans. Her tears of joy became the rains of our survival.

And when her dancing slowed, and the Lady sought a companion to share the wonders of the world, Spirit created the God as her lifemate and companion. Because she so loved the earth, Spirit made her companion half spirit, half animal, so that together the Lord and Lady could populate our planet. The Lord's power moves through her, and she showers the earth and all upon it with her blessings. Together, the Lord and Lady gave birth to the birds, animals, fishes, and people of our world. To protect and guide the humans, the Lord and Lady created the angels and power spirits. These energies walk with us always, though we often cannot see them. To each bird the Lady gave a magick song, and to each animal the Lord bestowed the instinct to survive. The Lord is the master of the animal and vegetable kingdoms, and therefore wears the antlers of a stag crowning his great head. This aspect of half man, half animal shows his joy in both the human and animal creations of the Spirit, and he revels in this image.

As the humans began to grow and prosper, the Lord and Lady saw the need for healers among their own kind. And so they drew forth energy from the realm of the angels, the realm of the power animals, and the realm of the humans to create the Witches. The Witches brought with them the wisdom of the Lord and Lady, the ability to heal, and the art of magick. The Lady taught the Witches how to cast a magick circle and talk to Spirit, and the Lord taught the Witches how to communicate with the spirits of Air, Fire, Earth, and Water, and commune with the animal and plant kingdoms.

At first, the humans accepted the Witches, and treated them fairly; but because the Witches were different, other humans began to fear the Wise Ones of the Lord and Lady. Thus the Witches became the Hidden Children, conducting their rites of positive energy in secret lest they risk capture and death at the hands of fearful humans.

As the world grew darker with ignorance and hate of human creation, the Lady took the body of the moon to represent the gentle light of her perfect peace, and the Lord took the vibrant rays of the sun as his symbol of strength in perfect love. And once a month, when the moon is full, the Witches celebrate and remember the blessings our Mother has bestowed upon us. We call forth her energy to help us take care of ourselves, our families, our planet, and our friends. Four times a year, as the sun cycles through the seasons, the Witches celebrate the festivals of fire and honor the Lord and his love for us. At the four quarters of the seasons, the Witches honor the cycle of life and the gifts of the earth.

The Lady has many names—Isis, Astarte, Bride, Diana, Aradia and thousands more—and the Lady walks within and beside each woman of every race. The Lord has many faces, from the strong Cernunnos to the delightful Pan. He guards and guides us and resides in each man of every race. When thunder roars in the heavens and lightning cracks from the ground, the Lord and Lady dance the divine myth of creation so that we may remember them and know that we are never alone. When the sun rises each morning, we bask in the joy of his love for us, and when the moon moves through her phases, we understand the cycle of birth, growth, death, and rebirth, as is the nature of our kind.

When it is our time, the Witches enter the **Summerland**. From the Spirit that moves and flows through the Lord and Lady, we continue to learn the mysticism of the universe so that we may return, life after life, to serve our brothers and sisters. In each lifetime, Spirit guides us through learning experiences, preparing us along the way for our individual missions. Sometimes we are born among our own kind, and in other instances we must seek out our spiritual family. Many of us do not remember our chosen

Summerland n. A Wiccan version of Heaven, this is where souls go after physical death to celebrate the afterlife and continue our spiritual education.

path until we reach adulthood but others, from the time they form their own thoughts, know instinctively of their heritage.

We are the Witches, the representatives of wisdom's growth on our planet. We are the Hidden Children, back from the dead. We are the People, the power, the change—and we have incarnated in every race and every culture. We are the angels of earth.

Reincarnation

One of the primary building blocks of the Wiccan faith includes the belief in reincarnation. When Witches die, we believe that we go to a place called the Summerland. In this realm of joy and learning, we reunite with those we love and begin to reassess our life on earth. When we are ready, we return to the earthly plane to continue to work out our Karma. Memories of former lives often surface when one studies the Craft, though we must keep in mind that who we were isn't as important as who and what we are *now*. Our task is to complete our personal missions so that we can become better people and enrich our souls. Witches universally believe that we are responsible for our actions, and we must accept that responsibility with clear thinking and an honest heart. If we become lost in following what once was, we can't complete what we can be.

The Cone of Power

You will often hear Witches discussing the cone of power. This cone of energy manifests when a single Witch or a group of Witches work magick or ritual together.

Imagine a group of people standing together in a circle. People who can dance well stand at strategic points in the circle. A candle sits on the floor in the middle of the circle, named for a magickal intention such as healing, prosperity, et cetera. The group of people dance around the candle in a deosil (jes-il, clockwise) pattern until they believe they have created enough energy to send into the universe to make the change they desire. If the group of people have gathered to banish something, they begin dancing deosil (clockwise) to unite themselves in a common cause, and finish widdershins (counterclockwise), a predetermined amount of rounds of each. Then the people form a line with hands and rush toward the candle shouting the thing they want (or don't want). Does this sound silly? Did you notice that I *didn't* say these people were Witches?

Any group of people can use song, dance, chanting, or prayer to create energy, whether those people participate in a rock concert, go dancing at a school fling, watch or participate in a sports event, sit in a church service, or whirl around in a square dance in the school gym. Most of the people involved in any of these activities don't realize that they are raising energy, and so that energy dissipates into the universe without focused cause or good use.

Witches draw power from several sources, including Spirit, the Elements, the Ancestors, and the Angels. Any individual in any religion can draw power from these same sources. Witches use their own power—the power of the mind—to manifest what they need, whether they participate in a group environment or work alone.

Daily Devotions

Most Witches practice what we call daily devotions, where we take at least five to ten minutes twice a day to reaffirm our faith and talk to Spirit. Sometimes we do our daily devotions at our altar (you don't need to cast a magick circle for this) or we may walk outside and do our devotions there. It doesn't matter where you do your devotions, as long as you do them.

Your devotions can begin with a prayer you have written yourself, or you can just relax and talk to God in your own way. Some Witches sing, hum, or chant. You don't need to be a Witch to practice daily devotions. Any religion has room for such a practice.

You might begin by saying:

Blessed are my feet which walk the path of the Lord and Lady.
Blessed be my knees that kneel at the sacred altar.
Blessed be my heart that beats the drum of compassion.
Blessed be my lips that they may speak the truth.
Blessed be my eyes, so that they may see the wisdom of Spirit.
May the love of the Lord and Lady be within and around me
as I begin my journey through life this day.
So mote it be!

The Magick Circle

The knowledge of the **magick circle** is one of the greatest gifts given to us by Spirit. Conjuring a magick circle represents a mental art of the Witches, a technique learned early in our training. The magick circle functions as our church, our holy ground, and our place to hold power until we are ready to release that power. This circle also keeps negative energies away from us while we work, so that we may be pure in our intentions. Thanks to misinformation and Hollywood garbage, many people believe that the magick circle represents evil or holds evil. To these people, I say simply: "Get real. I've got better things to do with my time."

magick circle n. Powerful sacred space that represents Wiccan holy ground or a Wiccan temple.

Casting a magick circle is very easy, and you will find, as you study, that there are many ways to conjure your mental temple. Let's watch Angelique, my seventeen-year-old daughter, as she casts a magick circle.

Angelique walks to the center of the room, takes a deep breath, and relaxes into perfect calm. She then walks to the North of the room and holds her dominant hand out from her body, index finger pointing out and down. As she begins to walk the circle in a clockwise direction, speaking the words of the circle casting, she imagines a beautiful hedge springing up as her finger glides along through the air. Angelique says:

I conjure thee, O great circle of power,
so that you will be for me a boundary
between the world of men and the mighty spirits,
a meeting place of perfect love, trust, peace, and joy
containing the power I will raise within thee.
I call upon the guardians of the North, the East, the South, and the West
to aid me in this consecration.
In the name of the Lord and the Lady
thus I do conjure thee, O great circle of power!

By the time Angelique finishes saying the words, she has walked the circle three times. The circle does not have to be as big as the room, the circle can be as small as she likes, as long as she remains standing (or sitting) within the boundaries. Now Angelique walks to the North quarter of her circle, pounds her hand on the ground, and says:

As above, so below, this circle is sealed!

Angelique has just affirmed that her circle is a large bubble, reaching above her head and below her feet.

Once Angelique has cast the circle, she tries not to walk in and out of the energy she has cast. Over time, you will become sensitive to the energies of the circle boundary and feel the difference of having a circle and not having one. If Angelique needs to go get something outside the circle, she will "cut a door" with her hands (like parting a curtain) and then close the circle from the other side (like letting the curtain fall back into place). She'll get what she needs, and then open the circle and close the circle again. Angelique will try not to leave the circle too often, because each time she cuts the door she weakens the circle's structure.

When Angelique is ready to take the circle down, she will walk counterclockwise, starting from the West, moving South, East, then North, drawing the energy back into her finger. When she reaches the West again, she will pound the ground with her hand and say:

> This circle is open, but never broken.
> So mote it be!
> We are the people, we are the power,
> and we are the change!
> Merry meet and merry part,
> until we merry meet again!

You should perform most magickal work and ritual celebrations within a magick circle. After you read the next section about proper preparation, why don't you try casting and releasing the magick circle? Nothing will jump out of the woodwork and bite you, honest!

Properly Prepared

In the Craft, no one may enter a magick circle unless they are properly prepared. This means that a person has either dedicated themselves to Spirit, been initiated into the Craft by other Witches, or is willing to set aside any differences or negativity to work with the Witches. To be properly prepared also means that you are willing to talk to Spirit about your problems and your triumphs. Finally, properly prepared means that before you entered the magick circle (our church) you have cleansed your mind, body, and spirit of all negativity. Many Witches take a ritual bath to cleanse their bodies before they enter the magickal circle to show themselves and Spirit that they have washed away any impurities. Often, when a Witch enters a magick circle, another Witch anoints his or her forehead and sprinkles water on him or her, saying, "May you be cleansed, purified, and regenerated, and may the Lord and Lady instill you with their blessings. So mote it be!" to symbolize purification. A Witch working alone does the same thing. In a Catholic church, believers follow a similar practice with holy water, and then they genuflect to show their reverence to Spirit. In a Protestant church, believers often whisper in the sanctuary to show their reverence to Spirit. As you can see, different religions honor God in various ways.

The Oath of Secrecy

Many Witches, upon their initiation, or in their self-dedication ceremony, take an oath of secrecy. Does this mean that they can't tell anyone about anything in the Craft? No, obviously, because I'm telling you a bunch of stuff and I haven't ever broken my oath. So what does this oath entail, and why do you have to take an oath in the first place? If you are familiar with the term "confirmation" then you will understand the Wiccan Oath. In a confirmation, you tell Spirit that you believe in the existence of God/dess, and that you will work very hard to create harmony for yourself and for other people in the name of that belief. The same principles apply in the Wiccan Oath. The only difference in our Oath, and the oaths of some other religions, is that the Craft does not stipulate that you believe in only one kind of God. We think that Spirit has many faces, and all faces are holy.

Everything in the Wiccan Oath could be said in any religion, and has been said by them, in their own way, at one time or another. If you don't think there's magick in the structured religions, think again. Little old ladies with rosaries can pack a powerful wallop with prayer magick.

Gee. Bummer. No plastic on the floor. No documents signed in blood. No devil waiting to grind your head under cloven hoof. No diabolical chanting to make the hairs on your neck rise or your heart slam against your chest in terror. Guess you'll just have to go to the movies for that kind of stuff, huh?

The Signs and Symbols of the Craft

Just as the Christians use the cross and fish as their sacred symbols, and the Jewish faith uses the Star of David, the Wiccan faith has sacred signs and symbols that represent Spirit. The most misunderstood symbol, of course, is the five-pointed star, commonly known as the pentagram, point up. A pentacle is a five-pointed star, point up, with a circle around the star. The pentacle stands for Earth, Air, Fire, Water, and the Spirit of the human, encompassed by the never-ending love (the circle) of Spirit. Witches often wear this symbol for protection and an affirmation of their faith. Wearing the symbol where everyone can see it isn't necessary. The symbol carries more power if you keep it under your clothes and causes much less confusion for you if you keep the symbol hidden. Of course, if you wish to wear your pentacle outside your clothing, that's okay too. Some Wiccan traditions put the pentacle in the center of their altars, where others place this symbol in the North, representing prosperity. Still other traditions don't put the symbol on the altar at all.

In the movies, you may have seen the pentacle drawn on the middle of the floor with a candle setting at each point of the pentacle to represent the magick

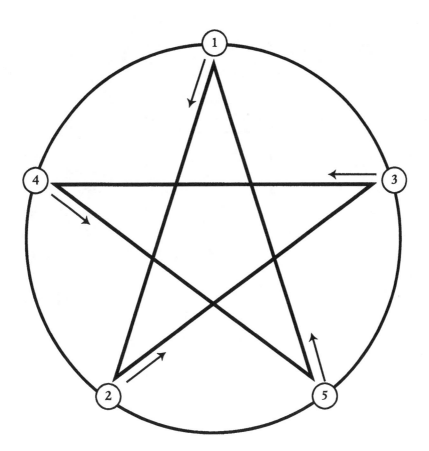

Invoking Pentagram

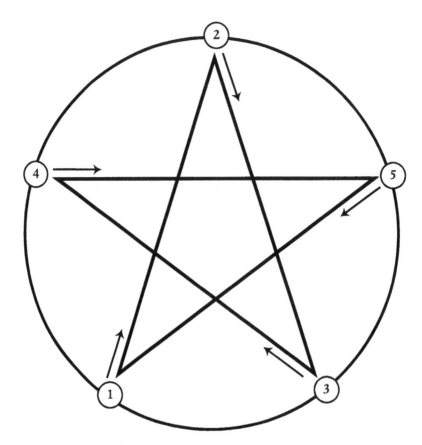

Banishing Pentagram

circle boundaries. In all honesty, most Witches don't do this practice. And to be very honest with you, I've never seen this done firsthand, and I've participated in hundreds of rituals all over the United States. Even most Witches who have ritual rooms set aside for their magickal work or wheel of the year celebrations don't paint the pentacle on the floor.

In magick, you can draw a pentagram several ways. The invoking pentagram is most commonly drawn starting at the top of the star (see the numbered diagram on p. 31), and the banishing pentagram is done the exact opposite (above).

Draw the invoking pentagram in the air, on a candle, or on a piece of paper to bring energies to you. Draw the banishing pentagram in the air, on a candle, or on a piece of paper to push negative energies away from you. You can also draw the pentagram to invoke the energies of Earth, Air, Fire, and Water, but I'm not going to go into those symbols in this book; however, I do want you to know that they exist, and are used by many Witches.

The use of the star, or pentacle, dates back beyond Christianity to the time of the stellar religions. Stars were also prominent in Egyptian beliefs (the Goddess Nuit, for example). Stars symbolize sacred or celestial fire and can be associated with the Wiccan need-fires or bale fires (the representation of stars on earth—therefore melding the energies of earth and heaven together—heaven being the fire, earth representing the wood used to feed the fire, and the sacred breath, oxygen, to grant continuance of both).

The sacred spiral, a very old symbol, represents the dance of divine energy within the world of the Witch. Drawn clockwise, the sacred spiral brings things to you; drawn counterclockwise, the sacred spiral pushes negative energies away from you. The spiral also signifies our ancient journey within, because if we do not know ourselves, then we can never seek to know what may be outside us. Witches often enjoy the spiral dance in ritual, which affirms our belief in the continuation of life through the patterning of a double spiral.

Sacred Spirals (counterclockwise and clockwise)

Equal-Armed Cross

The equal-armed cross represents another powerful magickal symbol. This cross stands for many ideals—the four seasons, the four directions, the four archangels, the four winds, the four quarters of the magick circle, and more. Drawn in the air or on paper from top to bottom and right to left with the right hand, the symbol represents healing energies. Drawn from top to bottom and left to right with the left hand signifies banishing negative energies. A Witch also employs the equal-armed cross to "seal" a magickal working so that negative energies cannot reverse the positive efforts of the magickal person.

The symbol of the Goddess (full moon in the middle flanked by crescent moons) signifies the feminine aspect of Spirit, women's mysteries, and the healing of the divine. Witches use this symbol to connect with the divine feminine and wear the image to show their faith in the Lady.

Goddess Symbol

As you can see, none of these signs or symbols speak of any evil intent, and shame on those who have told you differently!

The Book of Shadows

A **Book of Shadows**, commonly called the BOS, represents the spiritual testimony of a Witch. Before we begin on this topic, I need to tell you that no such thing exists as the Grand Grimoire. A Grimoire is another name for the Book of Shadows, but no such "grand" book exists. That idea came out of, you guessed it, a movie.

The Book of Shadow's importance does not lie in the words, though surely these words can function as a key to open your mind. The Book of Shadows can be the representation of work compiled by a group mind, such as a coven, a tradition, a clan, or a

Book of Shadows n. A collection of spiritual lessons, spells, magickal rules, and other information that is written down as a reference book.

single person. The BOS proves the survival of the tradition, clan, or coven, and of course, yourself. You must live the Craft to understand the import of the BOS, which is why most Witch traditions, clans, or families do not offer the Book of Shadows until the student has progressed several years in training designed just for them.

The BOS also represents the oath you took during your **Ceremony of Initiation**. The book becomes a physical link to the group mind; however, don't mistake the BOS for the group mind. It is not. If someone steals a BOS, the members of a tradition or clan are not as upset about the material as they are about the unethical act. To remove a piece of the group mind by dishonor is to break the oath taken during the Ceremony of Initiation. Members of the group will not have to sit and do bad mo-jo on you—the unethical circumstance will reap its own Karma.

Ceremony of Initiation n. A ceremony of honor conducted by a group welcoming an initiate into the Craft.

Books of Shadows don't often carry a copyright, and we have a good reason for this. After all, a BOS can contain many passages you have copied from preexisting works. Witches rely on each other for material, much as professional writers do. If you can remember to annotate where you got the information for future generations of Witches in your BOS, please do so. After all, we want to stay ethical. Items from others often mingle with original material. Depending on how often Witches have copied the book, material can be lost or gained. We've seen this in the nine-year cycle of the Black Forest Clan. The BOS our students receive may not be the one given five years ago, due to the growth of the group. This is another reason we don't have heart failure if the BOS goes where it shouldn't. By the time the BOS gets where the material wasn't supposed to go, the information will be outdated. The BOS becomes a representation of bits and pieces of people all over the world, each giving to the book.

You will find a personal BOS (one compiled by yourself) far more valuable than one from any tradition or clan, simply because of the effort you took to put that book together. Your BOS can contain personal experiences, dreams, drawings, calligraphy, revelations, et cetera. The book will represent the sum of your magickal life. You cannot appreciate a tradition's BOS or a coven's BOS until you have written your own—hence another reason you will not immediately receive this BOS if you belong to a coven, clan, tradition, or Witch family. You should begin by making your own. Anyone of any faith can make a personal Book of Shadows. Here you write down prayers you like, things you see that may be magickal or spiritual, poems you compose to express your feelings, or drawings you create to touch the spirit within you and the Spirit who loves us all.

Dedication and Initiation

Just how does a person become a Witch? Today, we have all sorts of Wiccan sects. Some Wiccans argue that the only way to become a Witch involves the initiation process performed for you by a Witch (meaning it takes a Witch to make a Witch). Other Wiccan groups feel that with self-study and honest observance of our laws and customs an individual can dedicate oneself to the Wiccan faith. The argument over initiation began about thirty years ago when the religion of WitchCraft experienced a sudden boost in popularity. At the time, there were not enough traditional teachers to meet the rising interest in the religion. To assist in this tidal wave of interest, several Witches came out of the closet and began to write about the Craft, feeding as much information as they could to a salivating public. These well-known and respected authors include Raymond Buckland, Sybil Leek, Janet and Stewart Farrar (pronounced Fair-er), Z. Budapest, Starhawk, Doreen Valiente, Patricia Crowly, Scott Cunningham, Marion Weinstein, Laurie Cabot, and others. Through these authors many individuals can piece together enough information on modern-day WitchCraft to begin their solitary (or group) practices. Thus, the birth of what we call "eclectic" Wicca, a form of Wicca where an individual does not belong to a particular tradition, group, or sect, took place. Today, we have as many eclectic practitioners as there are Traditional practitioners. Neither grouping can or should be considered better than the other.

As defined earlier, an initiation consists of a group of individuals who care enough about a person that they will perform the ceremony of change for them. The initiation procedure primarily belongs to the traditional Witches, though some eclectic covens and groups use the initiation procedure. If you belong to a traditional group that has a hierarchy (form of government), then you will most likely go through their initiation ceremonies. And yes, there usually is more than one ceremony. As you learn, you progress through specific levels of training. The highest level, that of eldership, represents a place of honor and skill reserved for older Wiccans. Confirmation and first communion are familiar ceremonies that coincide with the purpose and mystique of the Wiccan Initiation.

A **dedication**, on the other end of the broomstick, normally consists of a ceremony that an individual does for him or herself, to state, in ritual, that he or she believes in the laws and structure of the Craft, and that he or she will try his or her best to follow those laws. Most eclectic Wiccans have enacted some sort of dedication ritual. In a dedication, the individual tells the Lord and Lady (or Spirit) that he or she is ready to follow the Wiccan way. Some traditional groups also require a dedication period of a year and a day before the individual experiences the initiation ceremony. Neither the dedication ceremony nor the initiation requires a person to "give up" a previous or current faith.

dedication n. An individual's statement, through ceremony, that affirms his or her dedication to Craft laws and structure and to deity.

So just what happens in an initiation? Initiation ceremonies vary from group to group, yet four aspects remain the same: the purification, the challenge, the symbolic death and rebirth of the individual, and the oath. A dedication consists of two parts: the purification and the testimony of dedication.[1]

The High Priestess and the High Priest

In many books on Wicca and WitchCraft, especially those dealing with group activities, you will read about the High Priest and the High Priestess. Sometimes the High Priest and High Priestess of a group are married, and sometimes they are not. As no sexual activity occurs during one's fulfillment of duties as either the High Priest or High Priestess, it doesn't really matter if they have taken marriage vows or not.

The High Priest and High Priestess function as a team of spirituality, working toward the betterment of the group to whom they have pledged responsibility. Both perform ministerial responsibilities such as counseling, training, and the working of ceremonies and rituals. That's right, our High Priest and High Priestess perform the same function in our religious groups as do the ministers and priests in other religious structures.

Our Special Days

Esbats

The thirteen full moons of the year hold sacred energies associated with the Great Goddess and to the Moon. Traditionally, these thirteen full moons coincide with the thirteen Esbats of the year. These days, many Witches hold Esbats every week or at least twice a month. In some Craft traditions, these working

---

1. If you'd like more information on how to perform a dedication ceremony, I have provided those details in my book *To Ride a Silver Broomstick*.

nights, called Minor Feasts, offer an array of food after the ritual. Participants bring all sorts of things to eat and drink, including one hot item, such as soup, or other covered dish. Esbats performed on a full moon represent ritual working occasions at the time when the Goddess is at her full power. In some groups, individuals perform their Esbats alone, with the Sabbats reserved for group activity. In other Witch traditions, the entire group celebrates Esbats and Sabbats together. If you are a Witch working alone, you will celebrate the Esbats and Sabbats by yourself. Esbats represent celebrations of creative life force throughout the universe, and during them Witches often work petition and candle magick to achieve their goals. An Esbat, whether performed solitarily or with a group, gives the Witch personal time to link their spirit with deity. If you have not figured it out by now, a one-on-one relationship with Spirit is vitally important to any Witch.

In a group format, Witches choose the Esbat as a working session for coven business, for the teaching of Craft history or magickal practices, initiations, or for engaging in special magickal projects. Whenever possible, the coven or solitary works within a magick circle to contain the power generated by any workings performed. In a solitary format, Witches utilize Esbat energy to connect with Spirit, meditate, or work toward personal goals to enhance the Witch's life. Traditionally, Witches employ Esbats to perform divinations for the benefit of themselves, friends, and family members. No matter the solitary or group format, the consecration of **cakes and ale**, our communion, is customary at Esbats during the performance of ritual in a magick circle. These days, most Witches do not use alcoholic beverages, and prefer a natural beverage, such as fruit juice.

Witches perform Esbats indoors and outside, depending on facilities available and the type of ceremony planned. For coven and solitary magick, Witches find Esbats provide a powerful connection to the Goddess, especially if the ceremony falls within the sphere of Moon energy. Drawing down the moon by the High Priestess is a regular part of highly ritualistic Esbats in some traditions; in others, any coven member, or the entire coven, may participate in the drawing down the moon ceremony. At a solitary Esbat, a Witch usually draws the energy of the moon into him or herself.

cakes and ale n. The Wiccan communion that consists of a natural beverage and cake offered to each participant in a ritual.

If coven members wish to perform a special ritual, the Esbat is an appropriate time to do it. Handfastings (marriages) and Wiccanings/Sainings (christenings) may be done at Esbats, as well as Goddess-oriented rituals, the charging of talismans or amulets, or the consecration of tools, et cetera. As you can see, the Esbat provides the foundation ceremony for various magickal applications. Performing many different activities during an Esbat ceremony is usual for a Witch, especially if the Witch has spellwork or consecrations to do.

Traditionally, most early American Witches spent the evening of the full moon in prayer, personal celebration, and magickal workings to draw on in the coming month. They would mix herbs, make magickal cords, grind powders, and empower amulets and talismans.

Sabbats

In Paleopagan times (over 4,000 years ago), there were only two fire festivals, Beltaine and Samhain, to welcome and to bid farewell to the seasons of birth and death. At the appropriate hour, at the highest point on the land, the people would light the bonfires, one by one, until the entire countryside blazed with controlled fires. To many Europeans, the official ceremony began at the dying of the sun the day before the holiday and ended three days hence at sunset. These **fire festivals** were associated with planting, harvesting, and hunting ceremonies. Some Witches call the fire festival days the "days of power." As European history progressed, two additional holidays were added: Imbolgc and Lammas, creating the four fire festivals. German Pagans added the equinoxes and solstices, creating eight High Holy Days (rather than the original four).

fire festivals n. First consisting of Beltaine and Samhain. Imbolgc and Lammas were added at a later date. These four festivals are associated with planting, harvesting, and hunting ceremonies.

During medieval times, church chroniclers decided to turn the history of these Pagan events into a weapon of misinformation. They wished to discourage the faithful from entertaining thoughts of celebrating these Pagan holidays. The practice of rewriting current and historical events to meet specific needs is called historical revisionism. The church chroniclers practiced historical revisionism by collectively naming the eight Pagan holidays "Sabbats." The word "Sabbat" comes from the French derivation of *s'battre*, meaning "to frolic" or "to celebrate." Church officials contended that people who participated in the Pagan celebrations were frolicking with the Devil, and therefore Sabbats were evil. Many dictionaries and folklore compilations of today still incorrectly associate Sabbats with evil, which truly isn't the case, where others have begun to weed out the historical inaccuracies.

The Wicca of today celebrate the eight festivals much like our ancestors of the past. The Sabbats track the movement of the Sun through the year and are thought to bring good fortune and prosperity according to the segment of the year to which each holiday relates. This means that our Sabbats are seasonally driven, and that we use the energies of the changing seasons to enhance our lives. This cycle of growth and death is described as the Wheel of the Year.

Sometimes Wiccans will refer to Sabbats as "Major Feasts" because we always have tons of great food to eat after the holiday ceremony.

In the ceremonies of many Wiccan traditions, these rituals allow the male energy to come into balance with that of the female energy. The events include a re-enactment of a legend associated with the individual holiday. The re-enactment (or play) is based on a story or legend that contains a moral. Not every Wiccan group re-enacts the same legend for the same holiday, which can be confusing to the newcomer.

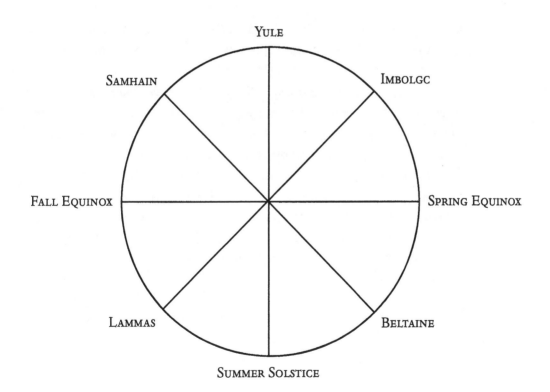

Wheel of the Year

In the next section I list the eight sabbats and mention some of the more common themes, but I do not explain the legends, as the legends would take up a book in themselves. I merely mention them so that as you go further in your studies and read other books on Wicca, you will have at least been introduced to them here.

The Greater Sabbats

The Four Greater Sabbats or Fire Festivals are as follows:

1. **Samhain** (pronounced *Sow-een, Sow-in,* or *Sav-ain*)—October 31 through November 11, depending on the tradition and schedule of the group. This is the "Witch's New Year" and the primary Sabbat from which all others flow. Some Witches say that Faery Hills open this night, and contact with them is a great possibility, for your good or ill. At this time the veils between the worlds of the living and the dead wane thin; therefore, this eve of celebration often lends itself to remembering those we have loved who have gone beyond the veil. Since Witches believe in reincarnation, we know that our loved ones have not ceased to exist, and that their spirits live on. In this way, Samhain also represents a celebration of continued life. Witches count Samhain as the third and final harvest celebration of the eight Wiccan holidays, and the holiday is the largest Major Feast of the Turning of the Wheel (however, the Witches harvest nothing from their fields or gardens this night). You might decorate your altar with pumpkins, Indian corn, hay, gourds, and other fare related to the season.

    In some traditions, the cauldron becomes the primary magickal tool for this Sabbat, and the ceremony may revolve around an invitation to the Crone (Wise Woman) to bring wisdom to the Witch or the legend of the Goddess Cerridwen, or the ceremony might also include the story of mourning for the dying God, much like a Good Friday service in the Christian religion speaks of the death of Christ. Totem energies range high at this time of year and ritual masks, depicting personal or group power animals, can be worn by those people who stand at the four quarters. Witches may use ritual drumming to summon positive energies or family spirits. Scrying and regression meditations also find favor this night. The practice of bobbing for apples at a Halloween party comes from our Pagan ancestors, who highly valued apple magick. Once the Witch caught the apple in his or her teeth, a little of his or her soul crept into the apple. The Witch either ate the apple for prosperity or buried the apple on the property to ensure continued bounty over the long winter months.

2. **Imbolgc** (pronounced *em-bowl/g*)—February 2 (sometimes called Candlemas). In this ceremony we honor the Goddess and her recovery of giving birth to the God, and the advent of the birth and growth of the land. Many Witches incorporate the Celtic Triple Goddess Brigid or Breid, who represents fire, water, healing, inspiration, and artistic endeavors into their Imbolgc rites. In some rituals, the High Priestess of a group will wear a crown of lights, signifying the Goddess' strength and her movement of the seasons into the light of the spring and summer months. Imbolgc represents the first day of the Wiccan spring. The Celtic God celebrated might be Lugh, the Solar God. The word "Candlemas" represents the many candles lit this night to signify the awakening of the earth. Sometimes, Witches call Imbolgc "The Festival of Light." The light of the candles corresponds to sympathetic magick, drawing the essence of the sun to the people. Place a bowl of melted snow on the altar to speed the spring season. The primary magickal tool of this Sabbat is candle magick.

3. **Beltaine** (pronounced *beel-teen* or *Beel-tawn-uh*)—April 30 or May 1, falls opposite of Samhain. Witches consider this holy day the second greatest Sabbat of the eight Wiccan ceremonies. As Samhain encompasses the celebration of death, Beltaine regales the festival of rebirth. This is the holiday of the bale fire that brings blessings into the home. When the Witches incorporated the cross-quarters into Western Wicca, the family stripped Yule's pine tree and the trunk went in the wood shed to be saved for the maypole. Ribbons of white (for the Goddess) and red (for the God), secured firmly to the top of the pole, flow out in gentle breezes of spring until the dancers take up the ribbons and weave them around the pole to the beat of lively music, rattles, or drums. Holding the ribbons first high, and then low, the red ribbons moving clockwise and the white ribbons moving counterclockwise, the participants weave security and bounty into their personal lives for the coming months. With the last few feet of ribbon, all the dancers move clockwise to seal prosperity and growth for the group throughout the coming season. You might decorate your altar with hawthorn, spring greenery, items made in the winter season for spring and summer use, holey stones (stones with a natural holes in them), flowers, et cetera. Menstruating women paraded over the fields on brooms to encourage fertility in the land. Beltaine is far from a solemn holiday, and is known for its feasting, laughter, and fun. East is the opening and closing quarter.

Romance and love play an intricate role in Beltaine celebrations, as on this holiday we envision the love between our Lord and Lady. Laughter, song, and dance take high precedence in our rituals for this occasion.

In many Craft traditions, hivings (so called for when a group grows too large and part of the group leaves to form a new group), degree ceremonies, open study groups, new training classes, the naming of a coven, the development of traditional or personal insignia, and other group-related projects begin with this holiday.

4. **Lammas** (pronounced *Lam-mahs*)—August 1, is primarily a Sabbat to honor Lugh, a representation of the Celtic Sun God. Sometimes called the Wedding Feast and in other instances the First Feast of Harvest. The first of the three harvest Sabbats, and third-largest feast, this holiday gives thanks to Spirit for the abundance of the earth. The Sabbat's Gaelic name is Lunasa. Witches usually place food from the land or sea on the altar and set up a large dining table near the ritual site. Unlike many other Sabbats, Lammas usually becomes an all-day event with a picnic, games, and generous chatter. Altar decorations include food from the fields, wedding ribbons and flowers, et cetera. North American Witches view this festival as the primary grain harvest, and the ritual of bread baking often becomes incorporated in the festivities.

Lammas represents the Wiccan Thanksgiving, and is the birth holiday for the modern American Thanksgiving. This celebration, enacted by the Puritans only twice in the New World, represented the European Pagan practice of Harvest Home.

The Lesser Sabbats

In Wicca, Witches also celebrate the lesser or cross quarter Sabbats plus the four fire festivals mentioned earlier. These lesser Sabbats are:

1. **Winter Solstice** or **Yule**, known as Finn's Eve (falls around December 21 or 22—the exact dates of the solstices and equinoxes change each year). At the Winter Solstice the Witches celebrate the rebirth of the God as he returns to bring warmth and fertility to the hearts of humankind. The Old Custom believed that lights and candles were used to lure him out of the womb of his mother. It is a custom to leave all the lights burning, or an oil lamp on the altar, for the duration of this night. In one legend associated with this holiday, the Oak King (of the waxing year) fights and suppresses

the Holly King (of the waning year) at this time. Witches see the Holly King as Father Christmas, wearing his color of red with holly in his hat, driving a sleigh of eight (Sabbat) deer (symbols of the horned God).

Witches envision the Yule tree as the "wish" tree, where all your wishes for the new year hang in the arms of the universe. The pine tree represents the Goddess, as this tree doesn't die through the winter season. Save a small part of the trunk for next year's Yule fire. The larger portion of the trunk might find its way to an outside magick circle, where the Witch pounds the trunk into the ground around the circle to form a magickal barrier through the years, or, as mentioned earlier, the family might save the trunk for the maypole of spring.

The wreath is a symbol of the Wheel of the Year, and items placed on it should represent those things that you wish to bring into form by the next Yule celebration.

You may think that Witches are trying to copy their Yule to the celebration of Christmas, but this isn't the case. Early Christian scholars could not come up with an accurate date for the birth of Christ. Since the position of the Church was to convert the Pagan population, the Church superimposed the birth date of Christ over the original Pagan celebration.

2. **Spring Equinox** or **Ostara** (March 21 or 22), known by Wiccans as Ostara (pronounced *Oh-star-ah*). Sometimes called "Lady Day," this holiday represents the return of fertility to the land. The holiday finds more influence through the Nordic, Greek, and Roman deities than anything else.

    In some Wiccan traditions, for one week prior to this date, each Witch should take into account all the injustices they have done to their families and friends. The individual writes down his or her negative acts and, throughout the week, must seek to create balance with those whom they have injured through apology, paying back past due loans, et cetera. On circle night the Witch brings the list, with what the Witch has done to Karmically right each problem, into the celebration. In ritual the Witch burns the paper, wiping clean his or her Karmic slate.

    Quiet family celebrations may include the coloring of eggs, especially if the Witch has children. The school system dictates the time children have off, so many adult Witches move their Ostara celebrations closer to those of the modern-day religions to include their children in celebrations.

3. **Summer Solstice** (June 21 or 22) is when Witches celebrate the strength of the God in all his passion and glory. On this day, the God reaches his peak. Another bale fire holiday, Summer Solstice celebrations may include the nine traditional woods to create the blaze. The Oak King and Holly King who fought at Yule return to fight again. This time the Holly King becomes the victor in battle and reigns until Yule. Witches make protective solar amulets during this season to take care of both family and traditional concerns. All sacred plants (as in the Druidic tradition) have reached their magickal peak. Witches will harvest these herbs on this day.

Familiars and family pets find a special place of honor at this festival, and Witches bring their pets into the magickal circle for blessing and protective magick.

4. **Fall Equinox** or **Mabon** (September 21 or 22)—The name "Mabon" comes from the Welsh God who symbolized male fertilization in the Arthurian myth. Like Ostara, Witches did not observe this Sabbat until the Norse invaded the islands. Mabon has a twofold principle, where the holiday centers on the celebration of cutting things out of your life and also honoring the female dead of the family. Some Celtic Witches believed that since the God was reabsorbed into the womb of the Goddess, only women inhabited Tir-na-nog, and that place became known as the Land of Women. Witches might make new wands and staves of willow, a practice handed down from our Druidic ancestors.

Fall Equinox is the second fall harvest of the Wiccans, and items on the altar include autumn leaves, fruits of harvest, pumpkins, dried corn, et cetera.

* ⋆ *

On the Equinoxes, day and night are equally long; these are days of great power in terms of universal balance. The Winter Solstice, the shortest period of daylight of the year, marks the rebirth or re-emergence of the sun. The days will then progressively lengthen. At Summer Solstice, the sun is at its peak, and this burning orb represents the God's great and kingly powers. All nature spirals to its highest point at this time. Witches view the Solstices as festive days, where the Equinoxes become days of reflection and self-examination.

The greater and lesser Sabbats form an eightfold spoke around the Wheel of the Year that represents the journey of life. We are all part of the Great Design of the Universe, changing and returning to a beginning; to celebrate the Sabbats is to place yourself actively on this wheel. In a Sabbat, including the consecration of cakes and ale (communion) is standard plus some form of ritual activity that marks the drama of the season.

The Feast was a traditional custom of both Esbats and Sabbats in Britain. Usually the keeper of the covenstead (home or collection place of the Witches) or the person whose house where all are assembled would be responsible for providing meat or stew cooked there, while other Witches would bring wine, bread, and other foods. When meeting outdoors, a major function of the coven cauldron involved the heating of stew or soup brought along for the Feast. Sometimes Witches held the Feast during the ritual; other times, Witches released the circle first. Making the music at the Feast fell to the musicians in the coven. All others would dance. Some elements of this tradition remain in modern covens, as participants normally bring food and several groups beg the talents of their members in song and dance. In some covens, each member participating in ritual brings something to present at the altar—flowers, greens, pine cones, gourds, candles, incense, or other appropriate altar decorations brought as gifts to the Gods.

Solitary observance of Sabbats and Esbats is often quite different from group celebrations. Some solitaries mark the Sabbat by decorating their home and altar, cooking a special meal, doing a small working at the altar, et cetera. Many solitaries save the bulk of their magickal work for the full moon, and spend this night taking care of their own magickal needs. A Witch working by oneself may choose to perform an entire ritual Esbat or Sabbat alone.

Sacred Space

Witches work and talk to Spirit in sacred space or sacred space and a magick circle together. Sacred space represents our temple, but it is not a magick circle. We cast our magick circle in the sacred space. This temple of sacred space can be a physical area or a nonphysical one. Yes, you can *even* create sacred space in your mind. I've gotten lots of letters from teenagers whose parents refuse to listen to them about their interest in the Craft, and therefore forbid them to have a holy place in their rooms. Rather than feel like you can't practice the Craft in physical sacred space, create a sacred space in your mind. We teach the big Witches to do this too, as the mental arts have great importance in Craft training. Imagining sacred space is a good way to begin your mental training.

To create physical sacred space we choose an object that represents the four elements. Let's say that Falynn, my fourteen-year-old daughter, wants to create sacred space. She chooses incense to represent Air, a candle to represent Fire, a bowl of water to represent Water, and salt for the Earth. She holds her hands over each object and asks that Spirit cleanse, consecrate, and regenerate the object in the name of Spirit. She might say:

> Holy Mother, I cleanse this water of all negativity in this world
> and in the astral. I consecrate and regenerate this water
> in the name of the Lord and Lady.

Then Falynn would do the same things for the other representations of the elements. She can start with any element—the order doesn't really matter.

Once Falynn has done this, she will take three pinches of the salt and add them carefully to the water. When she finishes, she will stir the water three times with the index finger of her dominant hand in a clockwise direction. Then she will hold her hands over the water and say:

> In the name of the Mother and the Father
> I ask for the blessings of love,
> harmony, and peace upon this water.

As Falynn says the words, she imagines that the water begins to glow with white light. Once the white light gets very big in her mind, she will stop. Falynn has just made holy water.

Why don't you take a moment and collect your four representations of the elements? I'll wait, I promise.

⋆ ⋆ ⋆

Now that you've collected your things, cleanse and consecrate them just like Falynn did, then make your holy water. Wasn't that easy? You just did your first Witchie thing! I'm proud of you. If your parents or guardian doesn't let you use incense or candles, think of something else that will represent those elements to you. It's okay. Anything will do if you handle the objects with reverence. For example, you could use a feather instead of the incense, and a red ball to represent Fire.

Once you have cleansed and consecrated your objects, you are ready for the next step, creating your sacred space. Beginning with your North object (the salt for Falynn) you will move around the room in a clockwise circle, sprinkling just a bit of this salt as you go. Let's see what Falynn is doing. There she is. She's sprinkling the salt, saying:

> I cleanse, consecrate, and empower this sacred space
> with the element of Earth in the name of Spirit.

When she gets back to the North, she says:

> So mote it be!

This is the Wiccan way of saying "this is finished with my blessing."

Falynn picks up the East representation (the incense) and she does the same thing, walking around the room in a clockwise direction, saying:

> I cleanse, consecrate, and empower this sacred space
> with the element of Air in the name of Spirit.
> So mote it be!

Now Falynn picks up the candle, walks clockwise around the room, and says:

> I cleanse, consecrate, and empower this sacred space
> with the element of Fire in the name of Spirit.
> So mote it be!

Finally, Falynn will walk clockwise around the room holding the bowl of water, sprinkling a bit as she goes, saying:

> I cleanse, consecrate, and empower this sacred space
> with the element of Water in the name of Spirit.
> So mote it be!

Then Falynn walks to the center of the room, holds her hands above her head, palms facing upward, and says:

> In the name of the Lord and Lady,
> in the name of the Great Mother and Good Father,
> I cleanse, consecrate, and empower this sacred space
> with the element of Spirit!
> So mote it be!

Falynn has just completed creating sacred space. You can also use this procedure to rid a room of bad energies. Most Witches create sacred space at least once a month, whether they are doing magick, prayer, or meditation. Your mom or dad is right when she or he tells you that you have to keep your room clean. Negative energy will collect even in the cleanest room, but it's ever so much worse in a dirty one.

Witches also create sacred space before an Esbat or a Sabbat, or before casting a magick circle. Now that you've read what Falynn did to create sacred space, why not try this procedure yourself? Even if you aren't interested in becoming a Witch, I can't think of any reason you cannot create sacred space to bring harmony into your life, and the practice is absolutely acceptable for any religious philosophy.

The Altar

Most Witches have an altar in their sacred space. To a Witch, the altar represents his or her place of power, the spot that belongs to God. The Witch focuses his or her energies in many magickal workings on or near the altar. Every time a Witch walks by his or her altar, he or she automatically thinks of God. Your altar can be a night stand, a dresser, a little table, even a trunk—when you begin in the Craft it doesn't matter what your altar is, what matters is that you designate an altar for yourself and what your altar becomes.

My daughters and both of my sons, plus the big Witches in the family, use flat stones as our altars. We set these stones on tables or on the floor. You can keep your altar out all the time if you have permission, or put your altar away if the altar offends or upsets someone in the house. If you use a piece of furniture for your altar, then you can put your altar setup away when not in use. An altar setup consists of all the things a Witch puts on his or her altar. Witches who work in established, traditional groups have altar setups that pertain only to that group. These setups contain a representation of the four elements, a wand, a chalice, and other items. I'm not going to cover the traditional altar setup in this book as the teen Witch doesn't need them to begin studying the Craft. If you pursue the Craft, you'll learn about these tools later in your training. Right now, I'd like you to learn just the way I teach my own students here at the Black Forest Hearthstone. I'm more interested in teaching you how to become a better person, and to do that, you don't need the tools of the Craft, at least not right away.

Solitary Witch n. A Witch who works alone.

Solitary Witches don't have to follow the traditional group rules, and therefore many design their own altar setup.

What sorts of things go on an altar? Lots of times a Witch will have statues of the Lord and Lady, or a picture of something that they feel represents the

Witch's idea of God. Often we have a representation of each element, candles to see by (called illuminator candles), and any object that has importance to us. We try not to let our altar get too cluttered. To keep the altar from getting crowded with our special things,

shrine n. A sacred place that holds a collection of objects representing deity.

many Witches have a shrine area in their sacred space too. Although Witches offer prayers at a **shrine** they do not normally use the shrine surface in the same way they use the altar.

Since the altar holds great importance in our religion, we don't put anything on the altar that isn't holy or sacred—no cups of juice, cans of soda, homework papers, half-eaten cookies, books from school, makeup, sports equipment, or bits of odd clothing. We also don't let anyone play around on our altar, fiddle with what we've put there, or allow other people to remove things from it. This, I know, can be hard if we have curious parents, siblings, or friends. Over the years, I've had several teens tell me that their parents have desecrated their altars by coming into their rooms and destroying their holy things. These parents, sadly, act on their own fear. It never occurs to them that by burning books, breaking altar setups, and throwing out holy things that they have committed one of the most painful acts of cruelty that a human is capable of—dishonoring another's religious faith. These parents don't understand that their teen will never forget this act of destruction, and may not forgive them for a long time, if ever. I've had letters from adults who, when they were teens, have been victims of this type of negative behavior. Believe me, they have not forgotten, even if the destruction occurred twenty years ago. It saddens me to hear these kinds of stories. I understand that the parents or guardians acted on their own fear, but I am disheartened that they haven't found the strength or understanding in their own faith to be able to see the world around them clearly. One eighteen-year-old young man turned to his livid father, surveyed his smashed altar and holy things broken and tossed about the room, and said quietly, "How would you like it if I went into your church and did the same thing?" His father's jaw dropped. I realize the difficulties in teaching teen Witches to honor the faiths of others when our own faith so often becomes the victim of violence from those we love.

If you think you will have a problem with others where you live, keep in mind that your altar doesn't have to look like an altar to be an altar. For years I kept the main altar in my own home looking like an unusual collection of interesting items, just so visitors to the house would not give me or my family any grief. As

I grew stronger in my faith and interacted more in my community, I could tell others the good things about my faith. Now, I don't have any trouble, and have my altar in plain view of everyone from the mail-person to the mayor of the town. This movement from secrecy to total openness took several years. We'll talk more about how to deal with others in connection to your faith further on in the book.

Of course, not all parents will have difficulties with your interest in Witch-Craft. Some parents are open from the beginning, where others carefully read Craft material (like this book and others recommended in the suggested reading list) and then allow their teens to continue discovering the fantastic world of religion and Spirit. Hundreds of parents and guardians have turned to the Craft themselves once they have all the facts, and practice with their teens!

When there's no argument about having an altar, some Witches have large stone or ornate wooden altars. I've even seen portable altars that look like leather briefcases until you unfold them, slide the legs down, and set them up. Depending on the tradition or group a Witch belongs to, he or she may place a permanent altar in the North (for shamanic workings), in the East (for ceremonial workings), or move the altar with the cycle of the seasons. Some Witches prefer to place their altar in the center of the room, working around the altar as they work their magick, thereby increasing the power they raise by their continuous movement.

personal altar n. A surface designated by a Witch to represent his or her place of power.

As with sacred space, you don't have to be a Witch to have a home altar. Any faith will benefit from the construction of a **personal altar**.

What would a teen's altar look like? Let's check out the altars of some teen Witches that I know. Alicia's parents have always exercised free thinking and, after reading material on the Craft, have no difficulties with Alicia's interest. Her parents encourage her to look beyond conventional structured religion and often help her find special objects for her altar. Alicia's mother is head of the local library and her father is a professor at a nearby college. Alicia uses her bedroom dresser for her altar. She lives near the ocean and she loves anything that relates to the sea. At night, the gentle surf lulls her to sleep. She also uses the sea sounds to help her relax when meditating. Alicia embroidered an altar cloth (a cloth Witches use to cover the surface of the altar) with images of mermaids, seahorses, and waves. Because Alicia uses an altar cloth, she puts large nonflammable tiles underneath the two candle holders she chose in the shape of mermaids. Alicia positions these candle holders and tiles near the back of the altar. To represent the East and the element of air, Alicia found some nice seagull feathers on the beach. For South and fire, she chose a small candle holder that uses little candles. This candle holder has waves painted around the base. For the west, Alicia uses a seashell that holds about ½ cup water. On the North section of her altar, Alicia has another seashell that holds about ¼ cup salt. In the center of the altar, Alicia sets a pentacle she made out of tiny seashells. This pentacle took her hours to make, but Alicia knows that time spent making any magickal object builds power into that object, so she didn't mind all the hours she spent making it. Sometimes, Alicia leaves the gifts she finds from the sea on her altar, to show the Lord and Lady that she loves them.

Robert's parents both practice the Craft. His mother and father run a large open circle in the city. Robert's mother is an ER nurse and his father is the CEO of a large company. Robert has a major thing for wolves. He thinks wolves have an incredible mystique about them. Robert made a small table in shop class with an image of a wolf burned in the center. Robert uses small lanterns in place of illuminator candles. For incense, he burns a sage stick in a fire-safe bowl. For a representation of the God, Robert set a small set of deer antlers near the back of his altar. His ceramic water and salt bowls have pictures of a huntress and a stag dancing across the outer edge. Robert hung a large tapestry of a wolf on the wall behind his altar. The music of the woods dances through Robert's soul. He often places stones, moss, and other treasures on his altar as an offering to Spirit.

Julie's circumstances are a little different from those of Robert and Alicia. First, Julie shares a room with her younger sister, which gives her limited privacy. Secondly, Julie's father forbids the burning of candles in her room. He's afraid that Julie's younger sister, who is a handful, will knock a candle over and burn the house down. Julie's dad is a manager at the local Navy base. Her mother doesn't work outside the home. Although Julie's father doesn't have a problem with her interest in a different religion, Julie's mother doesn't understand the fascination. She feels that Julie should practice Catholicism, like she does. The family experienced strained relations when Julie tried to set up her altar. To keep emotions flowing smoothly, Julie put a statue of Mary on her desk and does magick with her rosary beads. She still attends mass, and sees the energy of the Mother as she manifests through Mary and the female saints. Although Julie would like to have a standard Wiccan altar, she knows she will eventually reap the rewards for her patience, and uses what she can right now. Julie loves her mother and doesn't want to upset her. In time, as Julie's spiritual-ity grows, her mother may see the difference in her behavior and allow Julie to practice more openly. Meanwhile, Julie hung posters of various Goddesses on her side of the room, mingled with scenes of unicorns, tigers, and medieval cas-tles. When Julie wants to meditate, she waits until her little sister falls asleep (if ever) and puts on the headphones to her CD. Julie does a lot of needlework, and uses the tiny stitches to make her own special kind of magick. No one ever knows the difference. Julie can't leave out bowls of salt and water because her little sister constantly touches all of Julie's stuff, nor does she use incense as her parents have forbidden any type of fire in her room. Instead, Julie brings in fresh flowers when she can, or sets out a bowl of potpourri.

Matthew has always shown artistic talent. He draws, paints, works with pot-tery, and does other artistic endeavors. He will be going to college in the fall, majoring in the fine arts. Matthew has a sister, but she has her own room, so at least he can set his altar up in relative privacy. Matt's dad doesn't live with the family. His mother is a supervisor at a grocery store. Matt's mom doesn't mind his interest in the Craft, and has read some books on the subject herself. Matt's father, on the other hand, would try to remove Matt and his sister from the home if he knew of Matt's interest. Matt's mom and dad don't get along, and Matt knows that his father would use Matt's newfound interest in the Craft to get back at his mother, so Matt keeps a very low profile whenever his father talks religion (which thankfully isn't very often). Matt's altar contains a collec-tion of his artwork. He has pictures, pottery, and other types of crafts depicting his vision of Spirit. Matt enjoys bright colors and intricate designs. If anyone walks into Matt's room, they think his altar represents nothing more than a col-lection of his artistic talents.

Let's peek at our last little Witch—Tabitha. Tabitha's mother and grand-mother are called family tradition, or fam trad, Witches. This means that they have a magickal/religious tradition handed down through the family for gener-ations. Usually such a tradition carries little organization, as the information traveled through the family by word of mouth. Fam trad Witches practice a great deal of folk magick. Folk magick consists of household tools, a smattering of moon and plant lore, favorite chants, charms, and songs, and, surprisingly enough, carries a hefty magickal wallop. Our Tabitha just turned ten, so her altar and magickal practices may be different from the older kids simply because of her age. When Tabitha practices ritual, she puts her favorite stuffed animals at the quarters. She has a bear in the North, a deer (I believe it's Bambi) in the East, a bull (from her uncle who visited Spain last year) in the South, and a horse (from her Chincoteague Island vacation last summer) in the West. Her center totem animal is a stuffed wolf shipped to her at Yule from her **Goddess Mother** who lives near Niagara Falls. Sometimes, Tabitha creates her magick circle with all of her stuffed animals, while she stands in the middle and surveys her imitation fur and foam circle. Sometimes she casts her magick

Goddess Mother n. A Wiccan Godmother.

circle with a big feather. A friend of her mother's wrapped the base of the feather with rawhide and strung some pretty beads on the rawhide's ends. Tabitha also has a stick hung with lots of tiny bells. When she wants to send messages to people, or to Spirit, she calls the element of Air and uses the stick. This is an ancient Druidic practice handed down from mother to daughter.

Tabitha's daddy is teaching her to play the drums so that she can join the family in the drumming circle they have each month, but Tabitha has a baby brother and can't bang on the drum after he goes to bed. Her mother permits Tabitha to use the rattle she made herself if she promises not to shake the rattle near the door to her brother's room. It was easy to make the rattle. Tabitha took two plain paper bowls and threw a handful of dried beans into one bowl. Then her mother stapled the bowls together. Tabitha decorated the bowls with crayons and markers. She has a magick rattle for love, one for healing, and a special one for protection.

Tabitha's altar sits in the corner of the dining room, opposite the family altar. She took a footstool that her big sister made in shop class and set a big, flat stone from the pile in the backyard on top. Tabitha puts whatever she wants on her altar. She likes to work with clay and other crafty things, so something new often appears there whenever she finishes a project. Hanging over her altar she has a pretty picture of a woman that she cut out of one of her mom's fashion magazines. For now, that's her idea of the Goddess. Tabitha leaves interesting things on her altar to symbolize her gifts to the Lord and Lady. If Grandma gives her two candies, she will eat one and give the other to the Lady. Sometimes, after dinner, she will leave part of her dinner roll on the altar as a gift to the Lord. As part of family custom, at Yule she will put three pennies on her altar to acknowledge that all wealth comes from the Lord and Lady, and at Thanksgiving she places six kernels of dried corn on the altar to say that she understands the hardships that the Puritans went through, and that Spirit helped them to survive. She asks the Lord and Lady to help her family through the coming winter months. Tabitha shows us that any holiday, or any day of the week, can be made into a special, private, holy occasion.

I've just shown you five different altar setups designed by teenagers or kids like yourself. I included the family information so that you can identify with teens just like yourself. Why not take some time now and design your own altar?

✦

My goodness! I've covered an awful lot of information in this chapter, so you may want to go over the different subjects again, especially if you plan to practice the religion and science of WitchCraft.

✦

3

Ritual

I who am the beauty of the green earth,
and the white moon among the stars,
and the mysteries of the waters,
and the desire of the heart of man.
I call your soul to arise and come to me.
For I am the Mother of nature,
who gives life to the Universe.
From me all things proceed,
and to me all things must return;
and before my face, beloved of Gods and men,
let your innermost divine self be enfolded
in the rapture of the infinite.
Let my worship be within the heart that rejoices;
for behold, all acts of love and pleasure are my rituals.
Let there be beauty and strength,
power and compassion,
honor and humility,
mirth and reverence within you.
And you who think to look for me,
know that your search and yearning shall never find me,
unless you know the mystery;
that if you cannot find what you seek within yourself,
then you will never find it outside yourself.
For behold, I have been with you from the beginning;
and I am that which is attained
at the end of desire.[1]

Guess you thought that Witches were all magick, mo-jo, and mumbled mantras, huh? Magickal practices make up only a small part of what we really do. Our prime directive involves making ourselves better people, enabling us to throw off the chains of past difficulties, unhappy circumstances, and unfortunate situations to rise like the bale fires of old—to rise and blossom into spiritual people who gently persevere, rather than wanting the power of others.

Every type of positive religion incorporates ritual into the structure of their belief systems, including Wicca. Witches have all sorts of ritual, from the complex to the basic. In this chapter we'll talk about two types of ritual, basic and spontaneous.

Basic Ritual

You can use the basic ritual formats in an Esbat, Sabbat, or other circumstance where magick or ceremony comes into play. I've put together three basic rituals for you: General Working, Esbat Ritual, and Sabbat Ritual.

General Working

1. **Do the Altar Devotion.** Consists of cleansing and consecrating any items on the altar in the name of the Lord and Lady. The energies are then symbolically mixed together and blessed to create a focused point of power. This is a mental as well as physical action.

2. **Creating Sacred Space.** Carrying the four elements (Earth, Air, Fire, and Water) in a clockwise, circular pattern individually around the room (or outside area where a ritual will be performed) to purify the space where you will be working. Blessings are usually silently requested. This is a mental as well as physical action.

3. **Casting the Circle.** Physically walking in a clockwise (deosil) circular pattern to create an invisible circle of energy that encompasses the individual (or group) in an energy bubble. A blessing (either verbal or mental) is usually requested in the form of a circle casting rhyme or statement. This is a mental as well as a physical action. *Note:* Witches may use several variations of movements to cast a circle.

---

1. Originally written by a very famous and passionate Witch and author, Starhawk, who rewrote the words set forth by Doreen Valiente (another equally talented and famous Witch) who found the material in Leland's *Gospel of the Witches*. You will find the full version of *The Charge of the Star Goddess* (quoted in part on the preceding page) in Starhawk's book titled *The Spiral Dance*.

4. **Calling the Quarters.** Standing at North, East, South, and West (respectively) and inviting the energies of that element into the circle. Blessings and assistance are usually requested verbally. *Note:* Element correspondences and what is called differ from Witch to Witch or group to group. This is a mental as well as a physical action.

5. **Invoking the God and Goddess (or both).** Standing in the center of the circle and requesting that the Lord or Lady (or both) enter your circle. Blessings and assistance are verbally requested. This is a mental as well as a physical action.

6. **Performance of the Magickal Work.** All preliminary actions involved in spellcasting, as well as performing the spell, are done here. In a holiday ritual the reenactment of a myth or a legend falls here. If a reenactment and a magickal working are planned, the reenactment is performed first, followed by the magickal working.

7. **Raising Energy.** Mental focus on the desire through singing, drumming, clapping, humming, breathing, et cetera. The technique will vary from individual to individual or group to group. *Note:* Sometimes groups will also raise energy before the invocation to promote harmony within the group.

8. **Thanking the Lord and Lady.** A verbal thank you and request for a blessing. Most Wiccans do not ask the God or Goddess energy to leave unless the ritual calls for the departure of these spiritual energies.

9. **Closing the Quarters.** Releasing (or sending away) the quarter energies requested in #4 above. This is a mental and physical action that is said verbally.

10. **Releasing the Circle.** Moving in a counterclockwise (widdershins) circular direction around the room or area to remove the circle put in place in #3 above. This is a mental and physical action stated verbally or silently. The energy collected from the circle is then put into the altar, one's tools, or the spellcasting vehicle (such as a candle). *Note:* Sacred space is not usually released.

11. **Grounding and Centering.** A mental exercise (that can contain physical movement) to remove excess energy within the body and mind that has been raised during the ritual. *Note:* Sometimes a Witch will ground and center at other points in the ritual as he or she feels the need.

If you don't understand any of the above steps, don't worry. I will show you how to do all these things throughout the book.

Ritual has always been an active part of human spirituality. Wiccan ritual gives the seeker a clear communication to Spirit; in other words, you don't need a middleman to get to Heaven (or Summerland, as may be).

Let's run through a General Ritual with Autumn, a sixteen-year-old Witch. Since Autumn is working alone, she is called a Solitary. Let's say Autumn wishes to design a ritual to help her in her school studies. Granted, Autumn knows she will have to continue to do the work expected of her, but she feels she needs the edge to get through this next marking period. She needs confidence in herself, and would like to clear away any blocks that may keep her from doing the best that she can. Since this is the beginning of a project, Autumn will choose to do her ritual as close to the new moon as possible, because the energy of the new moon lends well to beginning any new project, goal, or desire.

From new to full moons, Witches perform workings to bring things toward them. From full to new moons, Witches work to push things away. So, just for the sake of clarification, if Autumn had to begin her ritual from full to new moon, she would work on *banishing* blocks in her path, getting rid of low self-esteem, etc. If she works from new to full, then she would word her ritual a little differently. She would work on *bringing* confidence, wisdom, and a clear path toward herself.

Now that Autumn has chosen the moon phase she will work under (new to full) she may also wish to tie her work to a special day of the week. Look at the simple table below to decide when Autumn might do her ritual.

Magickal Correspondences for Days of the Week

Sunday	Success, Family, Sibling Relationships, Career
Monday	Intuition, Dreams, Psychism, Child Protection
Tuesday	Conflict
Wednesday	Communication, the Arts, Partnerships
Thursday	Career, Finances, Wealth
Friday	Love, Passion, Friendships
Saturday	Banishing Negativity

These seven days and their meanings are part of what Witches call **Magickal Correspondences**. Many Witches try to include as many magickal correspondences that match their working as possible. These correspondences can be confusing to a new Witch, so in this book we're just going to stick with the days of the week and the moon phases. Which day of the week would you choose for Autumn's ritual? Very Good! Sunday or Wednesday would be the right choice! Either day will do.

Magickal Correspondences n. Items, objects, days, colors, moon phases, oils, angels, and herbs used in ritual that match the intent of the celebration or ceremony.

Autumn is lucky because the new moon falls on a Sunday, so she has two correspondences that match. What if the new moon doesn't fall on the day she chose? Autumn would go with the moon phase as her first choice, and trash the day; or, she could choose the Sunday or Wednesday closest to the new moon. The day could fall before or after the new moon—it doesn't really matter, since Autumn's intent is pure.

Okay, Autumn has chosen the moon phase and the day, but what about the time of her ritual? More advanced Witches often use **planetary hours** to pinpoint the exact time they wish to do a specific ritual, but planetary hours can get complicated, so now what? If she doesn't use planetary hours, will that hurt her ritual? No. Autumn's priority focuses on choosing a time when nobody will disturb her, or when she doesn't have other responsibilities to fulfill. This may mean that Autumn must do her ritual when she gets up in the morning.

planetary hours n. A system of hourly division associated with planetary energies.

She has cheerleading practice from 6:00 P.M. to 8:00 P.M., and after that she has the chores around the house to finish that she couldn't get done because she normally does her homework from 3:00 P.M. until dinnertime. For Autumn, then, her ritual time will be in the morning, rather than at night.

Autumn now has the moon phase, the day, and the time chosen for her ritual. What does she do next? Before doing her ritual, Autumn must decide exactly what she will work for. Since Autumn will be working at the start of the new moon, she will ask for wisdom, patience, and clear thought in her studies. If she is having trouble with only one subject, she may attune her request only to that subject. It's best to write down exactly what you want on a piece of paper, to be sure you get the words to match what you really want. The English language can be a tricky animal, and we must be careful what we wish for. Remember to phrase your words in a positive way.

Let's see what Autumn wrote: "I have patience, wisdom, and clear thought in all my school studies, especially Algebra. I am blessed with confidence and I earn good grades in school. With harm to none, so mote it be." Gee, why did Autumn write that? She put her request in the present tense, as if she had already attained what she desires. Did she do something wrong? Nope. Always word a magickal request as if that request has already manifested.

Autumn now associates one mental picture that depicts her desire. If she has trouble seeing a picture in her mind, she may draw a picture of her upcoming report card with the grades she wants on that report card. Then she will draw a picture of herself with a big smile on her face—yes, a stick figure will do nicely, beside the report card.

Since Autumn is sixteen, her parents permit her to burn candles in her room. Look at the table below, and choose what color of candle Autumn might choose to burn as a part of her ritual.

Magickal Correspondences for Candle Colors

White	All purpose
Red	Passion and Creativity
Blue	Peace, Wisdom, Integrity
Orange	Work, Career
Brown	Friendship
Green	Healing and Money
Violet	Spirituality
Black	Banishing Negativity
Yellow	Intellect
Silver	Psychism

Notice that Autumn has several choices here: white (which is the all-purpose candle), blue (for wisdom), orange (for school work), or yellow (for intellect). She could choose one color, or all four colors, if she likes. Autumn's purse is a little empty this week, so she's going to try to find some white candles in the house somewhere. It took her awhile to find some. She checked in the kitchen drawer, but someone has already used several of those candles. One new candle had a crack halfway down. Autumn knows that you should have a fresh candle for any magickal or ritual working so she couldn't choose the used ones, and she can't work with the broken one because the crack will interrupt the flow of energy in the candle. Finally, after one heck of a search, Autumn discovered a box of emergency candles on the basement shelf. They're a little yellow because of age, but they'll do—she grabs two of them. As Autumn checks her supplies to make sure she has everything she needs, she realizes something is missing. Ah, yes! If she plans to incorporate candles into her ritual, she needs oil to dress the candle, because candle dressing enhances the energy flow. Years ago, when Witches didn't have the scented oils, they would use olive oil to empower their candles and anoint their foreheads in group ritual. Autumn checks the few supplies she keeps in a chest in her room.

What if your parents will not permit you to burn candles? No sweat. Remember the picture that Autumn drew representing what she wanted? Just draw that picture on colored paper, or on white paper with colored markers. I once did a magickal working with an orange crayon because that was all I could find. Hey, it can work.

All rightie then! Autumn has her moon phase, her day, her time, her statement of intent, her drawing, and a candle. Now what? Autumn decides what type of ritual she will do. Does she want to do the General Ritual, or would she like to perform a full Esbat? This choice depends on two things: the time available to her and the severity of her intent. Autumn thinks that a General Ritual will do, since she really doesn't have the time to do an Esbat, which is a much longer and more involved ritual.

The night before the ritual, Autumn gathers the things she thinks she will need for her ritual in the morning because she knows she doesn't have much time. She sets out her four representations of the elements: salt, water, incense, and one white candle. She places her drawing and her statement of intent in the center of the altar, with the other white candle beside the papers. Then she covers the whole altar with a piece of cloth to protect her collection from negative energies and dust, which carries negative energy.

ritual purification n. The practice of cleansing the body and mind prior to performing a ritual.

In the morning, Autumn will take a shower before she does her ritual. Yes, baths or showers are very common for **ritual purification**. What if Autumn can't do that because she will wake the whole household? She will at least cleanse her face and hands before she begins.

Once Autumn has finished her ritual purification, she will devote the altar. Autumn checks to make sure that she put her element representations in the right place on the altar. The bowl of salt goes in the North, the incense in the East, the fire candle in the South, and the bowl of water in the West. These items show that Autumn works in harmony with Earth, Air, Water, and Fire plus Spirit. She will cleanse, consecrate, and mix these energies together.

First, Autumn lights the incense. She holds her hands over the incense and says:

> I cleanse and consecrate thee in the names of the God and Goddess.
> May their blessings reside within thee.

She then puts her hand over the small fire candle, holds up the candle, and says:

> Creature of Fire,
> work thy will by my desire.

She puts the candle down, holds her hands over the flame (not close enough to burn herself) and says:

> I cleanse and consecrate thee in the names of the God and Goddess.
> May their blessings reside within thee.

Next comes the cup of water. Autumn holds her hands over the cup of water and says:

> Creature of Water,
> I cleanse and consecrate thee in the names of the God and Goddess.
> May their blessings reside within thee.

Finally, Autumn moves her hands over the salt, positioned at the North end of the altar, and says:

> Creature of Earth,
> I cleanse and consecrate thee in the names of the God and Goddess.
> May their blessings reside within thee.

Autumn has just done the cleansing, consecration and empowerment of the four Elements. While she says the words, she envisions white light circulating around each element. This is the positive energy of Spirit.

Autumn hasn't quite finished her altar devotion. She takes three pinches of salt and puts the salt in the water bowl. She holds the water bowl up and imagines that Spirit enters the water. When she feels that the water has reached empowerment, she places the bowl back on the altar. Autumn has just made holy water.

With her dominant hand, Autumn draws four clockwise circles in the air over the altar, then taps the altar four times with the heel of her hand. She has just sealed the altar.

Now she will move on to creating sacred space, just as Falynn did earlier (on page 48). Once she has completed that function, Autumn is ready to cast her magick circle.

Autumn stands in the middle of the room, takes a deep breath, and relaxes into a calm state. If she has trouble doing this, Autumn can imagine that she is a tree with roots that go deep into Mother Earth. Now Autumn looks up, smiles, takes another deep breath, and begins to walk the circle clockwise (deosil—pronounced *jes-el*) with the index finger of her dominant hand pointing out and down. She will walk the circle three times while saying:

> I conjure thee, O great circle of power,
> so that you will be for me a boundary
> between the world of men and realms of the mighty spirits—
> a meeting place of perfect love, trust, peace, and joy,
> containing the power I will raise within thee.
> I call upon the angels of the East, South, West, and North
> to aid me in the consecration.
> In the name of the Lord and the Lady
> thus do I conjure thee,
> O great circle of power!

Then Autumn pounds (or taps lightly so she doesn't wake anybody) the floor with her hand, and says:

> **This circle is sealed.**

Time now to call the quarters. Beginning in the North, Autumn will call each quarter, moving in a clockwise direction. Witches have all sorts of quarter calls from which Autumn could choose, but she wants to keep this ritual simple; after all, she has to get ready for school. With head bowed, arms folded across her chest, and legs spread in a sturdy stance, Autumn begins her North quarter call. As she speaks, she slowly raises her head and opens her arms:

> **Angels of Earth,**
> help me today in my ritual to help me improve my studies.

That was simple, wasn't it? Autumn will move to each quarter, saying the same thing, except she will call the Angels of Air at the East quarter, the Angels of Fire at the South quarter, and the Angels of Water at the West quarter.

When she finishes she will move to the center of her circle, hold her arms above her head, and say:

> Lord and Lady, precious Spirit, lend me your wisdom, confidence, and clarity of thought as I work this ritual to improve my studies.

At this point, Autumn will focus on the actual working part of her ritual. First, she picks up the unlit candle that will represent her purpose. She holds the candle tightly between both hands, closes her eyes, and asks the Lord and Lady:

> Cleanse, regenerate, and bless this tool for this ritual for self-confidence and good grades in school.

She imagines white light surrounding the unlit candle. Then, with her eyes still closed, Autumn thinks of the intent of her ritual, that of gaining self-confidence and getting good grades in her studies. Autumn conjures up the picture of success and holds that picture in her mind as long as she can. Once the picture slips from her mind, she will put the candle in a fire-safe candle holder. Next, Autumn picks up her drawing of success, closes her eyes, and asks the Lord and Lady:

> Cleanse, regenerate, and consecrate this drawing of success.

Again, she envisions the picture surrounded by white light, just as she held the same visualization for the candle. When she loses the picture in her mind, Autumn opens her eyes and places the drawing under the candle holder. The more ritual Autumn practices, the longer she can hold the picture of success in her mind. Autumn knows this, so doesn't worry about "how long" to hold that picture in her mind. The length of time will come naturally.

Activities that Autumn has done so far—from choosing the appropriate day, moon phase, what she wants to say, candle color, et cetera—lend positive energy to her ritual. Although the entire ritual may take her only ten minutes to complete, she's already invested time and energy into the working through her thought process. Now comes the part of the ritual where Autumn will raise energy to instill her desire into the universe.

Just as we have many ways to cast a circle and call the quarters, so too many procedures exist for raising energy. In fact, Witches call these ways of raising energy the Paths of Power. Some of these vehicles are:

- Meditation
- Invocation
- Praying
- Whispering, singing, monotonous chanting, or sing-song chanting
- Trance and astral projection
- Herbals, oils, and incense
- Movement or dancing
- Drums or rattles
- Ritual

Often, a Witch will use more than one path of power in any given magickal working or ritual. For example, Autumn had already chosen an oil and her favorite incense. She invoked the Lord and Lady, asking for their assistance in the ritual. Since Autumn chooses to do her ritual early in the morning and doesn't want to wake everyone in the house, most of her ritual involved whispering. Amazingly, whispering magick carries clout too.

Although Autumn used three of these paths in her ritual so far, she hasn't yet focused on the main event: the raising of energy. She has gathered the energy, but she hasn't "raised" the energy. Now Autumn must choose which path to use in this final stage. Drums, dancing, or rattles are definitely out—too noisy. She can't do meditation because she does have a time limit, which also knocks out trance and astral projection. Autumn chooses monotonous chanting, prayer, and movement to conclude the magickal aspects of her ritual. Autumn picks up her drawing and begins to walk around the circle in a clockwise direction, chanting softly:

> She changes everything she touches;
> everything she touches changes.

As she continues the chant she moves faster and picks up the beat of the chant. When she feels she has finished, she puts the paper under the candle holder and holds her hands over the candle, imagining her success. Then she says:

> As I light this candle, my will be done!

Autumn lights the candle (with a lighter, as the sulfur in the matches adds negativity to a ritual). Autumn stands with her feet spread apart and her arms outstretched, palms up (called the Goddess Position) and imagines her goal whirling about her. She imagines the energy of the quarter angels coalescing over her candle. Slowly, she raises her arms, envisioning the energy that she has created moving up into the air. When Autumn feels she is ready, she will raise her arms up over her head and "let go" (just like she might let go of the string of a balloon filled with helium) of the energy that she has collected. When she has let go, Autumn says:

Holy Mother, take this, the energy I have raised into the Universe,
and allow my petition to manifest.
Bless and protect me on my journey through life.
May this working not reverse, or place upon me any curse,
and may all astrological correspondences be correct for this working.
With harm to none.
So mote it be!

Autumn imagines the Goddess taking the energy and casting that energy into the universe. Autumn then imagines the Lady smiling and sending her blessings to Autumn.

Why did Autumn say, "May this spell not reverse or place upon me any curse?" She didn't do anything wrong, so why should a backfire be a concern? For two reasons: magick (energy) always follows the path of least resistance, and we are only human and sometimes we make mistakes without meaning to. Therefore, we use this little saying, first written by Sybil Leek, a very famous British Witch. Autumn asks that "all astrological correspondences be correct for this working" because she wants the unseen universe to work with her desires, not against them. Finally, Autumn asks that her work "harm none" because she doesn't want anyone hurt by her magick, even by mistake.

Autumn takes a deep breath and puts her arms down. She closes her eyes and envisions herself as a large tree with deep roots that burrow into the ground, gathering strength and calm from Mother Earth. Witches call this procedure grounding. Now Autumn finds the deep calm within herself. Witches do this by concentrating on deep peace from the navel area. Witches call this procedure centering. Whenever a Witch does any type of magickal application or ritual, they always ground and center afterwards. If Autumn had the time, she would practice magickal daydreaming (where she would make a movie in her mind about the progression of herself through her goal), but she doesn't have the time right now, so she'll do that before she goes to bed tonight.

Autumn now walks to the center of the circle and thanks the Lord and Lady for their participation in her ritual. She then walks to the West, holds her arms out, and closes that quarter by saying:

> Angels of the West, Element of Water,
> thank you for your participation in this ritual.
> Go if you must, stay if you like.
> Hail and farewell.

As she speaks, she closes her arms across and next to her chest and bows her head.

From the West quarter, she moves to the South and says:

> Angels of the South, Element of Fire,
> thank you for your participation in this ritual.
> Go if you must, stay if you like.
> Hail and farewell.

On to the East quarter:

> Angels of the East, Element of Air,
> thank you for your participation in this ritual.
> Go if you must, stay if you like.
> Hail and farewell.

The North quarter:

> Angels of the North, Element of Earth,
> thank you for your participation in this ritual.
> Go if you must, stay if you like.
> Hail and farewell.

Autumn knows that when you call the quarters in one direction (here it was clockwise beginning in the North, then to East, then to South, and finally to the West) you close the quarters in the opposite fashion (here she walked counter-clockwise and, as required, started in the West, moved through the South and East, finishing in the North). Remember, the North quarter was the first quarter she called, so the North quarter has to be the last quarter she releases.

With the quarters released, Autumn only has to take up the circle. Witches never, ever leave a circle or open quarters just hanging there. Once you have begun a magickal procedure, you must always complete that procedure.

Just as Autumn called the quarters in reverse, she must now "take up" the circle in reverse. Since she cast the circle clockwise, she must now release the circle counterclockwise. Various Witches do this differently. Here, Autumn holds out her dominant hand, begins at the North quarter and, as she walks counterclockwise, envisions the circle coming back into her fingers and into her hand. When she gets back to the North quarter, she can put the circle energy into the candle, into her altar, or into Mother Earth. She then taps the floor (or in another, less quiet case, pounds), and says:

> This circle is open, but never broken.
> We are the people, we are the power,
> we are the change!
> So mote it be!

So there you go. Autumn has just completed her ritual to help herself gain self-confidence and bring energy into her studies. Since she doesn't want to leave the candle burning while she is at school, Autumn can put out the candle now (not blow, snuff please—if you blow out the candle, you blow away the magick). Tomorrow morning, she can light the candle again (without the magick circle or ritual format) and simply envision her picture of success. When she loses the picture from her mind, she can put out the candle. Autumn can keep up this practice for an odd number of days (3, 7, 9, or 11, as odd numbers carry magickal significance). She will put what is left of her candle in her purse, so she can carry it to school with her, or she can let the candle burn until it is "all" (as we say here in Pennsylvania Dutch lingo, meaning "there isn't any more").

Each evening before she goes to bed, Autumn will continue to daydream of her success. If she starts to think negative thoughts, she quickly replaces them with a keyword, such as "success" or "victory" or whatever. Keywords can even be silly, if you like, as long as you connect that keyword to your venture. Autumn will continue this magickal daydream until she has reached the successful conclusion of what she wants. Does she have to do that daydream every day? Well, that would help her a lot, but Autumn is human, after all, and will probably forget a time a two. This won't hurt the magick.

Some Witches say to do your magick and then forget it. In a sense, they are right. Don't do the magick and then worry whether the ritual or magickal application will work or not; rather, think of positive reinforcement only. If you start to think negative thoughts, you will damage the chances for your success.

Autumn will not tell the kids at school about the ritual she did this morning. Witches follow this rule: To Know, To Dare, To Will, and To Be Silent. To Know means that Autumn reaches to learn as much as she can about herself and the world around her, those things seen and unseen. To Dare means she has the courage to act out her success wishes. To Will means that Autumn has set her mind in a specific direction to manifest a particular goal. To Be Silent says that Autumn understands that many people are either afraid of magick or have no belief in magickal applications. If they make fun of her, their negative reactions will damage her efforts.

You can use the general application that Autumn employed for her desire. Take your time to work out what it is that you want: friendship, prosperity, healing, whatever . . . just remember this one, very sacred Witch Rule: *Never, ever ask for something that someone else already has (as in to take away ownership) and never, ever, ever, ever, ever do a ritual that would interfere with another's free will. Meaning— love workings directed at a specific individual are OUT!* (Witches have only one exception to this rule: Healing rituals for someone are okay.)

Autumn worked this ritual for herself, but what if she wanted to work a ritual for someone else? Witches have another rule: Never work magick for anyone without their permission. That means that, although Autumn's best friend has gotten herself into a jam, Autumn can't do a working to change things without asking the friend. Autumn can, however, do the following:

Pray. Witches pray, and pray a lot. Autumn could go to her altar, light a candle, and ask that Spirit help her friend in the best way possible for what her friend needs.

Love. Witches do send pure love energy to people. Autumn could envision her friend encased by the loving energy of Spirit.

Be Supportive. Being a Witch doesn't mean that we are all magick and ritual. We must use our other talents too, like giving a listening ear when our friends or family members need someone to hear them.

Think of regular ways to help our friends. Let's say a friend of yours wants to go to the prom, but she can't afford a dress. With her permission, you could work magick to help her get an attractive dress and simultaneously ask your friends for help. (Maybe someone's sister has a dress that would fit your friend?)

Talk to your guardian angels. Never think that it is wrong to ask your guardian angel for help for yourself, for a member of your family, or for a friend. Guardian angels always want to help you, all you need to do is ask. Remember, though, that your angel can't help you if you don't ask first. That's the rule.

⋆⋆[⋆]

Oh, my stars and garters! I just showed you how to do magick, didn't I? I most certainly did. You can use this general ritual for all your magickal applications while you learn the art, science, and religion of the Craft. In the next chapter, I'll talk more about magick and spellcasting. I presented the ritual to you first, because I want you to understand that WitchCraft isn't about casting spells and doing mo-jo—the Craft represents a religious experience and all the magick Witches do involve Spirit.

Your Friends, Magick and Ritual

While you learn the Craft, try not to fall victim to your cajoling friends who want you to do magick for them. Let's face the broomstick: you are studying something new, and mistakes will happen. Rituals and magick will bomb. I'll get into that a little later but, trust me, every good Witch has failed miserably at one time or another. Really, the best way to help your friends when they ask you to do magick for them is to tell them to do the magick themselves. We work the best magick for those things we ultimately want. If Karl wants a new radio for his car, this won't equate to a deep desire of your own, would it? No, it wouldn't. Karl needs to work his own type of magick to get that radio. Often, friends will ask you to do magick for them because they doubt that magick is real. If they don't believe magick is real, then they lend negative energy to what you might break down and do for them. It's far better to just give them the book, tell them to read the material, and then, if they feel comfortable with the information, to work their own magick. This is what the experienced Witches do.

Oh, and just to let you know. Autumn's report card for that semester boasted several As and two Bs. She brought her algebra grade up from a sixty-six percent to an eighty-nine percent. Not bad. Not bad at all. Obviously, Autumn did more than a ritual and her magickal daydreaming. She also completed all her homework, handed that homework in on time, and studied for her tests. A Witch gains wisdom through using all of his or her talents.

Esbat Ritual

We did pretty well on the general working outline, so let's peek at an outline for an Esbat. Much of the following outline will look familiar to you as we used many of these steps in our general working on page 58. Remember, if you don't understand any of the steps, don't worry. I will show you these things throughout the book.

1. **Do the Altar Devotion.** Consists of cleansing and consecrating any items on the altar in the name of the Lord and Lady. The energies are then symbolically mixed together and blessed to create a focused point of power. This is a mental as well as a physical action.

2. **Creating Sacred Space.** Carrying the four elements (Earth, Air, Fire, and Water) in a clockwise, circular pattern individually around the room (or outside area where a ritual will be performed) to purify the space where you will be working. Blessings are usually silently requested. This is a mental as well as physical action.

3. **Casting the Circle.** Physically walking in a clockwise (deosil) circular pattern to create an invisible circle of energy that encompasses the individual (or group) in an energy bubble. A blessing (either verbal or mental) is usually requested in the form of a circle casting rhyme or statement. This is a mental as well as a physical action. *Note:* Witches may use several variations of movements to cast a circle.

4. **Calling the Quarters.** Standing at North, East, South, and West (respectively) and inviting the energies of that element into the circle. Blessings and assistance are usually requested verbally. *Note:* Element correspondences and what is called differ from Witch to Witch or group to group. This is a mental as well as a physical action.

5. **Drawing Down the Moon.** Accepting the energy of the moon into your body. This is usually a silent, physical action. I say silent because it is difficult to concentrate on mentally and emotionally accepting the energies of the moon into oneself while speaking aloud. Many Witches turn to a window (if indoors) where they can see the moon. The moon's energy is associated with the Goddess (though in some cultures the moon was seen as a vehicle of the God, and the sun as a vehicle of the Goddess). When

you call on the energies of the moon, you are calling on the energies of the Goddess to physically, mentally, and emotionally become a part of yourself. In a solitary ceremony (a Witch alone) the individual performing the ceremony draws the moon into him or herself. In a group environment, the High Priestess usually draws down the moon; however, drawing down the moon can be performed by the entire group.

6. **Performance of the Magickal Work.** All preliminary actions involved in spellcasting, as well as performing the spell, are done here. In a holiday ritual the reenactment of a myth or a legend falls here. If a reenactment and a magickal working are planned, the reenactment is performed first, followed by the magickal working.

7. **Raising Energy**. Mental focus on the desire through singing, drumming, clapping, humming, breathing, et cetera. The technique will vary from individual to individual or group to group. *Note*: Sometimes groups will also raise energy before the invocation to promote harmony within the group.

8. **Meditation.** Silently thinking about what this ritual means to you, or what you choose to accomplish with the performance of this ritual. Meditational themes are your personal choice (or the choice of the group).

9. **Communion.** This is the act of honoring the gifts of deity by eating blessed bread and drinking fruit juice. Communion also helps to ground you after raising energy, as bread contains carbohydrates, a natural grounding mechanism. The communion creates group harmony. After you take a bite of bread, you say, "May you never hunger" when you pass the bread to the next person. After you take a drink, you say, "May you never thirst." Both statements are seen as blessings of positive abundance given to the person next to you. Communion is a solemn part of any Esbat or Sabbat.

10. **Thanking the Lord and Lady.** A verbal thank you and request for a blessing. Most Wiccans do not ask the God or Goddess energy to leave unless the ritual calls for the departure of these spiritual energies.

11. **Closing the Quarters.** Releasing (or sending away) the quarter energies requested in #4 above. This is a mental and physical action that is said verbally.

12. **Releasing the Circle.** Moving in a counterclockwise (widdershins) circular direction around the room or area to remove the circle put in place in #3 above. This is a mental and physical action stated verbally or silently. The energy collected from the circle is then put into the altar, one's tools, or the spellcasting vehicle (such as a candle). *Note*: Sacred space is not usually released.

13. **Feast.** The feast helps you to ground your energy and promotes group harmony. Feasts are usually potluck affairs, not a junk food binge. If the Esbat or Sabbat is performed before supper, then the feast becomes the main meal of the day. If the Esbat or Sabbat is performed late at night, the feast is considered an extra meal of the day. *Note*: Some Wiccan groups hold the feast before they release the circle to promote group harmony; however, that puts a time limit on the event as some individuals need to leave earlier than others.

14. **Clean Up.** Witches encourage all members of a group to clean up the ritual site and the feast area to promote group harmony. This also helps to teach new members that a messy area contains negative energy, and needs to be cleaned.

Do you notice the differences between an Esbat and a General Ritual? First, there are more steps, right? In an Esbat, the Witch includes a period of meditation and communion.

What do Witches really do at an Esbat if they don't run around naked, take drugs, make goo-goo eyes at the devil, and whomp up bad mo-jo? I thought you'd never ask. Wiccan Esbats encompass a Witch's work with his or her belief in Spirit, either alone or in a group format. No one Esbat ever seems to play out the same, and believe me, I've been present at hundreds of them. Witches usually do a ritual to honor Spirit and do their magickal work too. These Esbats can focus on a variety of topics, including healing, career plans, motivational aspects of self, relationship matters, protection for self or others, or personal achievement and success. These rituals may be open or closed. Open means that anyone may attend, where closed shows that the workings involve members only. Of course, if you work alone, then your Esbat would be considered a closed one. Sometimes the Witches hold an open healing circle, where anyone can attend despite their religious preference, and all manner of topics might find resolution.

Why would Witches hold a closed ceremony? Does that mean the Witches do no-nos and don't want anyone to find out about it? Sorry to reign in your imagination, but the purpose of the closed ceremony hinges on what Witches call the **group mind**. It takes several months to develop a stable group mind, where we all like each other and trust each other. Initiated Witches work in

group mind n. The establishing of perfect love and perfect trust among a group of individuals.

what we call perfect love and perfect trust. Uninitiated Witches and people who do not practice the Craft work in perfect love and perfect peace. Remember when I told you that Witches do not bring anger, jealousy, or hatred into a circle? That applies to our environment of perfect love and perfect trust. If one Witch is mad at another

Witch, for any reason, then that Witch must either stay out of the magick circle or put his or her differences aside while in it.

As I told you earlier, originally Witches held Esbats once a month, during the full moon (every twenty-eight days), so that the faithful could celebrate when the moon's effects on the earth drew the most power. During the full moon we connect with our Goddess, whose heavenly representation, as you read earlier in the creation story, becomes the moon. Sabbats, on the other hand, represent the movement of the sun and the cycle of the seasons. The sun, then, stands for our vision of our God. In very old Wiccan Traditions, the sun represented the Goddess and the Moon represented the God. Either way, these heavenly bodies find importance in our belief system, and we see them as manifestations of the divine, or Spirit. Just as other religions teach that all things come from God, so do the Witches.

During an Esbat, Witches work to help themselves and other people. We usually stand in a circle rather than sit on chairs or in pews, like in churches. Our religious ceremonies are active, and each person has something to do.

Like a general working, several things happen before an Esbat, whether a Witch works in a group or alone. First, the Witch has to decide the focus of the Esbat. Will the Witch concentrate on the empowering energy of the Goddess or will he or she add a magickal working? If a Witch wants to do a magickal working, then choices of tools, intent, and other correspondences might come into play. Again, at some point in the day, as close to the Esbat (or rite) as possible, the Witch takes a ritual bath, or bath of purification. Personally, I prefer showers. This bath or shower involves the purification of body, mind, and spirit. Many Witches meditate on Spirit while they bathe.

Before the Esbat officially begins, one Witch, usually the leader of the group, or yourself (of course) if you are working alone, makes sacred space, devotes the altar, and casts a magick circle. In this book we aren't going to work with any tools. We're going to use what our ancestors used—our hands. I'm not going to go into too much on the tools of the Craft because teens have enough trouble getting their families to accept their new religious belief. If you bring a big knife home (the athame, our knife that is used only in ritual) and tell your mother that you are going to cast a magick circle with that glittering blade, she's going to have heart failure. Besides, most Witches who have reached adeptship don't use tools anyhow, because they don't need them. This is not to say that our tools (when we do use them) aren't sacred. You'll learn more about our tools as you learn more about the Craft. Each tool does carry a special meaning, important in your future training.

Back to the magick circle. In my travels, I've discovered many ways to cast a magick circle. Sometimes the Witch walks around the room or designated place outside three times while saying special words, and other times the Witch may walk around only once. Two people can cast a circle together. You can even cast a circle with your guardian angel. The magick circle keeps negativity out and holds the power of the Witches in until you are ready to release that power.

A Teen Esbat

Let's say four teenagers, Annette, Julia, Tom, and George, want to perform an Esbat. What would they do first? They should talk among themselves about what they wish to accomplish in the Esbat. Do they want to work for healing, prosperity, good relationships with others, or all of the above? Perhaps they simply wish to honor the Goddess. If they need any supplies, one of the four should be responsible for gathering those supplies and another of the four should know where to get the supplies should the person responsible for obtaining them not show up. A Witch rule of Giant Pentacle: Always have back-up plans, just in case. Here, everyone agrees to bring the supplies to Annette's house Tuesday, although the ritual won't take place until Friday night. That way, all the supplies will be there and no one will have to run and find anything. George agrees to bring the illuminator candles for the altar. Julia has a fire-safe cauldron and tea candles. In this Esbat, the quarter candles will match the colors of the quarters: North—green; East—yellow; South—red; West—blue. Tom agrees to pick these up at the grocery store. These four teens recheck the date, time, and place where they will hold the ritual, just to make sure everyone knows what's going on. Sometimes, Tom has the tendency not to listen, and later gets upset because he doesn't know what's going on. Annette makes darn sure to repeat the facts to Tom so that he gets it.

There's been a minor disagreement here. Although the group as a whole has decided they want to honor the Goddess and empower themselves with her energy, they can't decide what type of magickal working they wish to do. To solve this problem, Julia suggests they use petition magick and a cauldron with a tea candle in it. That way, each of them can put in a personal petition, and it doesn't matter that the requests differ. Excellent idea, Julia. You get two Witchie points!

The last item under discussion concerns the FOOD. Yes, what food will each of them bring to eat after the Esbat? Why is food so important? Carbohydrates ground you. Also, the teens need to discuss who will bring the fruit juice and the cakes for the communion. Annette volunteers for this. She's a whiz in the kitchen and has decided to bake cookies in the shape of little moons with powdered sugar on top. For the feast, George has agreed to bring pizza, Julia will provide the sodas, chips, and dip, and Tom says he'll bring a bag of assorted veggies and a dip to go with them. Maybe he can even get his mom to make brownies. No one ever comes empty-handed to an Esbat, and I, your Ms. Witch Manners Mother, need to tell you that copping out with a mere bag of chips will get you nowhere at a big Esbat feast. Don't ever be El Cheapo on the food—that's impolite to the others who have put time and effort into making something.

The night of the Esbat arrives and, thankfully, everyone gets there on time. The teens will be using Annette's family room in the basement. Annette's family respects her rituals, so no one will worry about being interrupted. Annette has moved the furniture around a bit so that the middle of the large room remains free of things to trip over. In the center of the room she has placed a round coffee table. On top of the coffee table Annette sets a large, flat stone, just to make sure that no candle drips or sparks from the cauldron will burn anything.

Everyone helps Annette set up. George puts the quarter candles in their appropriate spots around the room: green for North, yellow for East, red for South, and blue for West. He makes sure that the group uses fire-safe candle holders. He double-checks the position of all the holders so that no one will knock them over during the ritual. He also makes sure that nothing flammable hangs above where the candle flame will rise. Tom sets the feast food on a card table out of the ritual area. Julia arranges the cakes on a silver tray, beside a silver goblet. She sets the tray under the altar along with the bottle of fruit juice. Annette arranges the altar, positioning the illuminator candles, the bowl of salt in the North, the incense in the East, the fire candle in the South, and the bowl of water in the West. She sets a cauldron in the center of the altar. Julia places the anointing oil on the right side of the altar, and their group Book of Shadows, along with the ritual that she has written for tonight, on the left side of the altar. Tom collects the drums and rattles from a wooden box in the corner of the basement and places them near the altar, but out of tripping distance. Finally, Annette asks each person for their petition. Remember that earlier the group couldn't decide exactly what they wanted to work for, so each person wrote down a request on a piece of paper. Annette takes these papers and places them on the altar now.

Temple Summoner n. Coven's right-hand man. A skilled individual who assists the High Priest and High Priestess.

In a standard coven, the **Temple Summoner** (usually male, but not always) or the **Maiden** is responsible for the ritual site setup. In smaller groups, such as our teen friends, giving anyone titles isn't necessary. Really, it's better if everyone shares in the duties.

The teens can begin their ritual one of two ways: either one teen will create sacred space, cast the circle, do the altar devotion, and then cut the door for the others to enter, or all the teens can play a part in the launching of the ritual. In tonight's ritual, everyone will have something to do.

Maiden n. Coven's right-hand woman. A skilled individual who assists the High Priest and High Priestess.

First, Julia will create sacred space. Everyone takes their positions for the evening. Julia will stand in the North, Tom will stand in the East, George will be in the South, and Annette will be West. The teens often switch positions (but not during a ritual) so that they can experience the energies of each quarter and learn to work with these forces.

While Julia creates sacred space (as Falynn did earlier on page 48) the others stand quietly, contemplating tonight's ritual. After Julia has finished, Annette will devote the altar (as I showed you earlier on pages 50-55).

When Annette has finished devoting the altar, George will step forward and pick up the anointing oil. Moving clockwise, he will go to each person, touch each individual's forehead with a skin-safe oil (never, ever use cinnamon oil—it burns) and say:

In the name of the Lord and Lady,
may you be cleansed, purified, and regenerated.
May all evil flee from thee.
Blessings of the Lord and Lady upon you and in you.
So mote it be.

The person he has blessed responds:

So mote it be!

George replaces the anointing oil back on the altar and takes his place in the circle. Now, Annette will cast the magick circle. Julia, Tom, and George will step forward so that Annette can move freely around the perimeter of the circle.

Annette stands in the middle of the room, takes a deep breath, and relaxes into a calm state. If she has trouble doing this, Annette can imagine that she is a tree with roots that go deep into Mother Earth. Now Annette looks up, smiles, takes another deep breath, and begins to walk the circle clockwise (deosil) with the index finger of her dominant hand pointing out and down. She will walk the circle three times while saying:

I conjure thee, O great circle of power,
so that you will be for me a boundary
between the world of men and realms of the mighty spirits—
a meeting place of perfect love, trust, peace, and joy
containing the power I will raise within thee.
I call upon the angels of the East, South, West, and North
to aid me in the consecration.
In the name of the Lord and the Lady
thus do I conjure thee,
O great circle of power!

Then Annette pounds the floor with her hand, and says:

This circle is sealed.

If Julia, Tom, and George were in another room while Annette cast the circle, Annette would now use her hands to part the circle (like opening a curtain) so that the others could walk in. Witches call this cutting a door. You don't have to cut a door if you work alone or if as in our ritual tonight, Annette cast the circle around those present. If anyone walks through a circle without cutting the door, the power of the circle diminishes. The more times someone walks in or out of a circle without cutting a door, the weaker the circle becomes. We have two exceptions: children and animals, who can move freely within and without a circle, as Spirit much loves both. Anyone who enters the circle should walk in a clockwise direction, as moving counterclockwise will also weaken the energies within. Witches call counterclockwise movements within the magick circle widdershins.

Therefore, during the ritual tonight, whenever anyone moves within the circle, they must walk clockwise—never back and forth, or counterclockwise.

If Annette had to cut the door and allow people into the circle, Annette would smile at them, then one at a time, draw a star on each person's forehead with body-safe oil and say the same words George said earlier. She would add to each: "Welcome into our circle." After the last person steps through the door, Annette closes the imaginary curtain.

Like the basic ritual I showed you earlier, in a traditional Esbat, the High Priestess or others in the coven call the quarters. This means the participants open the way, through words and gestures, for the energies of their choice to come into the circle to help or protect in the magickal working. These energies have associations with each quarter. In this book, we are only going to work with the angels and the elements, but Witches also call in devas, power animals, and other positive energies.

In our teen circle, George, Tom, Julia, and Annette will each call a quarter. One never, ever orders quarter energies to do anything. We always practice good manners in a circle, to each other, to deity, and to the energies from whom we request help. A rude Witch is a crude Witch, so to speak.

Julia stands in the North, and therefore she will lead off the quarter calls. George, Annette, and Tom stand in their own quarters of the circle, but turn to face the direction of North. Julia, with her back to the center of the circle, faces outward, hands crossed over her chest, takes a deep breath, and calms herself inside before she begins, saying:

> **Hail Spirits of the North, Powers of Earth.**
> **Be with us here tonight.**

Slowly, Julia opens her arms, as if opening a curtain.

> **Bring your strength, prosperity, and stability into our circle.**
> **Please witness this rite and guard our sacred space.**
> **So mote it be!**

Annette, George, and Tom echo:

> **So mote it be!**

Tom, standing in the East, turns to face the outside the circle, just as Julia did at her quarter. Julia, Annette, and George now turn to face the Eastern quarter. With the same hand motions, Tom says:

Hail Spirits of the East, element of Air.
Bring us your intellect, your wisdom, and your positive thought.
Please witness this rite and guard our sacred space.
So mote it be!

Julia, Annette, and George echo:

So mote it be!

Annette stands in the South, and now it's her turn. She faces the outside of the circle while the other three face the Southern quarter. Following the same motions as the first two, she says:

Hail Spirits of the South, element of fire.
Bring us your courage, your passion, and your creativity.
Please witness this rite and guard our sacred space.
So mote it be!

The others echo:

So mote it be!

George, the final participant, faces out to the West, and Julia, Tom, and Annette face the Western quarter. George says:

Hail Spirits of the West, element of Water.
Bring us your transformation, your love, and your joy.
Please witness this rite and guard our sacred space.
So mote it be!

The others repeat:

So mote it be!

Witches have many ways to call the quarters. This has been just one example to give you the idea of how a Witch calls a quarter. Keep in mind that each person, as they call the quarter, becomes the quarter. If you call water, then feel the water, see the water in your mind, and enjoy the essence of transformation, joy, and love that you call. If you call fire, then *be* that fire. Be the passion, be the creativity, be the strength. Although I've just shown you what four people can do, lots of Witches, including myself, often work alone. We cast the circle, move clockwise around the circle, and call each quarter by ourselves.

Now what? Sometimes Witches chant or sing a song to create group mind. The chanting, singing, or drumming allows each person to be in sync with the others (if you are working alone, you're getting in sync with your higher self). Since this is an Esbat, the group chooses this chant: "Moon, moon, Mother Moon; Mother Mother moon moon." They begin softly, then raise their voices louder and louder, until they feel the power has been raised.

Okay, what's next? Usually, someone calls the Lord and Lady into the circle. Let's pick Annette and Tom. Witches call this practice **invocation**, where we invite the Lord and Lady to be with us during the ceremony. Of course, just as we have many ways to cast a circle or call the quarters, we have many procedures to invoke Spirit.

invocation n. The process of inviting the Lord and the Lady to enter the circle and join in ritual.

If we work alone, we would hold our arms out, feet spread apart, and ask the Lord and Lady to enter the circle. Witches call this stance the Goddess Position. When we feel confident in working with Spirit energy, we call the Lord or Lady into ourselves. Because we've got four teens together tonight, Annette and Tom will call the Lord and Lady together. Annette puts her right hand on Tom's heart and Tom puts his right hand on Annette's heart. Annette takes her left hand and covers Tom's right hand (which is on her heart). Tom does the same thing with his left hand, putting his hand over Annette's hand that rests on his heart. Sound complicated? It isn't, really. Together they now ask the Lord and Lady to enter the circle. If they are confident, they will ask the Lord and Lady to enter each other.

If Annette and Tom have asked the Lord and Lady to enter the circle, then everyone can turn to face the moon (if inside, face the direction of the moon), hold their arms up, and ask the Lady to fill them with her loving energy. If Annette and Tom have drawn the Goddess and God into themselves (respectively), the following occurs. First, Annette walks to each person and, facing them, puts her hands (palms down) above their head. Then she draws her hands down over their heads and stops at their shoulders. She has just gifted them with the blessed energy of the female Spirit, or the Lady. When she has finished with the last person, Tom does the same thing, except he gives them the blessings of the Lord. Witches call this procedure "drawing down the moon" or "invoking Spirit." You can also draw down the moon with Wiccan tools, such as the wand, or non-Wiccan tools. One of the most wonderful Esbats I ever held involved each person drawing down the moon with a long-stemmed rose.

Now the real work of the Esbat begins. We are halfway through the ritual. What comes next? If we check our outline, we see the next step would be: Performance of the magickal work. If we celebrated this Esbat alone, then here we would make talismans, amulets, knot magick, herbal magick, et cetera. Groups can do these functions too. We just have to remember that with the addition of each person, your time factor will increase. For example, if each person said some words of honor or made a specific petition for something, then lit a candle and placed that candle in the cauldron that contains sand, each person will spend approximately two to three minutes on the process. With four people, as in our teen circle, this would be eight to twelve minutes. With a larger group, let's say fifteen people, then we would be talking about thirty to forty-five minutes. Gee, that would take a long time. In rituals with large groups, it's best to keep things simple or you'll be there all night. With smaller groups, you do have more room for magickal projects. Alone, there is always plenty of time. For this reason, most Witches do more involved magick in Esbats where they can work by themselves.

Tonight, the teens have put their papers with their requests on the altar. Each teen moves to the altar and picks up their paper (remembering to move in a clockwise direction to pick up the paper) and returns to their position in the circle. Quietly, each person attaches a mental picture of success to their petition.

Annette steps forward, faces the altar, and says:

> There is one power, which is the God and the Goddess.
> I hereby call upon the bountiful energies of the universe
> to aid us in manifesting our petitions.
> Our lives are filled with abundance,
> and all our needs are met.

It's time to raise energy to handle those requests. As with all parts of a Wiccan ritual, we have many ways to raise energy. We talked about some of these practices earlier: singing, drumming, dancing, meditating, chanting, et cetera. Since Annette lives in a Wiccan household, it's okay for the group to make noise. Each person steps forward and takes the drum or rattle of their choice, then drops their petition paper in the cauldron. They return to their places and wait for Annette to start the beat. The teens can drum and rattle for as long as they like. When the group first began working this way, they didn't drum for too long because they were unfamiliar with the instruments. Now, however, they've gotten pretty good, so they may drum, changing the beats, for up to a half hour. Usually, the lead person starts slowly, then speeds up until the drumming goes faster and faster. The teens concentrate on sending the energy around the room in a clockwise direction, each thinking of their mental picture of success as often as possible. Remember, there is no end to the creativity a group can employ to raise energy. Drums were the choice this evening, but the group could pick another vehicle next time. When the drumming finally stops, Annette will step forward and burn the papers, saying:

> **Paper will give way to flame,**
> **the essence of the word remains.**
> **Fire destroy and fire create**
> **let what's written be our fate.**
> **Fly to the heavens, fiery bird.**
> **Bring back the fact behind the word.**
> **So mote it be![1]**

The group adds:

> **So mote it be!**

Annette says:

> **May this spell not reverse, nor place upon us any curse.**
> **May all astrological correspondences be correct for this working,**
> **and may we harm none.**
> **So mote it be.**

The group adds:

> **So mote it be!**

By this time the teens are laughing and having a good time. You see, raising energy in the circle often finds release in laughter, which is magick all by itself, anyway. Laughter makes the energy go faster and disbands any negativity in a room. To bring the energies of the circle into a smoother balance, the teens might take ten minutes to do deep breathing exercises or meditate on their thoughts of success.

After the meditation, the teens get ready for communion. Just as this process is a solemn one in any church, so communion in the circle gives honor to the Lord and Lady. In a large circle, the Temple Summoner retrieves the cakes and

---

1. Written by Jack Veasey.

the Maiden fetches the goblet and apple juice. At the appropriate time, they will hand the communion items to the High Priest and High Priestess. In a smaller circle, we don't need all this formality.

Since Annette and Tom brought the Lord and Lady into the circle, they will be our prime players in the communion. Tom picks up the goblet, goes down on one knee, and holds the goblet out to Annette. Annette holds her hands over the goblet, palms down, and says:

> From the moon to the earth,
> from the earth to the roots,
> from the roots to the vine,
> from the vine to the berry,
> from the berry to juice—
> may the Lord and Lady bless and consecrate
> the contents of this cup.
> So mote it be!

The group responds:

> So mote it be!

Annette keeps her hands in place, imagining a white light glowing all around and through the goblet.

Tom rises and Annette pours the contents of the goblet into paper cups. She gives a cup to each person, saying:

> May you never thirst.

The person responds:

> May you never thirst.

Annette returns to the altar and picks up the tray of cakes. She goes down on one knee in front of Tom. Tom holds his hands over the cakes and says:

> From the sun to the earth,
> from the earth to the roots,
> from the roots to the stalk,
> from the stalk to the grain,
> from the grain to these cakes—
> may the Lord and Lady bless and consecrate
> the meal upon this tray.
> So mote it be!

The group responds:

> So mote it be!

Tom keeps his hands over the tray, envisioning white light surrounding and entering the cakes. Annette rises and Tom offers a cake to each person, saying:

> May you never hunger.

They respond:

> May you never hunger.

Tom returns to the altar and sets the tray down.

The ritual is almost over and soon the feast will begin. Annette and Tom now thank the Lord and Lady in their own words, then put their hands slowly in the air to release the divine energies they have called. If they want to, Annette and Tom could hold hands together, raising them slowly, to do this task.

The teens now take their original places at the quarters. George, who is West, will release his quarter first, as West was the last quarter called. He turns to face the outside of the circle, with arms open. The others turn to face the West. Slowly closing his arms to rest across his chest, George says:

> Spirits of the West, element of Water.
> Thank you for your participation in this ritual tonight.
> Go if you must, stay if you like.
> Hail and farewell!

The group responds:

> Hail and farewell!

Julia now faces South, and the group turns to face the Southern quarter. With her arms open, and slowly closing, Julia says:

> Spirits of the South, element of Fire.
> Thank you for your participation in this ritual tonight.
> Go if you must, stay if you like.
> Hail and farewell.

The group responds:

> Hail and farewell!

Tom faces the East, with arms open. He slowly closes them, saying:

Spirits of the East, element of Air.
Thank you for your participation in this ritual tonight.
Hail and farewell.

The group responds:

Hail and farewell!

Annette faces the North, with arms open. She slowly closes them, saying:

Spirits of the North, element of Earth.
Thank you for your participation in this ritual tonight.
Hail and farewell.

The group responds:

Hail and farewell!

Annette steps forward. Since she cast the circle, she will release the circle. With her dominant hand, index finger pointing out and downward, she walks around the circle, counterclockwise, envisioning the energy collecting in her hand. When she finishes, Annette can take this energy and place the force in the altar, in any tools, or into the ground. Then she pounds the floor with her hand, or stomps her foot, and says:

This circle is open, but never broken.

The group says:

We are the people, we are the power, we are the change!
Merry meet, merry part, until we merry meet again!
So mote it be!

With laughter and chatter, the group descends upon the feast.

Some rituals you will read in books are far more scripted than this one. Here, you learn the basics and take the ritual from that point on, allowing your creativity to blossom. In some Wiccan Traditions, this doesn't happen, as group Esbats and Sabbats contain highly choreographed areas, including long passages of memorization and scripts to follow.

Sabbat Ritual

For a Sabbat, your basic ritual outline would look something like this:

1. Prepare Sacred Space
2. Do the Altar Devotion
3. Cast Circle
4. Call Quarters
5. Draw Down the Moon or Invoke the God and Goddess
6. Ritual Enactment of Festival
7. Performance of Magick (Fire Festival)
8. Circle Dance or Raising of Power
9. Communion
10. Thank Spirit for Participating
11. Release Quarters
12. Release the Circle
13. Feast
14. Clean-up

Notice that some differences appear between the Esbat ritual and the Sabbat ritual. First, the magickal operation (if any) in a Sabbat takes second banana to the holiday enactment. Second, Witches usually reserve meditation activities for general rituals or Esbats. Finally, many Sabbat activities involving group activities don't always take place at night. Since Sabbats link to solar energies, many groups spend an entire day celebrating a Sabbat, especially in the warm months where seminars, drumming, and picnics fill the day. Sometimes the events can begin with a Sabbat ritual; in other cases, the events may end with a ritual.

When you write a Sabbat or Esbat, let your emotions in and out! Look your feelings straight in the eye. Ritual should be an expression of yourself and all the nuances of you and your belief in Spirit. If we talk about the battle between the dying Oak King and the victory of the Holly King, we can allow pent-up emotions created by our fears, our self-sacrifice, and our rage to surface in the words, countered by our emotions of winning, of victory, and of goal attainment. If we speak of the love of the Goddess, her bounty and her adoration of life, then we can allow our feelings of wanting the fulfillment of love and our love for others to surge through the ritual. The best rituals written and performed are those that you create yourself, not those you get out of a book. Yes, many books exist, brimming with Pagan and Wiccan rituals. In a pinch, I've used those myself. Nevertheless, I recommend that you work with those rituals as guidelines to teach yourself how to write a ritual, and to understand the various mythos of Wiccan theology. The ritual should be an extension of yourself. That's what makes rituals so special. There is no "wrong way" to write a ritual, if that ritual seeks to harm no one and affirms and celebrates life.

Spontaneous Ritual

Spontaneous ritual does not follow any type of format. This type of ritual represents your creativity. A spontaneous ritual is your gift to Spirit. A spontaneous ritual normally includes the casting of a magick circle and the calling of the quarters. From that point on, whatever you do, if you practice pure intent and work with Spirit, the body of the ritual is up to you. For example, Michelle, a very talented and budding artist, likes to cast a magick circle, call the quarters, and then work on her projects. There's nothing wrong with this at all. When she's tired, she'll release the quarters and the magick circle.

A magick circle can travel with you. Donny, an excellent photographer, blesses and empowers his camera equipment and film at his altar before he goes out on a shoot. He also casts a mental magick circle around himself while at the site, asking Spirit to help him take the best pictures possible.

Kerri, a cheerleader, prays at her altar before every game or competition, asking Spirit to help her do her best. While at the event, she will cast a mental circle around herself and her teammates for strength, protection, and excellence, because the Goddess says, "All acts of love and pleasure are my rituals." Here, Kerri loves to perform, and dedicates her gifts to the Mother.

Most Witches do spellwork in a general ritual format, an Esbat format, or a spontaneous ritual. It doesn't really matter which format you choose, as long as you feel comfortable with that format.

Letters from Teens on Ritual

In this section I'm going to deal with some questions or concerns teens have had over the years on the subject of ritual.

1. *I'm afraid to do ritual because I think that I may conjure something I shouldn't. What should I do?*

   You can't conjure things you don't call. No demon will appear looming in the dark. No floating dishes, gyrating toys, or flying furniture will need permission from you to land. No bumps, raps, or echoing laughter will assault your ears and scare your dog. All these things happen in the movies. They will not happen in your ritual. To ensure that your fear button doesn't turn on, call only what you know and understand. For example, let's say you find a cool book that has all sorts of mumbo-jumbo dancing across the page. You can't read the names, and have no idea what sort of energies the incantation might call. Don't use it. Never work with any material that you don't fully comprehend. If you are very nervous, then work with your guardian angel always, by asking aloud before you begin.

2. *I've read lots of books, but I've never tried anything. I want to be a Witch so bad, but I don't know how to start.*

   Design a basic ritual and do that ritual. The Craft is like riding a bike. When you first start, you will wibble and wobble around a lot but, like anything that you practice, you'll get better. You've got to muster the courage to begin anything new. The Craft is no different. Time and study become the basic tests to decide whether the Craft is for you.

3. *I have trouble keeping a picture in my head for any length of time, and sometimes I have trouble making a picture in my head at all.*

   Don't rush yourself. Take your time. To practice, look at a picture in a magazine, then close your eyes and try to see that picture in your mind. Don't worry if you can't hold the picture for very long. Again, practice makes perfect, and this procedure, called visualization, takes lots of practice.

4. *I haven't done any ritual because I'm afraid that I won't do the ritual the right way. I feel I need a teacher, that the books won't help me.*

   If you feel you need a teacher, you've missed the point of the Craft. Most experienced Crafters will not teach students unless the student has experienced a few years of self-study. Taking someone "cold" into the faith requires a lot of time and energy by the teacher. Most Wiccan teachers don't want to teach someone for a few months, and then discover that the student has lost interest because the Craft involves lots of work. The main thrust of Craft philosophy urges you to stand on your own two feet. In the Craft, we believe that when you are spiritually ready for a teacher, the universe will present you with the teacher who will be best for you.

5. *I want to join a coven. Can you please tell me who in my area could teach me or who might let me join their coven?*

    Because of the laws of guardianship, ninety-five percent of adult Crafters will not teach WitchCraft to minors, unless those children live in magickal homes. Your parents, whether you like it or not, do have a say about what adults you associate with or activities in which you participate. If your parents don't understand the Craft, or don't like the idea of you learning the Craft, they can legally stop you. This goes for anything in your life. If your mom doesn't want you to participate in basketball, you can't go play on a sponsored team without her permission.

    Most Witches also feel that if you do not come from a magickal home, you need time as an adult to search the world around you for the kind of spirituality that is right for you. Even if you are over twenty-one, you might not find immediate acceptance into a coven environment.

6. *My friends and I want to create a coven. How do we do this?*

    I don't recommend coven government for minors. A circle of friends to practice magick and ritual with—hey, that's fine, but I feel that the workings of a real coven require experienced adults. Every coven should have an elder—someone who has worked a great deal in ritual and magick, who understands the mechanics of human relationship, and who has had some training in group work and counseling. No one, whether they are adult or minor, can become a High Priestess or High Priest overnight, or pick up a book and suddenly decide that's the role they want for themselves. Most of the Witches I know have worked for years in self-study and group training before they attempted to begin a coven. Teen years, as we all know, can be extremely volatile times. Locking yourself and a few friends into a coven format, to me, isn't a wise idea.

7. *My parent(s) won't let me do ritual. How can I practice the Craft if I can't do ritual?*

    You can pray. You can do ritual in your mind. You can meditate. It's harder when no one allows you to do all the bells and whistles, but it can be done.

The Seeker Ceremony

No matter what your religion, you can write a ritual and do that ritual to encompass a Seeker Ceremony for your religious belief. Although I've designed this book specifically for young Crafters, any person can commit their energies to learning any religion. Don't feel you have to align yourself to the Lord and Lady right away just to work within the boundaries of the Craft. You may wish to practice the various aspects of the Craft for a full year, or even longer, before you decide to take any further steps. No one can tell you when to perform this type of dedication ceremony. This decision is one you must make by yourself. In my book *To Ride A Silver Broomstick* (which is the next learning step after this book) I provide a dedication ritual for you. Meanwhile, I've designed a Teen Seeker ritual to help you in your search for spiritual enlightenment.

A Teen Seeker Ritual

When to Perform: When you feel ready. You might like to choose a special day, such as your birthday, a Wiccan holiday (Beltaine is a good one), or other day that has importance to you. Some kids like to wait for a full moon, a new moon, or a Sunday. Your timing doesn't really matter. Your choice to perform the seeker ritual does.

Where to Perform: Where you want. Some kids like to go to the beach, the forest, a favorite fountain, et cetera, or you could stay in your backyard, or do the ritual in your room.

Supplies: These depend a great deal on the permissiveness of your parents. In reality, you don't need any supplies to tell Spirit that you feel ready to walk the path of spiritual enlightenment, but humans like to use things to represent important moments in their lives. You may like to put a little cauldron on your altar with a tea candle, or you might like a certain kind of incense. The choice of supplies will be up to you. You might like to buy yourself a small token to represent the ceremony—a necklace, bracelet, or a small item to carry in your pocket.

What to Say and What to Do: This, again, is up to you. Although I provide a ritual outline here, I recommend that you say what comes from the heart—that's the best way to talk to Spirit, whether you choose to do the seeker ritual or a ritual of healing for a friend.

The Day of the Ceremony: Gather all of your things together, such as your incense, what you would like to wear, the token for yourself, any items you will use to place at the quarters or on your altar, et cetera. Place everything on your altar and ask for the blessings of the elements. You can pass incense over the items for East, a red candle for South, holy water for West, and a bit of salt for Earth, saying:

> I cleanse and consecrate these items
> in preparation for my seeker ceremony.
> May no evil or negativity abide in thee.
> May the blessings of the Lord and Lady (or Spirit)
> descend upon this altar and these things.
> So mote it be!

If you plan to transport your props to another site, pack them carefully in a picnic basket, a duffle bag, backpack, et cetera. Include something to eat and drink for communion, but be careful of spills.

The Ritual: Set up the ritual site and your altar. If you have chosen to do your ritual outside, be sure to walk the area and ask the faeries and devas of the land to accept you and to protect you while you do your ritual. Remember that the altar can be temporary. When you feel ready, do the altar devotion, then cast your circle, saying:

> I conjure thee, O circle of Power,
> so that you will be for me a boundary
> between the world of humans and the realms of mighty spirits—
> a meeting place of perfect love, trust, peace, and joy.
> I call upon the elements of the East, the South, the West, and the North
> to aid me in this consecration and to help me to raise
> and contain the power herein.
> In the name of the Lord and the Lady
> Thus do I conjure thee,
> O great circle of Power!

Remember that you can cast the circle by walking clockwise three times around while reciting the words, or walking around only once.

Tap the ground and say:

> This circle is sealed.

Move to the Northern quarter and say:

> Guardians of the North, element of Earth,
> welcome to my seeker ceremony.
> Angels of Earth, lend your strength and stability to this ritual,
> gift me with your special powers.
> Enter here, and join me on this momentous occasion.

Move to the Eastern quarter and say:

> Guardians of the East, element of Air,
> welcome to my seeker ceremony.
> Angels of Air, lend your wisdom and intellect to this ritual,
> gift me with your special powers.
> Enter here, and join me on this momentous occasion.

Move to the Southern quarter and say:

> Guardians of the South, element of Fire,
> welcome to my seeker ceremony.
> Angels of Fire, lend your passion and creativity to this ritual,
> gift me with your special powers.
> Enter here, and join me on this momentous occasion.

Move to the Western quarter and say:

> Guardians of the West, element of Water,
> welcome to my seeker ceremony.
> Angels of Water, lend your transformation and love to this ritual,
> gift me with your special powers.
> Enter here, and join me on this momentous occasion.

Move to the center of the circle and say:

> Holy Mother, Divine Lord,
> I welcome you into this circle cast for my seeker ritual.
> Come to me and bless me on this momentous occasion.
> Gift me, please, with your special powers.
> I have come this day *(eve)* to proclaim my interest
> in the Craft of the Wise.

Kneel and place your hands on the altar and say:

I, *(your name),* do solemnly swear by my Mother's lineage
and all that I hold sacred and holy
that I will honor and respect Spirit
and the brothers and sisters of the Craft of the Wise.
I will work hard to serve Spirit in every way,
and I will try to learn all aspects of the Craft.
I will not use my knowledge of the Craft to cause harm,
nor will I require the payment of money, goods, or services
when I pray for people or work magick for them beyond a fair exchange
of energy. When I have learned sufficiently,
I may choose to dedicate myself to the Lord and Lady,
or I may walk away and follow another spiritual path.
I will do my best to work in harmony for myself and for others always.
I will respect other religions as I respect my own.
Spirit has now witnessed my oath.
On this day, *(name the day),* I claim my power.
So mote it be.

Stand up, and light the tea candle in the cauldron. Take the token you have purchased or found for yourself and hold the item out, over the altar, and say:

Bless this token of my faith,
O Lord and Lady.

Take the token to each quarter, and ask for the energies of that quarter to bless and energize the token. Return to the altar, hold the token out again, and say:

This token represents my testament today.
I will wear it in honor of the Lord and Lady.
So mote it be.

As you put the token on your person, say:

At this moment I am reborn in body, mind, and spirit!
So mote it be!

Now you seal your ceremony with your personal communion. Hold your hands over the drink and say:

From the moon to the land,

from the land to the vine,

from the vine to the berry,

from the berry to the juice,

I consecrate this drink in the name of the Lord and the Lady.

May their blessing shower upon me through eternity.

So mote it be.

Drink some juice, then pour the rest on the ground (or into a bowl) in a libation to Spirit. The bowl is called a libation bowl.

Hold your hands over the cake (cookies, bread) and say:

From the sun to the land,

from the land to the stalk,

from the stalk to the grain,

from the grain to this bread,

I consecrate this food in the name of the Lord and Lady.

May their blessing shower upon me through eternity.

So mote it be.

Eat some cake and drop the rest to the ground or in a bowl in a libation to Spirit.

Spend some time in meditation.

Move to the center of the circle and say:

Great Mother, Divine Father,

I thank you for attending my seeker ceremony.

Guard and guide me until I decide to become

part of the community of the Craft of the Wise,

or choose to seek another path.

Help me to do the divine work given to me,

and help me in all my choices.

So mote it be!

Move to the Western quarter and say:

> Guardians of the West, element of Water,
> thank you for your participation in my seeker ritual.
> Peace be with you and harm none on your way.
> Angels of Water, thank you for your special gifts.
> Go if you must, stay if you like.
> Hail and farewell!

Move to the Southern quarter and say:

> Guardians of the South, element of Fire,
> thank you for your participation in my seeker ritual.
> Peace be with you and harm none on your way.
> Angels of Fire, thank you for your special gifts.
> Go if you must, stay if you like.
> Hail and farewell!

Move to the Eastern quarter and say:

> Guardians of the East, element of Air,
> thank you for your participation in my seeker ritual.
> Angels of Air, thank you for your special gifts.
> Peace be with you and harm none on your way.
> Go if you must, stay if you like.
> Hail and farewell!

Move to the Northern quarter and say:

> Guardians of the North, element of Earth,
> thank you for your participation in my seeker ritual.
> Angels of Earth, thank you for your special gifts.
> Peace be with you and harm none on your way.
> Go if you must, stay if you like.
> Hail and farewell!

Begin at the West, and take up your circle. When you finish, pound the ground with your hand and say:

> This circle is open, but never broken.
> Merry meet and merry part, until we merry meet again.
> We are the people, we are the power, and we are the change.
> So mote it be!

You have just completed one of the most important ceremonies of your life.

Now you've discovered that nothing evil, insidious, or bizarre lurks at the heart of the Wiccan faith. I taught you ritual before magick, because magick fades to nothing without Spirit. Many people have a habit of reaching for magickal applications without understanding the spiritual energies that support such activities. I don't want you to make that mistake. Without the religion, magick falters and dies. Without faith, magick is nothing more than a process to occupy the mind, scattering thought-forms in a brisk, autumn wind.

⋆⁺⋆4⋆⁺⋆

Magick!

⋆⁺⋆The textbook definition of "magick" goes something like this: *Magick—Using one's will to create form.* Magick requires belief in a higher power, and faith in yourself. I've written scads of material on magick, and have read hundreds of books on the topic as well. I've thought about magick, talked about magick, and practiced magick for over twenty years. I've discovered that just as many religions exist in the world, so too many magickal systems present themselves from which the student may choose. I've learned that just as no religion is better than another, so too no magickal system outshines another. And I've learned that a magickal system isn't worth squat unless you plug that system into a religion.

Magick falls into two categories: folk magick and ceremonial magick. Sometimes Witches call these two systems low and high magick (respectively), but I don't agree. Low infers lesser-than, which simply isn't the case when we're talking about magick. Typically, the Craft student begins learning the applications of folk magick, then progresses to ceremonial form. Folk magick uses fewer tools, fewer words, and fewer steps than ceremonial magick. Most spell books on the market today consist of low magick applications. Once the student has mastered both systems, he or she chooses which system works best for him or her.

Whether you practice folk or ceremonial magick, both systems used in a positive way have the following in common: All magick contains prayer. All magick incorporates divinity. All magick concentrates on positive change. Which type of magick you use doesn't matter—it's how you use the magick that counts.

The actual performance of a magickal application may take as little as thirty seconds, once you gain knowledge, ability, and confidence in your work. For example, although I can usually stop a bloody nose in less than thirty seconds (a folk magick technique), it took a lot of study and practice on my part. I worked up to this level of skill through a series of steps. That's the point here. One major complaint I've heard from Witches is that modern magickal books do not carry advanced workings. Many young Witches fail to realize that the complication of the procedure carries less importance than the finesse of the procedure. Your skill makes the application fall into the beginner or advanced category.

manifesting magick n. Using your will to make something happen.

When Witches go through the training process they immediately learn two things: one, the theology and practices of the Craft; and two, how to raise their self-esteem. You can't work great magick if you don't believe in Spirit, or yourself. Yes, I know you can buy all those nifty-neatie spell books, but they aren't worth the paper they're printed on if you don't understand the fundamentals of making the magick in the first place. Magick represents your efforts of pushing energies or pulling energies. You push negative energies away from you. You pull positive energies toward you. Therefore, Witches work two kinds of positive magick—**manifesting** or **banishing**. To manifest something is to make that something happen. To banish something is to make that something go away.

banishing magick n. Using your will to make something go away.

To understand this aspect of the Craft, try this easy exercise. Breathe in and imagine the abundance of the universe coming toward you. Breathe out and imagine all the negative aspects of your life leaving you. Practice this simple exercise as much as possible every day, and you'll discover just how quickly you will begin to excel in basic, magickal practices.

Let's talk about a few of the magickal applications that Witches use, and in the process, I'll teach you some rules about how magick works.

Prayer

Prayer contains more magick than you can possibly imagine. In prayer, you talk directly to God. You tell divinity what's on your mind. What standard religions don't tell you, however, is that one doesn't just gush their problems to God and expect to get an answer. There are ways to pray.

Learn to talk to Spirit every day. Yes, that's right, just open your mouth and talk to Spirit. If you think people will look at you funny, then talk to Spirit in your mind. Don't boo-hoo to Spirit. All things happen to us because (a) we created the problem in the first place, and now we are dealing with the consequences; or (b) there is a special lesson that Spirit wants us to learn. Talk to Spirit like you would to your best friend. I talk to Spirit (and my guardian angel) all the time. I might say:

Please help me to understand what lesson this situation holds for me.
Please help me to be the best that I can be.
Please help me to say the right things, to write the correct words,
to assist in opening the hearts of others.

Don't stand there and stomp your foot and say, "If you don't answer me, I'll never believe in you again." Threatening Spirit is like busting your broom and expecting it to fly. Dumb. One doesn't make deals with Spirit. You don't say, "If you allow Cedar Cliff to win this football game against Delone, I promise I'll give up boyfriends for the next year." You just may get exactly what you asked for. I did. One does not bargain with Spirit and walk away unscathed from your promise.

Talking to Spirit before you make decisions is vitally important. Yes, I know that we have free will, and that often we want something so badly that we can taste it. Although we think that what we want might not be good for us, sometimes our desires overcome our logic. This, of course, leads us into trouble. It's taken me many years to understand that you need to talk to Spirit all the time. When I get up in the morning, I do my daily devotions and talk to Spirit. As I go through my day, I'll often whisper questions, statements, or whatever, to Spirit. The trick is to keep your questions, statements, and concerns positive. I realize this isn't always easy, but the technique works. I constantly ask Spirit to help me "walk my talk." Why do we need this constant exchange? People have the gift of free will. Every action you do, everything you say, changes your future (and the future of others) for good or ill. Rather than blunder through life thinking we know everything just because we have the gift of choice, we should ask Spirit to help guide our every step so that we can accomplish our missions, help ourselves, and assist others.

My daughter Angelique talks to Spirit in the mirror every morning. She gets up at 6:30 A.M. and, while she gets ready for school, does her daily devotions "on the go," then goes into the bathroom to apply her makeup. As she's putting her face together, she talks to Spirit. A prayer can be a request for help in a given situation. A prayer can be a thank you (very important) for help we have received. A prayer can be ten minutes long, or last only five seconds. Your intent here is important, not the length of time. You can put your prayer to music, draw a prayer, or make your prayer rhyme. Creative prayer works in harmony with the universe and carries more power. I often write prayers on paper. Witches call these prayer-papers petition magick. In the General Ritual in the last chapter you saw an example of petition magick. See how it all fits together?

Every magickal application, whether we are talking about spellwork, ritual, drumming, singing, et cetera, involves prayer—making a request to Spirit, honoring Spirit, or celebrating God all involve divinity. Every act of magick begins with a desire . . . and a prayer.

Singing and Musical Instruments

Music, whether we mean singing, playing a flute, or banging on a drum, involves the creation of sound. When we give that sound to Spirit, we manifest a kind of prayer. Rhythm lulls the mind into what we call the alpha state. The alpha state is natural to all humans. When you eat, watch television, drive, read, daydream, et cetera, your mind naturally goes into the alpha state. It is from the alpha state that our best magick unfolds. Let me put it this way: Say you are driving down the magickal highway of life. If you have lots of blocks on the road, expect your magick to get tangled and snarled. On this road, the blocks would be worries, anger, jealousy, et cetera. When we work magick we need to follow the old adage "Cool, calm, and collected." Witches never work magick when they are angry. Witches always relax, get their mind in order, and push away negative emotions to be sure they act in the best way possible. Let's not confuse this with procrastination. Don't put off working magick because you think things will be better later. Nope. That's just an excuse. On the other side of the broomstick, don't throw magick at things because you didn't have the brains to do the right thing in the first place. Using magick to bail yourself out of a situation that you allowed to get out of hand because you were too lazy to head off the trouble is like throwing propane on a house fire. Obviously, not the best move. Your magick will work, but often the worst has to happen for Spirit to straighten out the mess you made. Learn to move fast and ward nasty situations off rather than wait for the muck to descend on your sainted little head.

Oh, I got off the subject a bit, didn't I? Well, never mind. We'll hop right back on the Witch buggy and maneuver onto the main road. What was I talking about? Oh yes, magick and music. How could I have forgotten? Hmmm, yes, well, old people do that sometimes, segue, I mean. How long should you make magickal music? As long as you want to. You can play an entire song on your clarinet, or drum for ten minutes, or play a CD. What?? Absolutely. You can dedicate music written and sung by someone else to deity. Why not? Here at home I've taught all my kids to play the drums. We have djembes, doumbeks, bodhrans, and shaman drums. I've also got a large array of rattles and tambourines. The trick to drum trancing is to start quietly, then move the energy and sound faster and faster until you are ready to release that energy. If you work with a group of friends, have someone lead off, then that person will end the segment with a count of "one, two, three, four, five!" Everyone stops drumming and lets go on the count of five. Usually the drum with the deepest sound sets the tone for the segment, becoming the heartbeat of the magick. If you don't have a drum, don't worry about it. You can still drum. Take a plastic garbage can and set the open edges of the can on wooden blocks so the sound can escape through the open end of the can. You would be surprised at the neat sounds you can come up with. I heard about a fellow at a Pagan festival who cut the closed end of a big garbage can out, covered that end with yards and yards of clear packing tape, balanced the can between his legs so that the open end wasn't muffled, and used that garbage can for the deep sound of the heartbeat.

When I first went to festivals, I watched the drummers and examined the effect of the drums on the people. It was then I learned that the great power of music is not the words but the beat. I also learned that you can be a terrible drummer and still make magick. As with anything, practice makes perfect.

To begin with drums and rattles, think of a positive statement and make a beat to match. For example, you could say: "Spirit protect me," "Spirit heal me," or "I'll ace this test," et cetera. Of course, for the test you've got to study, right? Start slow, matching the beat to your words, and then go faster, and faster. Play as long as you like, then when you feel you've raised enough energy, stop and let the energy go. (Then study!)

Invocation and Evocation

In our chapter on ritual we talked about invocation, calling Spirit (or the God and Goddess) to help us with our work. Invocation and prayer can be synonymous, because when we pray, we invoke (call upon God) to help us in our lives. We might also call upon our guardian angel; therefore, we invoke the aid of this spiritual messenger. We can also invoke the energies of the elements, our ancestors, and totem animals. We summon the elements, stir the ancestral dead, and call the totem animals. Notice the difference in wording I just gave you. One does not order the ancestral dead or totem animals around. Whether you summon elements or not, you should always be polite!

To **evoke** something means to bring from within ourselves an energy or force outward into the universe. We can evoke loving energy from ourselves to those in need. We can evoke healing energy to help our children and loved ones. When we evoke energy from ourselves, we must be careful not to overextend and burn ourselves out. Witches become adept at invocation so that they do not use up precious life force needlessly. If you feel tired after a ritual, prayer, or a spell casting technique, then you have not invoked energy but evoked that energy instead. After any of these practices, you should feel revitalized and in harmony with the universe, not tired or cranky.

evoke v. What Witches do when they project energy from within themselves out into the universe.

Magickal Daydreaming

Earlier in the book I talked a little about magickal daydreaming. This path of power is one of my favorites because you don't have to be a genius to do the process. Daydreaming is a natural, mental outlet. We already daydream a lot, especially when we're young. Magickal daydreaming also represents a mental prayer to Spirit, and is a technique that you can do just about anytime, anywhere.

The only tool required for magickal daydreaming is your creative mind. As with other magickal applications, you can use magickal daydreaming alone or with other paths of power. In the general ritual you learned earlier, we employed magickal daydreaming as one step in the overall performance of the ritual.

Let's try some magickal daydreaming right now. List five things that you want desperately. This could be anything from finding a good job to learning how to be a good driver. A few rules exist in magickal daydreaming, as well as other types of magick:

1. Always daydream in a positive way. Do not daydream negative things.

2. Always daydream that you already have what you want, meaning daydream in the present tense.

3. Don't daydream for anything that belongs to someone else. The world is full of abundance. You need only tap into that abundance. You do not need to take something that someone else owns. That would be stealing.

4. All daydreams must be specific. No indecision allowed.

Pick the first thing on your list and write a positive statement about what you want. Witches call this positive statement of intent an affirmation. You affirm in writing (and by repeating the statement mentally to yourself as much as possible) what you want. My first daydream was to be a wise and empowered Witch. So, I wrote down on my piece of paper *I am a wise and empowered Witch.* I repeated that statement often in my mind every day, especially when I felt depressed or unhappy. I attached a daydream to the statement—a picture of myself happy and strong. I practiced this daydream with my affirmation for two years, every day, and you know, I daydreamed myself right into that position. Well, most of the time. I still do stupid things occasionally, but I'm only human, after all. To keep myself on the right path, I have continued to use this daydream—gee, for over fourteen years now.

My second daydream was to have an affordable, safe vehicle that was large enough to hold my big family. It took six years to manifest my dream, but I finally got the vehicle, and the car was exactly what I wanted. What is my point here? Magick will not necessarily happen overnight; sometimes it will take years to manifest what you want because magick, like electricity, follows the path of least resistance. That's why we must be careful what we daydream for and why, no matter how long it may take, we should never give up on our goals. Sometimes a lot has to happen in our lives to get us where we want to be. Learning to practice patience is a big part of Craft training. Many of your magickal workings will manifest within thirty days, usually from a full moon to a full moon, or a new moon to a new moon; but, if Spirit thinks the timing isn't right for you to receive your request (especially for big things), then it may take several months (even years, like in my vehicle daydream) to get what you want.

Don't think, either, that you can just daydream about something and it will happen without doing some sort of normal work. For example, when the time was right to get that car, I had to go looking for one, asking Spirit to give me the best deal. I drove around four towns, talked to a lot of sales people, and checked out the vehicle thoroughly before I signed my name on the dotted line. You have many gifts and skills, and magick will become one of those skills. Magick will not override your normal abilities.

One daydream crusher that hits everyone comes when you can't decide exactly what it is that you want. You vacillate, going from one thought to another. I did this with the vehicle daydream. I would see one kind of car in my mind, and then my husband would talk about another kind of car, and so I would get the daydream screwed up in my head. I also fell victim to believing that the daydream wasn't coming true because it was taking so long to happen. When I realized that part of my problem rested on my own indecision, then my daydream finally came true. This is true with all magickal applications. If you don't focus on exactly what you want, you're going to do nothing but chase the tail of your magickal robe. You'll be the little witch over there in the corner, running around in circles, spreading ineffectual sparklies everywhere and nowhere simultaneously.

Meditation

The biggest complaint that I hear from teens when they first begin to practice meditation is that the technique is too hard. Meditation isn't difficult to do; what's hard to master involves your patience factor. Meditation is magickal daydreaming taken a bit further. In meditation, you choose a specific time of day and carve out ten minutes to half an hour for practice. One does not become proficient at meditation in a short period. Truly, meditation for some folks takes up to a year or more to master. The hardest part of meditation is learning to sit still for any length of time. The second hardest thing in meditation is learning to gently focus your mind. The third hardest thing in meditation is learning when to let your imagination fly.

In theory, we have two types of meditation, that which focuses on a particular object or value (or non-value, like a blackboard), and that which uses the imagination. Both practices strengthen the mind and teach you to focus without straining yourself. With meditation comes the practice of **visualization**—learning to "see" a picture in your mind of a specific object (or non-object, in the case of the blackboard). When learning to meditate, I teach my students magickal daydreaming first, then progress into the more restricted process of focused meditation.

One of the biggest mistakes a new student makes when practicing meditation involves the "too much too soon" scenario. Students hope to sit, meditate for half an hour on their first try, and succeed—and that's the length and breadth of their magickal practice.

Wrong.

When we first try to meditate, by sitting still and concentrating on nothing (or a particular something) for any length of time, our bodies rebel big time. We itch. We want to move. All sorts of stupid things float through our minds, no matter how hard we concentrate on that "thing" or "non-thing." Don't worry about it—that's what is supposed to happen. You see, your conscious mind doesn't like trickery, which is exactly what you do when you learn to meditate. With meditation, you try to bypass the conscious mind with all its jabber and get to the heart of yourself and your talents, which lie in the subconscious mind. Your conscious mind enjoys playing games with you, and will try its best to foil your plans. Nevertheless, you're smarter, and you'll eventually succeed. Practice becomes the key.

visualization n. The practice of training your mind to "see" an object in your thoughts to bring it to you on the physical plane.

When I taught my children to meditate, I put some pleasant music (no, not loud stuff—that's for fun) on the CD player, had them sit comfortably, and told them to concentrate on a single object as long as they could. When they lost the thought, they were to choose another object. We practiced for only five minutes at a time. Over the summer, with practice, they could hold that image for five minutes. Trust me, even five minutes can be tough.

If meditation isn't that easy, why do we learn the process at all? First, learning to meditate gives your body a healthy advantage. Meditation will be a skill that you can use throughout your lifetime, no matter your religious practice. Today, stress management is more important than you could possibly believe. We now know that all illness begins in the mind—that mind, body, and soul interconnect. I realize you're young and that things like illness and stress might be far from your mind, but think again. Even through the ages of thirteen and eighteen, we experience all sorts of stresses in our lives: grades, peer pressure, volatile emotions, loneliness, a sense of losing the fun things in life because we are growing up, the excitement of the future. We know that some stress is good for us, but not always. The reason young people don't pay attention to stress is because usually you have a strong, healthy body, and it takes time for stress to begin breaking things down. When you are older, stress will bring on illness faster than when you are young. Meditation helps us to release our anger, our loneliness, and our fears so that we can become positive, healthy people. If you are sick, meditation helps you to get better by focusing on a healthy mind and body.

For Witches, meditation provides a vehicle for focused thought, which is important in prayer, ritual, and spellcasting. Once we learn to hang on to a visualization, our magick will work faster and better.

Guided meditation works much like magickal daydreaming, except you follow a script. You can write this script yourself or you can purchase all kinds of guided meditation tapes. Listen to the tapes first in the store, and buy the tapes only if you like the narrator's voice and what the visualization entails. Encourage your parents to use meditation. Believe me, they need peace of mind too.

Petition Magick

You've already read about petition magick in this book. Petition magick is by far the easiest of the minor magicks. The application requires a piece of paper and time to yourself. Witches use petition magick alone for a single application, or as an added procedure in more complicated spellworkings or rituals. Use petition magick for a little problem or a whopper. The size of the difficulty has nothing to do with the ease of the spell. You can do this type of magick in sacred space or a magick circle, depending on the nature of your request.

Sympathetic Magick

Witches work on the principle of "like attracts like." We call this universal law **sympathy**. For example, if you wanted to help your friend recover from an illness, you might place his or her picture in the center of your altar. This picture becomes the focus of your prayers and magick. Because the picture represents an image of your friend, then the principles of sympathetic magick move into the equation of your working. If you don't have a picture of your friend, look around for something that he or she has touched recently or, even better, something that belongs to him or her. When you touch things, you leave vibrations of your energy behind on that object. Items

sympathy n. A universal law that associates like objects with like objects.

handled by a person who experiences heightened emotion while they touch the item work best, though in a pinch any item will do. Witches also use hair clippings from the individual to create the sympathetic connection.

What if you don't have a picture, a lock of hair, or an item that your friend has touched recently? Not to worry. Enter poppet magick—the use of a doll, or object, to represent an individual (or your pet). Witches make poppets out of various materials, including clay and felt. Witches also use potatoes, cucumbers, and apples. I've also seen poppets made out of toothpicks and olives, or marshmallows and fondue sticks (hey, it worked)!

Color Magick

I love color magick because, like petition magick, this technique requires few tools. You need only a rudimentary knowledge of color to begin. Color and candle magick work together, because the same colors that you use for color magick relate to candle magick as well. Color magick works on the following principle: the vibration of color and how that vibration affects you and others.

Most Witches incorporate color magick in their spell and ritual work. My group, the Black Forest Clan, teaches students to use the colors that resonate with your personal energy. This will take some experimentation on your part. Use the lists below when in doubt, but don't view this information as the last word on color magick.

Color Magick Correspondence List

Color	Purpose
Black	Returning to sender; divination; negative work; protection
Blue-Black	For wounded pride; broken bones; angelic protection
Dark Purple	Used for calling up the power of the ancient ones; sigils/runes; government
Lavender	To invoke righteous spirit within yourself; favors for people
Dark Green	Invoking the goddess of regeneration; agriculture; financial
Mint Green	Financial gains (used with gold and/or silver)

Green	Healing or health; North Cardinal Point
Avocado Green	Beginnings
Light Green	Improve the weather
Indigo Blue	To reveal deep secrets; protection on the astral levels; defenses
Dark Blue	Confusion (to create—must be used with white or you will confuse yourself)
Blue	Protection
Royal Blue	Power and protection
Pale/Light Blue	Protection of home; buildings; young, et cetera (i.e., young males)
Ruby Red	Love or anger of a passionate nature
Red	Love; romantic atmosphere; energy; South Cardinal Point
Light Red	Deep affection of a non-sexual nature
Deep Pink	Harmony and friendship in the home
Pink	Harmony and friendship with people; binding magick
Pale Pink	Friendship; young females
Yellow	Healing; East Cardinal Point
Deep Gold	Prosperity; sun magick
Gold	Attraction
Pale Gold	Prosperity in health
Burnt Orange	Opportunity
Orange	Material gain; to seal a spell; attraction
Dark Brown	Invoking Earth for benefits
Brown	Peace in the home; herb magick; friendship
Pale Brown	Material benefits in the home
Silver	Quick money; gambling; Invocation of the Moon; moon magick
Off-White	Peace of mind
Lily White	Mother candle (burned for thirty minutes at each moon phase)

White   Righteousness; purity; East Cardinal Point;
                 devotional magick

Gray   Glamories

Use White to substitute for any color.

Colors for Days of the Week

Monday   White
Tuesday   Red
Wednesday   Purple
Thursday   Green
Friday   Blue
Saturday   Black
Sunday   Yellow

Candle Magick

Working with candles can be a simple or complex minor magick, depending on the rite or ritual you do along with the application. Use candle magick alone in sacred space or combined with other folk magick or ceremonial magick for practically any type of human situation. Candle magick works on the following principles:

- The color of the candle
- The type of oil you use to dress the candle
- The sigils (magickal symbols) you carve (or do not carve) on the candle
- The sort of divinity you call as you light the candle
- The herbs you sprinkle around the base of the candle

You do not have to use sigils or herbs if you don't want to. Many Witches load herbs into candles by carving out a hole in the bottom of the candle; or, if using a glass-encased candle, making a hole down one side in the wax and pouring the herbs and oils in the indentation.

You can make candle magick complicated, if you like. This involves the array of colors, deities, oils, and the use of astrological timing and other correspondences. Witches use five-day candle spells, seven-day candle spells, nine-day candle spells, tarot candle spells, rune candle spells, astrological candle spells, and planetary candle spells. Timed spells require a specific number of candles to burn on a certain day or number of days, at the same time each day for a set period. You can write a whole ritual around a candle spell. In short, there is no end to your ingenuity in working with candle magick. Candle magick is fun, inexpensive, and it works.

Recommended reading for candle magick information:

Practical Candleburning Rituals by Raymond Buckland (Llewellyn)

Advanced Candle Magick: More Spells and Rituals for Every Purpose by Raymond Buckland (Llewellyn)

Cord Magick

Magick with cords represents another simple magickal operation you can use alone or with other magickal applications, such as candle and petition work. Simple cord magick entails the following:

- Choice of cord color
- Choice of cord length
- Choice of a disposable cord, or one you will use again
- Choice of divinity

Normally, cord magick uses a red, white, or black cord (basic colors of early Goddess worship) thirteen inches in length, with the intention of giving the cord away or disposing of the cord when you finish. Of course, you can work with every color of the rainbow or something between—that choice lies with you and depends on your own experimentation.

Cord magick requires the magickal operation of charging, where you charge each knot with a chant or charm. A Witch seals each knot by drawing an equal-armed cross over the knot and dabbing the knot with oil or (yes) saliva. Disposal of the cord depends on the purpose of the spell. If you wish to banish negativity, you would bury the cord immediately, away from your home. If the application will center on healing or drawing something toward you, keep the cord until the desire manifests, then release the magick and burn the cord. You release the magick by drawing a star in the air over the cord while picturing all magick seeping away from the item.

As with petition and candle magick, the Witch must first write out exactly what they want, and then form a picture in their mind of the successful conclusion of the desire. As the Witch ties the knots, they concentrate on the picture of success.

Tie the knots in the following manner:

1——6——4——7——3——8——5——9——2

while saying the words below:

By knot of one, this spell's begun
By knot of two, my words are true
By knot of three, it comes to be
By knot of four, power in store
By knot of five, this spell's alive
By knot of six, this spell is fixed
By knot of seven, the answer's given
By knot of eight, I meld with fate
By knot of nine, the thing is mine!

Element Magick

This magickal application uses the five elements, as working Witches understand them: Earth, Air, Water, Fire, and Spirit. The elements are represented by the pentacle, which some Witches employ to command the four elements of earth. One never commands Spirit or deity. The magick of the mind, body, and spirit tie to the pentacle and to the elements. All must be pure and working in unison for the magickal operation to succeed.

Witches work a great deal with the elements. We have representations of them on our altars, our shrines, and in our sacred space. We call the energies of the elements in ritual.

Element magick can manifest as physical or mental. For example, in Pow-Wow (which is a German system of folk magick—not Indian stuff) the element of Fire takes the shape of a healing, or Divinity, stone that you find for yourself. The stone should not be a gem, but a plain, ordinary stone that has a smooth surface and fits neatly in the palm of your hand. Once cleansed, consecrated, and empowered, the Witch instills the candle flame and the energies of the flame into the stone. No actual fire need be available when you work with the Divinity stone once you have empowered it. Witches use the Divinity stone (or lightning stone) for banishing pain, closing wounds, and other healing applications. Once charged, the stone becomes the divine representation of the element of fire in that element's healing form.

Each pool, steam, mountain, lake, rock, comet, well, star, tree, flower, weed, et cetera, has its own energy vibration, just as animals and people do. Like vibrations meld together to create a collective unconscious. In the element world, these collective energies are know as sylphs, gnomes, salamanders, and undines.[1]

Sylphs	Air
Salamanders	Fire
Undines	Water
Gnomes	Earth

Just as we can align ourselves in a group healing circle, or in ritual, we can align ourselves with the collective unconscious or sympathetic energies of each element. Witches learn to align themselves with the energies of the elements as a foundation of their magickal training.

Each element, like people, contains a positive and negative energy force. For example, Earth creates a foundation for our homes, but Earth can be unyielding, like a mountain. Air can make us feel uplifted, excited, or energized, but Air can turn into a tornado and create havoc in its path. Fire warms our hearts and provides light for our inner darkness, but Fire can destroy and consume if we are not careful. Water gently lulls us into transformation and surrounds us with love and peace, yet Water can overcome us, ripping our homes from the land. Water can also become stagnant, or freeze into glacier form. These elemental vibrations move about our planet and through our lives every day, and we hardly notice them at all. These energies have always been with us, and so we take them for granted, overlooking their power.

The Witch learns the power of each element by working with that energy as much as possible. Although Witches "summon" the elementals, we have learned to politely ask these energies to help us when we work magick and ritual due to the raw energy potential.

---

1. It is believed that the elemental associations were created in the Middle Ages from records on Grecian mystery Traditions.

A quick reference for element magick would be:

Earth   Money, prosperity, fertility, healing, employment

Air   Mental powers, visions, psychic powers, wisdom

Fire   Lust, courage, strength, protection, health

Water   Sleep, meditation, purification, prophetic dreams, healing, love, friendships, fidelity

Many spells written for you in this book contain elemental correspondences. If you wish to continue your Wiccan training, you may want to read the following books to help you in your studies:

Earth, Air, Fire & Water by Scott Cunningham (Llewellyn)

Earth Power by Scott Cunningham (Llewellyn)

Herbs, Incense, and Oils

Witches use a variety of herbs, incenses, magickal powders, and oils to augment their work. Your olfactory senses send signals to your subconscious mind that allow you to relax, enhancing your mental prowess. Each herb, oil, incense, and magickal powder you use carries its own magickal properties, including gender, astrological correspondence, and elemental correspondence. If the study of these applications interests you, plan to spend time learning the various magickal and medical uses of each item. Most Witches begin learning about the plants indigenous to their area, then branch out into some more exotic flora.

A note of caution here. The American Medical Association forbids the distribution of herbals for ingestion unless you have a license for dispensing that product. You can't raise plants for medical purposes for friends. You can do so for yourself, but not for anyone else.

Witches use herbs in conjuring bags, poppets, dream pillows, loose, in candle magick, in incense, and medicinally in both fresh and dried forms. Necessary tools include storage containers, a mortar and pestle, and bags. Witches employ herbal magicks with minor magicks, such as candle burning, chants, charms, petitions, and meditation (to burn, not to ingest).

I realize that teens may have difficulty obtaining many herbs and plants listed in magickal books. The wonderful teacher, writer, and lecturer Leo Buscaglia once said "If the door is locked, look for an open window." Leo wasn't Craft, but he was very wise. If you can't find that "special" magickal herb, don't fret. After a long discussion with my own two teen Witches, we went for a trip to the grocery store with *Cunningham's Encyclopedia of Magickal Herbs* in hand along with our combined magickal knowledge (and, of course, my checkbook). (The one thing you'll learn about my books is that I never, ever give you a magickal application, ritual, or spell that I haven't first tested myself. Often several members of the Black Forest Clan will work the magick too, just to make sure that the results we say will happen will actually happen.)

Our magickal shopping spree ended in the following list that we designed for the teen Witch. You'll find some ingredients in the spells written just for you, the teen, in the next chapter. We figured that if you can't get to a magickal store or don't have the money for expensive, exotic herbs, we'd find herbs or materials that worked just as well. You can use items on this list as a substitution for an herb or item you can't get, or you can learn to make up your own blends, which I highly recommend. Many supermarkets contain floral areas, so I have incorporated a few well-known flowers normally sold in that section.

Grocery Store Magick List

African Violet	Spirituality, protection
Alfalfa	Prosperity, anti-hunger, money
Allspice	Money, luck, healing
Almond	Money, prosperity, wisdom
Aloe	Protection, luck
Apple	Love, healing, garden magick, immortality
Apricot	Love
Avocado	Love, beauty
Banana	Fertility, potency, prosperity
Barley	Love, healing, protection
Basil	Love, exorcism, wealth, flying (in airplanes), protection, sympathy
Bay	Protection, psychic powers, healing, purification, strength
Bean	Protection, exorcism, wart charming, reconciliations, potency, love

Blackberry	Healing, money, protection
Blueberry	Protection
Brazil Nut	Love
Cabbage	Luck
Cactus	Protection, chastity
Caraway	Protection, lust, health, anti-theft, mental powers
Carnation	Protection, strength, healing
Carob	Protection, health
Carrot	Fertility, lust
Cashew	Money, communication
Catnip	Cat magick, love, beauty, happiness
Cedar	Healing, purification, money, protection, stopping sexual harassment
Celery	Mental powers, lust, psychic powers
Chamomile	Money, sleep, love, purification
Cherry	Love, divination, victory
Chestnut	Love
Cinnamon	Spirituality, success, healing, power, psychic powers, protection, love
Clove	Protection, exorcism, love, money
Coconut	Water, purification, protection, chastity
Colored Pencils	Color magick
Coriander	Love, health, healing
Corn	Protection, luck, divination, money
Cotton Balls	Luck, healing, protection, rain, fishing magick, communication
Compact Mirror	Banish negativity
Crayons	Color magick
Cucumber	Chastity, healing, fertility
Cumin	Anti-theft
Curry	Protection

Grocery Store Magick List, continued . . .

Dill	Protection, money, lust, love
Eggs	Healing, removing negativity, fertility
Endive	Lust, love
Eucalyptus	Healing, protection
Fennel	Protection, healing, purification
Fenugreek	Money
Fern	Rain-making, protection, luck, riches, external youth, health, exorcism
Fig	Divination, fertility, love
Garlic	Protection, healing, exorcism, lust, anti-theft; relief from nightmares
Ginger	Love, money, success, power
Ginseng	Love, wishes, healing, beauty, protection, lust
Gourd	Protection
Grain	Protection
Grape	Fertility, garden magick, mental powers, money
Holly	Protection, anti-lightning, luck, dream magick
Horseradish	Purification, exorcism
Lavender	Love, protection, sleep, chastity, longevity, purification, happiness, peace
Leek	Love, protection, exorcism
Lemon	Longevity, purification, love, friendship
Lettuce	Chastity, protection, divinations of love, sleep
Licorice	Lust, love, fidelity
Lime	Healing, love, protection
Maple	Love, longevity, money
Marshmallows	Healing, friendship
Marjoram	Protection, love, happiness, health, money
Mayonnaise	Prosperity, cleansing

Mint	Money, lust, healing, travel, exorcism, protection
Mistletoe	Protection, love, hunting, fertility, health, exorcism of negativity
Mothballs	Stop sexual harassment
Mustard	Fertility, protection, mental powers
Nutmeg	Luck, money, health, fidelity, relief from nightmares
Nuts (Mixed)	Fertility, prosperity, love, luck, communication
Oats	Money
Olive	Healing, peace, fertility, potency, protection
Onion	Protection, exorcism, healing, money, prophetic dreams
Orange	Love, divination, luck, money
Palm, Date	Fertility, potency
Papaya	Love, protection
Parsley	Lust, protection, purification
Pea	Money, love
Peach	Love, exorcism of negativity, longevity, fertility, wishes
Pear	Love
Pecan	Money, employment
Pepper	Protection, exorcism of negativity
Peppermint	Purification, sleep, love, healing, psychic powers
Persimmon	Healing, luck
Pimento	Love
Pineapple	Luck, money, chastity
Pistachio	Breaking love spells
Plum	Love, protection
Pomegranate	Divination, luck, wishes, wealth, fertility
Popcorn	Wishes, luck, prosperity
Potato	Image magick, healing, separation

Grocery Store Magick List, continued . . .

Pretzels	Success, protection (Note: pretzels must be whole, and designed with a knot. Straight pretzels will not work.)
Radish	Protection
Raspberry	Protection, love
Rhubarb	Protection, fidelity
Rice	Protection, rain, money, fertility
Rose	Love, psychic powers, healing, love divination, luck, protection
Rosemary	Protection, love, lust, mental powers, exorcism, purification, healing, sleep, youth
Rye	Love, fidelity
Sarsaparilla	Love, money
Sassafras	Health, money
Savory, Summer	Mental powers
Safety Pins	Protection
Sesame	Money, lust
Shoestrings	Cord and knot spells
Spearmint	Healing, love, mental powers
Strawberry	Love, luck
Sugar Cane	Love, lust, sympathy
Sunflower	Fertility, wishes, health, wisdom
Tea	Riches, courage, strength, health
Thyme	Health, healing, sleep, psychic powers, love, purification, courage
Tobacco	Healing, purification
Tomato	Prosperity, protection, love
Tuna	Prosperity, abundance
Turnip	Protection, ending relationships
Vanilla	Love, lust, mental powers

Walnut   Health, mental powers, infertility, wishes

Wheat   Fertility, money

Wintergreen   Protection, healing

Witch hazel   Protection, chastity

Magickal Alphabets

In some Craft traditions, first-level students are required to learn one complete magickal alphabet so they can translate their entire Book of Shadows into a secret, magickal tome. Systems such as the runes can delve quite deeply into magickal applications and require a great deal of study. Never use the runes as an "alphabet" to spell translated words from English to runic, as each rune carries individual magickal properties. If you translate English to runic you'll get magickal soup. Witches use magickal alphabets with other applications, such as petitions, candles, and mental programming. You might like to try using the magickal alphabet I've provided here, called Theban, with the spells in the next chapter.

Most people think that Witches just throw some stuff in a pot and say something bizarre, like Shakespeare's

> Double, Double, toil and trouble;
> Fire burn, and cauldron bubble.
> Eye of newt and toe of frog,
> Wool of bat and tongue of dog.

As you've seen here, this isn't the case. If you looked very closely at the last two lines of this poem, and remember what I told you earlier in this book, eye of newt, toe of frog, wool of bat, and tongue of dog were all folk names for plants indigenous to Shakespeare's area. Hmmm, wonder what Shakespeare was really up to, huh?

English	Theban
A	
B	
C	
D	
E	
F	
G	
H	
I	
J	
K	
L	
M	
N	
O	
P	
Q	
R	
S	
T	
U	
V	
W	
X	
Y	
Z	

Are there other forms of magick? Yes, indeed. This small list of minor magickal applications represents only part of what you could study and learn, if you put your mind to the process.

Checking Your Path

Most working Witches check their favorite divination tool before doing any magickal application to be sure that they have made the best spiritual choice for the situation. If you do not yet have a divination tool, not to worry. Simply find two stones, as equal in size as possible. You can paint one stone white and one black. The black stone will represent a "no" answer, and the white stone will represent a "yes" answer. Put the stones in a little bag. When you wish to know if you should go with a particular plan of action, put your hand over the bag, and say:

Spirit of knowledge
Guide my hand to the correct answer.
Should I do the working of (*say what you plan to do*) **or not?**

Then pull out a stone (without looking in the bag, of course). If the answer is "no," then do not go on. Think of additional ways to handle the situation, and try again. If the answer was "yes," then you can proceed. If you are afraid of saying "Spirit of knowledge," then ask your guardian angel to answer your question for you.

Learning to Devise a Spiritual Plan

When Autumn worked her magick to help her study habits and grades in school, she devised a spiritual plan. You see, just throwing magick at a problem or goal isn't the ultimate answer. Witches think carefully before choosing a magickal technique. Witches consider an entire plan of action of which magick becomes a part. Yes, a spell can take only a few minutes to do, a prayer a moment or two to utter, but without a complete spiritual plan, you may be throwing snowflakes at a campfire. A complete spiritual plan includes:

- Logical thought about the goal or situation.
- Considering how your actions, both magickal and normal, will affect the outcome of the goal, situation, or other people.

- Building positive reinforcement around you.

- Reprogramming your mind to accept success through thought, word, and action.

- Involving Spirit as much as possible in what you do.

I know all this seems a little complicated for something like a simple spell but, if we learn to plan wisely, we have a better chance of success in all that we do.

Why Magick Doesn't Always Work

Every adept Witch has experienced failure. Through failure, we learn and grow. Don't think because you happily zap away that all will turn out the way you want it to. Remember, magick follows the path of least resistance and, if we are not careful and aren't specific with our requests, failure may come as a result.

Spirit also guides our failures and our successes. Let's say that you wanted a red car so badly that you were willing to do almost anything, but Spirit knows if you get that red car, you would drive dangerously, resulting in an accident that might take out the one person who can create the cure for cancer. (Okay, so I'm getting a little bizarre here, but bear with me.) Spirit may step in and stop your magick from manifesting, or you may have to wait a few years before you get that car. Sadly, because of our gift of free will, Spirit can't always stop the bad things in life from happening; but, if you work with Spirit all the time, you have a better chance of avoiding the pitfalls in life rather than bumbling merrily along without Spirit and getting into trouble all the time.

Here's another example. Laurie wanted to work at a particular clothing store in the mall. She followed a spiritual plan, kept her thoughts positive during the application and the interview process, and worked magick to obtain the job. She didn't get the job. Disappointed, Laurie wondered if she had done something wrong in her planning or magick. One week later, Laurie was accepted as a for-eign exchange student for the following semester. If she'd taken the job, she would have had to quit immediately. Spirit knows better than we do what will be right for us. I've always taught my students (and my children) that if your magick doesn't work or if your spiritual plan fails, do not lose confidence in yourself. Spirit knows what you do and do not need, and sometimes, when you are least expecting it, Spirit will step in and bring your work to a grinding halt. Sometimes Spirit does this to protect us, and other times Spirit knows that we have bigger missions, larger goals, and more important activities that we should be doing.

I've taught my children to ask Spirit during a magickal working "to make the best thing happen for me." This way, you allow Spirit to help guide you in your work and play.

I've also learned something else that's very important. If strange things start happening around you, don't look for black magick: look for the activity of Spirit. The universe is definitely trying to tell you something. You may be on the wrong path, you may have made an unfortunate turn somewhere, perhaps your friends aren't what you thought they were and their activities bring negativity into your life, or you may be spending time on something that is wasteful to your purpose. Sometimes, Spirit has to hit us over the head with a giant broomstick to get us to pay attention. Once we wake up, we can correct our activities and focus on what would be best for us, rather than on an illusion we decided to foster.

Drugs and Alcohol Don't Mix with Magick

I rarely pound my fist on the pentacle when teaching but, when the subject slips around to illegal drug and alcohol use in magickal applications or your daily life, I'm a real Bossy Witch of the West (well, East, since I live on the East Coast). Illegal drugs and alcohol do not, and never did, mix with magickal applications. I do not want to hear about the tribal vision questing excuse, which gets thrown up every time someone wants to talk about this issue. In modern times, we know how to lead our minds into trance states in a safe and healthy manner *without* the use of illegal drugs or alcohol. If anyone tells you differently, they're full of it. Illegal drugs and alcohol are crutches—nothing more, nothing less. Legal drugs, such as what your doctor prescribes, are a different matter entirely.

The Wiccan Way includes following the laws of the state and federal government. Yes, we have laws of our own, but these laws do not include ignoring the laws of the place where we live. If you get caught at school with drugs or alcohol, you face suspension and possible expulsion. Your nightmare will not end there, either. Depending on the mood of the arresting officer, you may find yourself in front of the District Justice and off to Juve Hall, pronto. Only a lucky few are sent to a rehab program. Trust me, even if you "only used it once," the school, your parents, and the police don't care. Off you will go. They will tag you and bag you. Using drugs and alcohol to get back at your parents is one of the stupidest things you can do. Oh yes, you'll hurt them all right, but drugs and alcohol will ruin *your* life, not theirs. I can't believe that anyone really wants to live a life of drug or alcohol addiction. When you take drugs or drink alcohol, you impair your thinking. Your personality can, and will, turn to major ugly. You start to lie about things. You won't remember stuff, and the sad thing is, you won't even realize it. Too late, someone around you may wise up and realize the toilet you've jumped into.

If you're a teen reading this and laughing at me, that's sad for you, because you're not thinking with a full deck anymore. You may think you are, but you aren't.

The drug problem around our teens today is more than immense. Drug addiction is indiscriminate. Rich or poor, this insidious aspect of our society has no preference. Sadly, it is often the rich and middle-class families who refuse to realize that their child may have a problem simply because of their social class. Wrong.

Let me share with you a story of a fellow author friend of mine.

Sienna has two daughters, both in high school. Sienna and her husband would be considered middle-class. They survive. They pay their bills. They do as much as they can for their daughters. Neither Sienna nor her husband takes drugs. They've been married for over twenty years. Heck, they don't even drink. There's no abuse and no extramarital associations. Pretty much your standard, American dream family. Not for long.

Of the two daughters, one was a junior, the other a freshman. Both girls are lovely creatures. Sienna, the mother, thought everything was perking along okay even though the two girls often fought with each other over silly things like makeup, clothes, and other teen concerns. One afternoon, three days before school was out for the summer, right as Sienna was finishing a book on a killer deadline, she received a call from the youngest daughter.

"They want to search my backpack," said Cindy (the freshman), "and I won't let them."

Sienna leaned forward and pushed the computer keyboard away from herself, trying to pull her brain out of the fictional story she'd been working on and into a suddenly frightening real world problem. "What do you mean? Why do they want to search your backpack?"

"Because they think I have drugs," came the tearful reply.

Sienna's heart stopped. Her hand gripped the receiver of the phone. For her, one of her biggest nightmares floated out of the wailing voice of her daughter and into her brain. Still, she had hope. Perhaps her daughter was worried about her rights? Maybe this was the issue. "So let them search it."

Silence.

"Cindy? Let them search the bookbag."

Silence and a muffled sob.

The nightmare caught Sienna by the throat and punched her right in the gut. "Do you have drugs in your bookbag?" murmured Sienna.

A tiny reply. "Yes."

Sienna quelled the urge to throw the phone against the living room wall. Instead, she said, "Let them search the bookbag. I'll be there in three minutes."

The nightmare unfolded, corner by corner, layer by layer. Cindy's older sister, Alexis, had become quite popular with many kids in the small school. Her network extended through every grade, every age, every social structure—including the druggie culture. She knew preps, skaters, jocks —it didn't matter to Alexis. Alexis felt that everyone deserved a chance at friendship. She had no idea that associating with people who have lost their self-esteem and have turned to drugs would be bad for her—after all, she didn't use drugs.

As Cindy faced the tornado of emotions of her parents in the principal's office, Alexis sat at home, unaware of the tidal wave that was about to hit her. You see, Cindy didn't point the finger at her friends—because friends don't dime out friends. She pointed the finger at Alexis.

Less than twenty-four hours before, Sienna had a happy family, at least that's what she thought. Now, she had a war zone that was to last for several months. The entire fabric of her family life dissolved like plastic in an inferno, all in a matter of seconds.

Sienna called Alexis from school. "Don't go anywhere. Your sister is in deep trouble."

"I wanted to spend the night with Lisa."

"We'll discuss that later. Just don't go anywhere."

"What kind of trouble?" asked Alexis.

"Drugs. Just don't go anywhere. Do you understand?"

"What!? No! Not Cindy!"

"Just don't go anywhere. Okay?"

Poor Cindy. The two girls who narked on her hadn't been noble. Sad but true. They weren't concerned for Cindy's welfare. They wanted to get even. The one girl, a senior, hated Alexis. If she couldn't get the older girl, the one she really despised, she could slice and dice the younger one. So, in her last hour of school as a senior, she grabbed a friend and off they marched to destroy the little sister. The other girl, fat and unhappy, had been teased horribly by Cindy's friends, and

Cindy, always present, had never made a move to stop them. Payback time. Clear and simple.

It is still garbled, after almost a year, how Cindy got the drugs, or from whom. Cindy claimed that she found the drugs in Alexis' room a month earlier. She said that one of Alexis' druggie friends (who had stayed overnight) had left them there. Later, Alexis remembered that this friend came to visit, and demanded to be taken to Alexis' room. When Alexis did not respond, the friend left in a huff. The so-called friend had left the drugs in Alexis' room.

Since Cindy wasn't very mobile (remember she was only fourteen) Sienna could not determine where the drugs originally came from; all she knew was that she was left with a life-changing mess. Alexis, hysterical that Cindy had pointed the finger at her, took less and less interest in the family as a whole. About to turn eighteen, the whole world in front of her, she chose to leave the family behind, spending as much time as she humanly could away from home. When the police questioned the girls, they asked to see Alexis first. They didn't question her about drugs but about another incident at the school. You see, once word got around that Cindy had been snagged, kids who didn't like Alexis told the police she was responsible for vandalism at the school, which wasn't true, but Alexis had to deal with the accusation just the same. Luckily, she was in class when the vandalism occurred, or she would have had more of a mess than Cindy.

Why did Cindy have the drugs in the first place? Good question. Eventually Sienna discovered that the ever-popular Alexis was too hard a role model for Cindy to beat. Alexis, more mobile because she was older, became a threat to Cindy's self-esteem. Sienna discovered that Cindy, through her friends, met with and became attached to a dealer (only sixteen) in school. Cindy's friends liked the boy and tried to get the two together as much as possible, without Sienna's knowledge. This boy came from an abusive home. Slowly, over many months, the boy added to the erosion of Cindy's self-esteem, telling her she was ugly, stupid, and low class. He told her that she needed to earn his respect. To do this, she had to take the drugs.

Lucky for Cindy, she was caught. Although she suffered through the humiliation and the near destruction of her family, she could now throw off her misconceptions of the competition between her sister and herself, and realize that she'd been a victim of self-abuse and teen abuse (which I'll cover a bit later). Cindy wanted to fit in. To be one of the crowd, she succumbed to dabbling in drugs, and in her desire to be noticed, she seriously damaged the group mind of her family. All this over two small flakes of pot in a little plastic container. That's all it took to get her suspended from school (which was lifted) and forced into a rehab program. You see, Cindy had reached the point of a "real" user at the time she was caught. Once the downward spiral began, she didn't know how to stop it. Cindy didn't realize that she could go to her parents and that they would have helped her. Teen abuse and taking drugs does that to your brain.

So, the universe decided to stop spinning and kick her off for a while.

Cindy's mother told her this: "If you're going in the wrong direction, and God has a special mission for you, and you won't listen, the universe will step in and throw you a punch like you never thought possible. The fact that you got caught means that God has a special plan for you, that She doesn't intend for you to muck up. You be glad you have something important to do. You think about that."

Luckily, Cindy hadn't been in trouble before and her parents loved her deeply. They stuck by her and helped her through. Perhaps, if you're like Cindy, you might want to think twice about what you're doing. It could save your life.

Illegal drugs and alcohol will also inhibit your magick. If you do illegal drugs or drink alcohol, your magickal expertise will go right down the proverbial toilet. Rituals will bomb, spells will backfire, and your spiritual plan will look like a piece of Swiss cheese.

Forget the illegal drugs and alcohol if you want to be a real Witch.

The Dark Side—Witches Don't Go There

Witches do not work magick to harm others and we know that no real power lies in evil. I've seen teens that look to the dark side, thinking that Witches who "do good" are weak, and therefore good poses no threat against evil. Think again. Although Witches understand that the world contains order and chaos, and that both energies work together in the universe to create our world, chaos does not mean evil, and Witches never, ever get involved with evil.

We had an eighteen-year-old teen around here awhile back by the name of Jefferson. Jefferson had read some bogus occult-related material. He wasn't interested in the truth; the excitement of dark things entranced him. Jefferson walked around town scaring people. He told kids his age and younger that he had power because he worked dark magick. Kids, being impressionable and uneducated in the real workings of the occult, believed him. Jefferson didn't understand that generating fear isn't power, but weakness. His boasting proved he had low self-esteem. In a way, it's sad about Jefferson, but no matter what anyone said to dissuade him, he kept on scaring people, making threats, and being a general pain in the magickal you-know-what. Day after day, Jefferson wove his negativity around himself, until one day—bingo, the fear he'd let loose on others caught up with him. Spirit set in, and off to jail went Jefferson.

Good riddance.

Did Jefferson learn his lesson? Probably not. Once people like Jefferson buy into the illusion that evil has power, it takes a long time for them to recover, if at all. If someone ever threatens you with black magick, laugh at them. The use of black magick needs your fear as leverage, or the magick doesn't work. If you are not afraid, then the negative energy can't touch you. "Fear," as the movie *Dune* teaches, "is the mind killer." Laughter will dispel negative energy, as laughter is a part of Spirit.

Magick Is Balance

All workings of magick and ritual create energies to pull life into balance. Sometimes, especially when we first begin working magick, our lives appear to slip and slide around, bringing problems we never expected or certainly wished to experience. When you work magick, you are telling the Universe that you are ready for balance in your life. In order for you to attain balance, your life and habits must change.

I've gotten letters from a few teenagers who say they will never work magick again because something they didn't want to happen did happen. They feel that if they had left magick alone, everything would have been okay.

Nope.

Things would have changed anyway, and probably for the worse.

Your life, from the time you are born until the time you die, is filled with cycles of change. If situations did not change, then life would become stagnant. Anything that remains stagnant dies. Change is a vital part of your being. Witches learn to embrace balance and respect change.

I've given you a lot to think about in this chapter. I hope that, by now, you realize how much work the religion of WitchCraft involves. The work is important. The work is for yourself and, ultimately, for those you love. This chapter on magick represents the tip of the broomstick—there is much, much more to learn and to know in the world of a Witch.

Let's go over the basic rules of magick one more time before we get into the next chapter (which, I know, you can't wait to do—me neither, but we've got to make sure you begin with a strong foundation).

Basic Witch Rules of Magick

- All magick should be a part of a spiritual plan.

- All magick should include Spirit.

- Do a divination with your yes/no stones before attempting any magickal operation.

- Remember that every action you do results in an action that will affect yourself and others.

- Remember Witchie rule #1: "Do what thou wilt, yet harm none."

- Remember Witchie rule #2: "Ever mind the rule of three, what you send out comes back to thee."

- Remember Witchie rule #3: "Never work magick to inhibit another's free will."

- Remember Witchie rule #4: "Always walk your talk."

- Remember Witchie rule #5: "Always have a back-up plan."

- Remember Witchie rule #6: "Always work the real world with the magickal world."

- While you are learning, do all magickal applications in a magick circle or sacred space.

- Witchie rule #7: "Stay away from drugs and alcohol."

- Witchie rule #8: "Never threaten or scare anyone with your magick."

- Witchie rule #9: "Embrace Balance—Respect Change."

I think that covers it. Witches will tell you that we have more, much more, information in the study of the Craft. I've given you enough here to get you started. Now, let's go on to some of the fun stuff!

★ ★ ★

⋆⋆⁵⋆⋆

Spells Just for You

⋆⋆I realize that you might have purchased this book just to get to the spells, and I know that some of you have skipped to this part of the book and ignored the first few chapters. If you have done this, then go back, *please*, and read the chapters before this one. If you don't, then your spellcasting probably won't work. You need the foundation in the earlier chapters to ensure your success with the spells herein. For those of you who have plugged faithfully along, I'm very proud of you! Now we get to do the fun stuff!

Just as science has rules, so does the art of spellcasting. If you break the rules, you may pay more than you had originally anticipated. Spells fall into five basic categories: Love, Health, Money, Protection, and Other (a catchall for spells that don't seem to fit anywhere else). Each category has its own set of rules. As I write this, I think lovingly of my own children and how, over the years, I've taught them spellcasting techniques. A little here, a bit there, until they have gained quite a repertoire of their own spellcasting techniques. I can tell you that when my children put their minds to the task, they can out-spell any adept Witch on the face of the planet. If you follow the instructions in this book, you should succeed just as well. I know you can. Any new technique takes time to master, and that practice leads to perfection. All the spells in this chapter fall into the category of targeted spells, meaning each spell was composed and tested for the purpose given. You can use any of the basic techniques in the spells I wrote for spells that you create your-self. The most successful spells come from the heart and mind of the spellcaster. Just remember to follow the rules.

In the last chapter we covered some basic rules of magick. Do you remember them? With each spell in this chapter, I hope that you follow a spiritual plan and do your divination with the yes/no stones to check your proposed work. I also suggest that you use the general ritual format or the spontaneous ritual format given in previous chapters when practicing any spellcasting technique. This includes the altar devotion, circle casting, and quarter calls. If you have forgot-ten, go back over the information again until you feel comfortable with the techniques. Begin your own Book of Shadows to record your progress and your work. Please don't just read the spell and do the operation for kicks, or look at the spell and decide to perform the application without the ritual format. My kids will tell you that working magick manifests as serious business. The art of spellcasting shouldn't become a slumber party activity because everyone wants to do something different for a change. If you treat your work with reverence and respect, you will reap fantastic rewards.

Once you understand the mechanics of spellcasting, you can take anything and make a magickal operation. In the end, the spells you design yourself carry more power than any spell you can get out of a book. Why? Those spells and magickal operations designed by yourself meld your creative energy with the forces of the universe. How do I know this? From watching my kids.

Jamie, my ten-year-old son, wanted money to go on a field trip to Philadel-phia. For whatever reason, he thought that money may not be forthcoming. He decided to do his own spellwork without telling anyone. One evening, Jamie took a small bottle and filled the container with water and Vicks Formula cough syrup (expectorant). He thought of money, lit a red candle (because he likes red), shook the bottle, and let the candle burn for about five minutes. Then he set the corked bottle on his altar. His reasoning? Water to help money flow toward him, and the expectorant cough syrup to get the universe to "cough up" the money.

Keep in mind that I didn't know what he'd done at the time. I knew someone in the house had worked magick because I could feel the energy flowing, but I didn't know who or why. I asked all my kids, "Who's been working magick?" No one 'fessed up. I especially asked the girls, as they've had more training. Noth-ing. I asked Jamie in passing, but didn't hold onto the idea since he enjoys our drumming circles more than learning the rules of magick. Or so I thought. I walked by the red bottle several times, thinking how pretty the bottle was, and wondered about the bottle's purpose. Nevertheless, I was so busy with everything that I didn't move into the thought for any length of time.

The day of the field trip came. I set twenty dollars on the table for those little extras kids like to buy when they go on a field trip. His biggest sister walked by the table and chipped in five dollars. The next sister went over to the table and gave him three dollars. His daddy took him out to the grocery store and got Jamie whatever he wanted for his packed lunch. While on the trip, one parent bought Jamie a ride on the horse and carriage.

Jamie returned smiling, with gifts for everyone. I still did not know he had worked magick. That night, I had circle. We decided to do trance drumming, with drums and rattles to work toward our goals. As I was discussing with the big people how they should focus on their goals and that they can make magick out of anything, Jamie piped up and said, "Sure! I did it with cough syrup and water, and I made lots and lots of money!" Jamie explained what he'd done and the whole crew learned a valuable lesson, with lots of laughs added in!

Jamie did follow the golden Witch rule: Never magick a person for something; magick the universe.

Timing

Many beginning Witches worry about timing. How long will it take my spell to manifest? How long do I have to wait before something happens? You'll have to wait as long as it takes. Don't have such a long face! Here are a few guidelines on timing:

- Magick follows the path of least resistance, so unless you have a reason for guiding the magick along a particular line of thought, just let the magick go. The more blocks you place in the way of manifestation, the longer it will take to make things happen.

- Small goals manifest faster than large goals. For example, I asked my students to choose ten goals. They were to narrow those ten goals down to three. For six weeks we worked on all three goals. Many students, whose goals were small, manifested their desires in four weeks or less. Normally, small goals require one week to thirty days to manifest (or one full moon cycle). If your small goal does not happen in thirty days, we work again. Witches call this technique moon to moon, as the cycle from a full moon to a full moon (or a new moon to a new moon) is approximately twenty-eight days.

- Larger goals require the building of your magickal techniques. Those students who had larger goals worked up to six months to manifest their desires. Each week we did a different kind of magickal application to add energy to their goals. One week we blew wish bubbles, envisioning our goals as the bubbles. Another week we made magickal popcorn. We empowered the unpopped kernels and, as each kernel popped, we shouted out our goals. The next week we braided cords, working our desires into the cords. The students saved their cords until their desires came true. The week after that, we drew pictures of ourselves as we would appear when our goals had manifested. Another week we made a noodle chain, empowering each elbow noodle as we strung the noodles on a string of yarn. The students put their goal chain on their altars at home.

  Each magickal category in this chapter has several spells that you can try. Choose one spell and do that spell, then use your creativity to create other magickal forms of expression to reach your goal.

- The old teachers said, "Do a spell, then forget it." These teachers meant do the spell but don't worry about it. Feeding negative thoughts into your spellwork will defeat your purpose. If you worry about the manifestation of the spell, then you create blocks in the path of that manifestation.

- Don't try to direct your spell too much. Let's say you need money, but you've tried every way possible in the regular world with no success. Now you want to do magick. If you think that the only way money will come to you is through the means you have already tried, you will fail. The wise Witch leaves the path to money up to Spirit. This would be the same for the path to love, the path to protection, et cetera. This doesn't mean that you should not keep working in the "real world" to help manifest your desires. If you were sick, you would go to the doctor AND work magick for healing. If you wanted to bring love into your life, you would work on being a pleasant person and not lock yourself in the house and expect Cupid to come down the chimney, dragging your lost love in tow. If you needed protection, you would talk to your parents about the situation that has occurred and why you feel frightened. If you feel, for whatever reason, you cannot talk to your parents, then talk to a reliable adult (and you know in your heart who the reliable adults are and who is a jerk). If you work money magick, you would keep looking for opportunities and work on your creativity.

With these little reminders in mind, you can move forward into the realm of spellcasting.

Each spell gives you the suggested moon phase, planetary, color, and daily correspondence. Try to follow these correspondences as best you can. Also keep in mind that your own creativity and needs carry important weight in spellcasting. If today is Sunday, and the spell calls for completion on a Monday, but you really need to do the spell TODAY, then go ahead and do the spell today. If the spell calls for a supply that you don't have, that's okay. Substitute something else.

Each of the following categories (Love, Health, Prosperity, and Protection) has specific rules that apply to that category. Please read over these rules carefully before attempting to do any of the spells.

Love

The Rules for Love Magick

Young people and adults alike think that you can catch the guy or gal of your dreams with WitchCraft. Even in modern times, songs like "Witchie Woman," "That Old Black Magick," and "Season of the Witch" have sparked our imaginations on the power of the femme fatale Witch. Well, you can snare a guy or gal with WitchCraft, but not in the manner you probably think. Witches have specific rules for love magick:

- Never, ever try to magick a person against his or her will. Often I receive letters from people who want to force someone against his or her will to love the letter writer. Witches don't do that. If you like Harold or Sally, you simply cannot cast a spell to *make* them love you and expect to live happily ever after. Even if your spell works, you will suffer the repercussions. Oh, you'll give anything to have that person love you? Think again. Breakups in relationships won through magick have consistently rated the most violent, the most devastating, and the most harmful of good magick gone bad. Only a fool magicks someone into loving them.

- Never, ever take someone's husband, wife, or significant other from them either with or without magick. Romping on someone's turf will get you into trouble. Good Witches do their best to stay out of that kind of dead-end relationship. A lover won from another by means of magick will lead you down the path of misery.

- You cannot own another person. A person doesn't "belong" to you like a piece of property. Witches never give away their "shields" to another person. You always retain your personal power.

You might think that I've just taken all the fun out of magick and romance, but I assure you, Witches have wondrous tricks to enhance their love lives without interfering with another's free will.

Love Correspondences

Ever hear the old adage "like attracts like"? Witches use their creativity to find items and energies that vibrate at the same "love" frequency. Let's look over some of these correspondences so that you can get used to thinking this way when whipping up your spells.

The phases of the moon most conducive to love energies are new moon to full moon (to make love grow), or on the full moon. How do you find out what the moon phase might be? Check in an almanac, on the weather channel on the television, in the local newspaper in the weather section, or in an astrological almanac.

The planet most associated with love energies is Venus, although spells incorporating the energy of the Sun (for success) or Mercury (for communication) fit well with a magickal working of this type too.

The colors of love are red (passion), white (purity), gold (family warmth), brown (friendship), and pink (enchantment). Be careful with pink, as the blend of red and white can backfire, especially if you have mixed intentions or you feel unsure of the working. I recommend pink for self-love, but not when doing other types of love spells. For other color associations, check the table I gave you earlier in the book (on pages 111-113).

The items of love can take any form. For example, the fruits and vegetables of love would be apples, cherries, apricots, beets, endive, figs, lemons, avocado, peaches, pears, peas, plums, radish, raspberry, and tomato.

The herbs and plants of love are aster, bachelor's buttons, lemon balm, barley, basil, cinnamon, clove, coltsfoot, coriander, crocus, daffodil, daisy, dill, elm, endive, gardenia, geranium, ginseng, hibiscus, lavender, maple, marjoram, myrtle, nuts, orchid, pansy, peppermint, primrose, rose, rosemary, rye, sugar, thyme, tulip, valerian, vanilla, vervain, and willow.

We can use the four elements in our love spells, too: Air for clarity and communication; Fire to raise passion; Earth to help plant our love and watch that love grow; Water to move our love energies in and around us, or to transform ourselves into a more loving person.

Symbols of love: A white or red rose; a red heart; swans; lace; pictures of angels; Xs and Os (for hugs and kisses); a chocolate kiss; mistletoe; a ring; a rainbow; a unicorn; red and white beads; a golden cup; or a red bow. I'm sure you could think of some love symbols that I've forgotten.

With all these correspondences at our fingertips, there's no end to the variety of spells we could manifest, especially if we use our creativity.

Come to Me Love Spell

Rather than targeting a specific individual, this spell calls out into the universe to bring the individual to you who would be best for you at this time in your life. You must specify a human, because a friend of mine cast this spell and got a cat. If you're looking for a lovable pet to match your lifestyle and energy pattern, then simply substitute the word "animal" or "pet" for the word "person."

Use your yes/no divination stones before casting the spell. Check to see if this is the right time in your life to do the spell. If you have changed the wording at all, use your yes/no stones to make sure the changes you've made will not harm anyone or yourself.

Do this spell only within the confines of a magick circle. Don't forget to do your altar devotion.

Moon Phase:	New through full
Day:	Friday
Planet:	Venus
Colors:	Red and white
Supplies:	Two candles, 1 red, 1 white; a ball of red yarn; red and white rose petals; white sugar; your name written on a piece of white paper in red ink; a small bowl; a needle or pin

Place all supplies on the altar. Cleanse, consecrate, and empower the items as shown earlier in this book. If you like, you could ask for the blessings of

Aphrodite or Venus (both love goddesses) on the work you plan to do, or you may wish to work with Spirit or your guardian angel. Hold your hands over your supplies until your palms begin to tingle or get warm.

Light the red candle. Put the white sugar, the rose petals, and the paper with your name in red in the small bowl. Gently stir the contents seven times, saying:

I stir

I change

I manifest

The human love from the universe that will suit me best.

Take the end of a needle or pin and carve the words "love" and your name on the white candle. Hold the candle tightly in your hand, and repeat the charm seven times.

Remove the piece of paper from the bowl and place the paper underneath the candle holder in the center of your altar. Sprinkle the rose petal and sugar mixture around the base of the candle in the shape of a heart.

Focus your eyes on the candle flame. Think of yourself happy, safe, and in the arms of a caring person. Do not, I repeat, do not target any particular person. Hold this thought as long as you can. When you lose the thought, open your eyes and say:

**Spirit, I ask the universe to send me the person
who will suit me the best.**

If you're thinking of just a friend, state that. If you want a deeper relationship, then say exactly what kind of relationship you are looking for. Take the ball of yarn, hold the loose end in your receptive hand, and begin unraveling the ball, repeating the charm, until you come to the opposite end of the yarn. As you pull the yarn toward you, envision yourself happy and loved.

Now roll the yarn back up again, repeating the charm, and envisioning yourself happy and loved. When you have a complete ball, set the yarn aside (do not throw the ball of yarn away until the love you have called comes to you). Thank Spirit, then snuff out the candles. Release your circle. Repeat the candle lighting part of this spell for seven days, always within a magick circle. At the end of the seven days, place the remains of the candle, the paper, and the heart-shaped sugar and rose mixture into a plastic baggie. Keep the baggie in a safe place until you encounter the love you asked for, then sprinkle the mixture in your backyard. Ask Spirit that, as the sugar and rose petals disintegrate, love grows in your life.

⁺✦⁺ Back Off Baby Spell ⁺✦⁺

In our Love Rules, I mentioned that you can't own a person, and that his or her decision on who they wish to love, or not love, resides only with them. What does a Witch do when a romance-wrecker comes sniffing at the heels of our loved one, attempting to lure our boyfriend or girlfriend away with lies and deceit? Do we just stand by and say, "Oh well . . ." and roll our eyes? Absolutely not! Although controlling the thoughts or feelings of any person isn't acceptable, we do have the right to protect our own feelings from the enterprising claws of vapid opportunists. Sometimes the universe will guide our boyfriend or girlfriend along a path that takes them away from us, despite our wishes or desires. If this is the case, the spell I've given you will not work, and you must accept the wise movement of the universe. I realize that allowing someone to walk (or run or sneak) away from us can, at times, release a volcano of torrid emotions (even if you're not a teenager). You may think a person is right for you, and really they are the worst. The old saying "Love is blind but the neighbors ain't" is disgusting but nevertheless accurate. If someone does walk away from you, then let them go. Butterflies, and people, are free.

I've designed this operation as a general protection and fidelity spell. You will ask that all your loved ones (not just your boyfriend or girlfriend) find protection from any chaos that might cross, through destiny, their path. By "destined" I mean a person hasn't chosen a particular lesson to complete before he or she incarnated on the earth plane. I truly believe that we have a choice before we come here on many things that we will or will not experience. We sometimes change our destiny in error while we are here because of our gift of free will.

You can also use this spell for yourself, in case you feel you have wandering eyes (or a wandering heart) but aren't ready to pounce on someone different.

Moon Phase:	Full
Day:	Tuesday
Planet:	Mars
Colors:	Red and white
Supplies:	Clover (fidelity); nutmeg (faithful feelings); 1 red licorice string (fidelity); a small piece of chocolate (love); a red ribbon 13 inches long and a white ribbon 13 inches long; a small square of white or red cloth (about 5 inches by 5 inches square), a small bowl; a pin or a needle

Check your yes/no divination tool with the following question: *Is it appropriate for me to do this spell at this time?* If the answer is no, do not go on.

Cast your circle and do your altar devotion. Set all of the supplies on the center of your altar. Cleanse, consecrate, and bless them in the name of Spirit. You may wish also to work with the Goddess Ana (the first mother).

Mix the clover, nutmeg, and chopped bits of red licorice in your bowl. Stir the mixture thirteen times, saying:

> **May all around me be faithful but free,**
> **should Spirit want this to be.**

Pour the mixture in the center of the white cloth. Take a pin or needle and scratch the words "faithful but free" into the chocolate. Put the chocolate on top of the mixture.

Twist or braid the red and white ribbon together and secure both ends with a knot. As you tie each knot, say:

> **May all around me be faithful but free,**
> **should Spirit want this to be.**

Take up the ends of the cloth so that you now have a little pouch. Tie the red and white ribbon around the edges of the pouch to close the bag. Secure tightly.

Hold the pouch in your hands, close your eyes, and repeat the above chant. You can rock back and forth, you could sing to yourself, it doesn't matter as long as you keep up the chant until your mind begins to wander. It helps if you just chant softly in a monotone voice, allowing yourself to drift into the rhythm of your voice. When you have finished, say the following:

> **With harm to none.**
> **May all astrological correspondences be correct**
> **for this working, and may this spell not reverse,**
> **or place upon me any curse.**
> **So mote it be!**

Thank Spirit for helping you, and release your magick circle. Carry this charm bag around with you until you feel the "danger" has passed. If you wish to keep the bag on you for a while, re-empower the bag with the same chant in a magick circle every full moon. When you feel you do not need the bag, bury the bag in your backyard, asking Spirit to keep love in your heart your whole life through.

✶✦✦ The Glamour Spell ✦✦✶

To appear glamorous to others you must *think* yourself glamorous. We are, after all, the sum of our thoughts. Being a teen isn't easy. Our bodies constantly change, go on revolt, get too big, or don't grow at all—leaving us frustrated and angry at ourselves. Peer pressure doesn't help. I am reminded of the cruelty of teens when my own kids come home, unhappy because someone made mean comments about clothing, hair, shoes, glasses, or whatever. It isn't just the kids, either. The things that come out of teachers' mouths astound me. Not all teachers are bad, but some shouldn't be in the school system. I have often told my kids, "If someone makes fun of you, it's because *they* have low self-esteem. They're trying to target you because they are ashamed of themselves."

When I was in high school I had a class on family values, which included discussions on health and sexuality. The teacher also covered the interaction between teens. This excellent woman taught me one very valuable lesson that I've never forgotten. She said, "Never look at the person who has the finger pointed at them—always look at the finger pointer."

Too often teens try to change themselves to suit others. This happens in adulthood too, when one's self-esteem drops in the toilet for whatever reason. Hair color and makeup companies skim millions of dollars from the teen market as young people try to look better because someone told them they don't look good enough. Clothes with sports logos or endorsed by athletes rage through the school halls like a multicolored tidal wave, destined to crash into anyone's budget with an unforgiving gouge. Why? Because the buyers feel that to look good, they have to be like everyone else, although the main anthem of any teen is "I'm different."

If you want to look more glamorous because other people are making fun of you—think again. So what if you can't afford the latest styles? Create your own. These days there's no end to what you could do with old clothes to make them look different and appealing. Everyone can learn to mend torn clothes and run a washing machine. Take a good inventory of yourself. How is your personal hygiene? Could this use some improvement? Do you brush your teeth? Keep your hair clean? For years I trimmed my hair myself because I couldn't afford to go to a hairstylist (still can't, it's shop and chop for me). I got pretty good at styling my own hair from looking closely at magazine pictures. Do you use deodorant? You may laugh, but sometimes parents of middle-school children don't want to see them grow up, so they refuse to instruct them on personal hygiene issues. No kidding, I've seen this often. If someone is making fun of you because you smell, maybe you *do*. Keep your gym clothes clean. Use a spray in your sneakers. There's nothing to be ashamed about. You're human, after all, and humans are half animal.

I knew a young man once whose clothes always smelled sour. Yuckie! I could never figure out why clothes would smell that way. Everyone stayed away from the boy (he was seventeen) because his clothes smelled. Years later, when I did laundry for my own family, I left a load of clothes in the washing machine after the cycle ended and forgot them there. Two days later, my daughter thought I had just washed those clothes and put the load into the dryer. Thinking the dryer had a new load of clothes that she washed that morning, I went downstairs and started to hang them up. I smelled that sour odor immediately and remembered, all those years ago, the boy who always smelled like he came out of the sewer. Either his mother didn't know how to do laundry or he was stuck doing his own clothes and never knew that you have to take the wet clothes out of the washer right away and either hang them up or put the clothes in the dryer (especially in the summer). I felt sad because something so simple, like taking care of the clothes properly, would have made that boy's life a whole lot better—if he had only known.

Now when we do the wash (my daughters and I), we empower a bottle of lavender softener for harmony and add the lavender to every load. We also hang the clothes up or put them in the dryer right away.

Then again, maybe those kids making fun of you are just being mean because they are jealous of you.

Does all this mean you shouldn't cast a glamour spell? Certainly not—but you should want to be glamorous *for yourself*, not for what others think about you or for what they say. When we feel glamorous, we feel empowered, strong, ready to take on the world. Glamorous doesn't necessarily mean glossy-slick like a magazine model. It took me years to make my husband understand that women don't dress up, fix their hair, or wear makeup for men—they do these things for themselves.

The first step of this spell involves some careful thought on your part. Pick ten people who you admire. Write their names on a piece of paper, then write opposite the names what you like the most about that person. The idea is not to become someone else but to look at those qualities you admire in others and shape those qualities into your personality.

Moon Phase:	Begin at new moon and work this spell for thirty days
Day:	Friday
Planet:	Venus
Supplies:	A mirror; a list of 10 good qualities that you would like to have

Cleanse, consecrate, and empower the mirror in sacred space at your altar. Ask for the blessings of Spirit upon the mirror. This will be your glamour mirror. Don't use the mirror for anything other than looking at yourself (meaning don't use this mirror for a protection spell). This mirror represents the glamour and beauty inside and outside of you. I also suggest that you don't lend the mirror to anyone. Witches have an unwritten code that we don't touch each other's magickal items unless we ask first. Magickal tools naturally attract little children, so if you have a little brother or sister, you may wish to keep your mirror in a safe place. If they touch the mirror, it won't hurt the magick—the God and Goddess love little children. Things do get broken by accident. If any quality on your list feels "questionable," you know, that funny gut-tickle-sinking feeling, check the quality with your yes/no stones. Perhaps you should wait for another time to work on that quality, or maybe that quality isn't right for you.

Each night, before you go to bed, look in the mirror and repeat the ten qualities you want to instill in yourself. For example: *I see the beauty within all things. I am a unique and loving individual,* et cetera. Do not look critically at yourself in the mirror. Each person has something beautiful about them. Perhaps you have attractive eyes, a pretty smile, or fantastic hair. Now, close your eyes and picture yourself as the glamorous person you want to be. Ask Spirit to help you change into a better person. You see, glamour isn't really on the outside—glamour consists of the fine qualities that shine through from the soul.

⁺✦⁺ Farewell Spell ⁺✦⁺

There does come a time in everyone's life when you don't want to be involved
with a specific person. Sometimes you learn that your boyfriend or girlfriend
isn't who you originally thought they were. Other times things just don't seem
to "click" between you as they did in the past. Friends come into our lives, share,
and then it's time for them to drift away. If your friend or love interest becomes
abusive, it's time to let them go. Angelique, my daughter, designed this Farewell
Spell, and she has used the spell several times with great success. The spell won't
hurt anyone. The purpose of the spell rests on passive separation rather than
aggressive action.

Moon Phase: Dark of the moon (the day before the new moon)

Day: Saturday

Planet: Saturn

Colors: Black and white

Supplies: A white candle; 1 black candle (If no one allows you to use
candles, then pick one white stone and one black stone,
about half the size of the palm of your hand, to use as a
substitute); a picture of yourself; a picture of the other
person; 1 black ribbon, 17 inches long; a pin or a needle;
a black marker; white paint or typing correction fluid

Check your yes/no stones with the following question: *Should I do the farewell
spell to separate myself and (the other person) today?* If the answer is no, consider
doing the spell another day. Perhaps the timing isn't right, or you may not need
to do the spell at all as circumstances around the situation are about to change in
your favor without magickal help.

Cast your magick circle and do your altar devotion. With a pin or needle,
write your name on the white candle. If you use a stone, write your name with
a black marker on the white stone. Write the other person's name on the black
candle with a pin or needle. If you use a black stone, write the name with white
paint or typing correction fluid (Wite Out or Liquid Paper).

Tie one end of the black ribbon around the white candle. Tie the other end of
the black ribbon around the black candle. Set the candles apart until the ribbon
stretches without any loops, but not so tight that you knock down the candles.
Place your picture and the other person's picture underneath the ribbon,
between the two candles.

Light the white candle and say:

> This candle represents me.
> I ask for the help of Spirit in casting this spell.

Light the black candle and say:

> This candle represents *(the other person)*.
> I ask for the help of Spirit in casting this spell.

Take a pair of scissors and hold them over the ribbon, and say:

> With these scissors I will cut this ribbon, which represents the mental
> and spiritual ties between myself and *(the other person)*.
> May we neither be harmed nor alarmed at this separation.

Take a deep breath, then cut the ribbon with the scissors.

Move the two pictures to the center of the altar (if they aren't there already) side by side. Put the white candle on top of your picture, and the black candle on top of the other person's picture. Let the candles burn for three minutes. During these three minutes, close your eyes and imagine you and the other person happily walking away from each other. Open your eyes. Move the two candles and the two pictures two inches apart. Let the candles burn for three more minutes. Do the same visualization. Now, move the candles and the pictures another inch apart. Repeat the visualization. Finish the spell by saying:

> With harm to none.
> May all astrological correspondences be correct
> for this working, and may this spell not reverse
> or place upon me any curse.
> So mote it be!

Thank Spirit for helping you in this situation, then snuff out the two candles.

The next evening, go through the same process of lighting the candles, then separating them. (Rule of magickal thumb: don't walk away from burning candles.) First two inches more, then an inch, and finally, another inch. Repeat this process for three to seven days. If the other person walks away from you within the first three days, thank Spirit again for helping you, then remove the ribbons and the candles from your property. If the person does not walk away, continue until the seven-day span has concluded, thank Spirit, and dispose of the items.

If the person has not moved away from you in thirty days, then repeat the spell until they do. The last time Angie did this, the other person's candle literally exploded. No, that person didn't get hurt, but they did move out of her life in less than twenty-four hours.

⋆⁺˟Don't Tread on Me Spell˟⁺⋆

Sometimes the boys or girls just won't leave you alone. Perhaps a friend (who isn't really a friend) spread a nasty rumor about you, and now all the boys are after you for the wrong reasons. Or maybe, if you're a guy, there's a girl or two who just can't get it through her head that you aren't, and never will be, interested in her, and now she's being a major pain about the whole issue. Although this could be considered a general protection spell, because we're talking hormones and sexual issues, I stuck this one under the love category.

Moon Phase: Dark of the moon (the day before the new moon)

Day: Saturday

Planet: Saturn

Colors: Green and black

Supplies: Glue; a 3 by 5 card; plastic or wooden box; 6 small makeup mirrors or those little mirrors you can get at a handicraft store (you will glue these on the outside of the box); a picture of yourself; a small plastic or rubber snake (green or black)—snake energy is very protective and healing

You do not need a picture of the other person for this spell. Before you work the spell, glue one mirror on each side of the box, including the top and the bottom, on the outside.

Use your yes/no divination stones to decide if the performance of this spell would be appropriate for the situation you currently face. If the answer is "yes," then cast your magick circle, call your quarters, do your altar devotion, and cleanse, consecrate, and empower your supplies. You may burn a black candle and a green candle if you like; however, this isn't necessary.

Hold the empty box in your hands and say:

> **Holy Mother, I have made this box of mirrors to protect me**
> **from** *(list the person's name or names).*
> **May the mirrors send back all negativity or energies I do not want.**

Close your eyes and imagine yourself surrounded with mirrors facing away from you. Open your eyes, put your picture in the box, and say:

> **I put my picture in my box and ask Spirit to protect me.**

Close the box. Glue the snake on top of the box, right across the mirror, and say:

> Don't tread on me!

Repeat this little chant as often as you feel necessary. The more times, the better. Finish by saying:

> With harm to none.
> May all astrological correspondences be correct
> for this working, and may this spell not reverse
> or place upon me any curse.
> So mote it be!

Thank Spirit. Close your quarters. Put the box in a safe place, where no one will move it and disturb your protective magick.

Call Me Spell

Ever wish someone would call you? Here's a simple spell to let someone know you would like to have a phone call from them. If they choose not to call you, then they won't. We don't want to mess with another person's free will.

Moon Phase: Any time

Day: Any day

Supplies: A piece of paper; a blue marker; and, as angels are known as messengers, you can use one of the following symbolic images: a butterfly; an airplane; a bird; or an angel

Draw the image you selected in the middle of your paper with the blue marker. Hold the blank paper in your hand and say:

> Element of Air, I would like *(the person's name)*
> to call me if he or she wills.
> Please help me in sending this message to
> *(say the person's name).*

Write the person's name underneath the drawing, with the following words: *I would like to hear from you. Please call me.* Sign your name.

Hold the paper in your hand and close your eyes. See the person you want to contact picking up the phone and calling you. Ask your guardian angel to send the message to your friend, then fold the paper three times and place the paper underneath the phone.

If for some reason a phone call is out of the question, you can write the person's name on the return address section of a white envelope, and your name at the center of the envelope. Write a letter to your friend, asking them to write a letter to you. Remember to put your image on the paper too. Fold the letter and put it in the envelope. Seal the envelope shut. Put the envelope in a safe place until you receive your answer.

Don't Call Me Spell

Susie has called you at least five times today, and your parents are sick of hearing the phone ring. If she calls again, you will be dead meat. Maybe you told Harold you don't want to see him anymore, and he's punching your phone number, hoping to change your mind. If you told him once, you've told him a thousand times. What to do? Try this little gem of a spell.

Moon Phase: Any time, but if you are having real trouble,
              use the dark of the moon

       Day: Any day, but if you are having real trouble, Saturday

    Planet: Saturn

    Colors: Black

  Supplies: A piece of white paper; a black marker; black pepper;
              a small envelope; if the person is really giving you trouble,
              try to find a picture of him or her

On the piece of paper, write the person's name (if you know it—if you don't, say something like: The person who keeps calling me and hanging up). Put a big "X" over their name. Underneath their name, write: *Please stop calling me.* Hold the pepper in your hand, and say:

Element of Earth, please keep *(the person's name)* from calling me.
Please build a wall of protection around me.
Lend me your power.
Lend me your magick.
So mote it be!

Sprinkle pepper over the person's name. Add their picture on top, if you have it. Fold up the paper so the pepper won't escape and put the paper in the envelope. Seal the envelope. Hold the envelope in your hands and say:

> Guardian angel. *(The person's name)* keeps calling me
> and I have no desire to speak to them.
> Please don't let them call me anymore.

Close your eyes. Picture the person picking up the phone, then putting it down without calling you. See them shaking their head, as if they are telling themselves they don't want to call you. Open your eyes. Place the envelope under your phone. Now, hold your hands over your phone and say:

> May only positive phone calls reach me.
> Negative messages fly away.
> Don't call back another day.

Repeat this chant until you feel comfortable. The more, the better.

If you are really having problems, do the above spell, then take a stone the size of your palm and paint the stone black. Write the person's name and phone number on the stone. When the stone dries, take it far away from your house and throw the stone where it won't catch in someone's mower or break a window. As you throw the stone, say:

> Guardian angel, whisk this person far from me,
> I blink, I turn, he's *(she's)* gone!
> So mote it be!

Peter, Paul, or Harry Spell (for Girls)
Diane, Debbie, or Crystal Spell (for Boys)

There will be times when you just can't decide whom you like best. Should you follow your heart or your head?

Moon Phase:	Doesn't matter
Day:	Sunday, Monday, Wednesday, or Friday
Planet:	Sun, Moon, Mercury, Venus
Supplies:	A stone, half the size of your palm from your backyard (any stone, really, that calls to you); white paint; red paint; a small paintbrush

Use your yes/no stones to make sure you should do the spell. Hold the stone you are going to paint in your hand and say:

> Element of Earth, bringer of stability.
> Lend me your power.
> Help me to see what person would be right for me.

Sit under the sun outside, or in a sunny window, and paint little red and white hearts all over the stone. Take your time. Let the hearts dry as you turn the stone to paint it so you won't mess up your hands. While you are painting, hum or whisper the following:

> *(The people's names)*, who is right for me?
> Guardian angel, sun above, bring to me the one true love.
> Let all others fade away.
> I walk with Spirit every day.

After you have finished, say:

> May this spell not reverse, or place upon me any curse.
> May all astrological correspondences be correct for this working.
> So mote it be!

When the stone has dried, carry it in your pocket or purse until your guardian angel shows you the right person. How will you know? Trust your angel. He or she won't let you down.

Happy Home Spell

Even in the best of homes, certain days (or even months) can get very hairy, especially if the adults in your home aren't getting along or a relative is causing problems. Maybe mom or dad is having trouble at work, and bringing her or his stress home. Perhaps a sibling, younger or older, has gotten way out of control and no one knows what to do. Time to call in the angels for a little help and spiritual cleansing. Of course, you can do this spell when things are going just fine and you want to keep it that way, too.

Moon Phase: If the moon is traveling from new to full, you want to bring love into the home. If the moon phase is traveling from full to new, you want to push negativity out of the home.

Day: Any day, but Sundays, Mondays, Wednesdays, and Fridays are especially good

Planet: Sun, Moon, Mercury, or Venus

Colors: White (purity), green (healing), blue (Spirituality)

Supplies: A bell; a white candle; an onion (cut in half); cloves of garlic (crushed—garlic works neither medicinally nor magickally unless you crush the cloves); a heart cut out of a white piece of paper; a red marker

Optional: A carpet deodorizer (you can use the powdered kind or the wax balls that you put in the vacuum cleaner bag)

In sacred space, cleanse, consecrate, and empower all your supplies. Take the onion, close your eyes, and say:

I empower you to collect all negativity in this house.

Imagine the onion turning into a giant vacuum cleaner, sucking up all the negative energy in your house. Take your time. Place the onion in the window in the room where most of the family usually gathers. Hold the garlic in your hand, close your eyes, and say the same thing. Do the same visualization. If a particular person is causing trouble in the house, take the crushed cloves (not too much or they will smell up the room) and place them under the rug, under the negative person's bed. If no one is causing a problem now, put the cloves of garlic around the outside doorstep of your front door. Mush them up really well so no one knows that they are there. Vacuum up the empowered carpet deodorizer (if your mom said that using the deodorizer was okay).

Write every loved one's name with a red marker on the white heart. Circle all the names with one big circle, saying:

I encircle everyone I love with positive energy, healing, and peace.
Let no evil enter our home.

Hold the paper in your hands, close your eyes, and visualize your family sitting together and very happy. Then say:

With harm to none.
May all astrological correspondences be correct
for this working, and may this spell not reverse
or place upon me any curse.
So mote it be!

Thank Spirit for helping you. Thumbtack the heart somewhere in your room. With your bell, go to each room in the house. Ring the bell three times in each room, saying:

> Guardian angel, please enter here and
> bring love and protection to my family.

Close your eyes and visualize the room growing brighter and brighter with angel light.

After you have finished (didn't forget the basement or the attic, did you?), thank your guardian angel.

Take It Easy Spell

Is your boyfriend or girlfriend moving just a bit too fast? You really like them, but you're not ready to rush into a commitment? Try this spell to cool things down.

Moon Phase:	Full
Day:	Friday
Planet:	Venus
Color:	Blue or white
Supplies:	A Popsicle or Italian Ice; a small piece of white paper; a paper plate; a blue marker

In sacred space, cleanse, consecrate, and empower all supplies. Write the person's name on the paper plate. Open the popsicle. Put the popsicle directly over the person's name on the plate, and say:

> *(Person's name)*, you're moving way too fast for me.
> I melt this pop to make you stop.
> So mote it be!

Close your eyes and envision the person being pleasant to you but not pushing you. Open your eyes. Hold your hands over the pop and say:

> Element of Water, lend me your power.
> Give me your magick.
> Help me sail smoothly through this situation.
> So mote it be!

When the pop has melted, throw the mess away and say:

Great Mother, help me in making the right choices about my life.
Don't let others rush me into something I'm not sure of.
Guardian angel, please give me your love and your guidance.
So mote it be!

Do You Like Me? Spell

Sometimes we really like someone but say nothing because we fear if we made an advance, we would experience rejection. Here's a spell to give you the green light (or the red one).

Moon Phase: Full
Day: Friday
Planet: Venus
Supplies: A small, new, red rubber ball

In sacred space, cleanse, consecrate, and empower the red rubber ball. As you bounce the ball, repeat the following spell:

From ground to air
From air to ground
I bounce the magick
Round and round.
Do you like me?
Do you love me?
I need to know the answer.

Dragon's eyes,
and angel wings.
Now I touch
the fairy ring.
Do you like me?
Do you love me?
I need to know the answer.

Earth and air
Fire and water.
My little ball
goes higher, and higher.
Mine is the magick
Mine is the power.
It's time to know the answer.

Repeat the last line as you bounce the ball. Keep bouncing the ball and say:

With harm to none, as I will it shall be done.
May all astrological correspondences be correct for this working,
and may this spell not reverse, or place upon me any curse.
So mote it be!

You should receive your answer shortly. If you do not have your answer in thirty days, repeat the spell.

Love Glo

There will be many occasions in your life where you either can't or shouldn't do a magickal operation in a situation, but you still feel driven to help someone who is unhappy or in trouble. Just send him or her a "Love Glo." Envision the person (or animal) surrounded by healing, white energy. Hold the visualization as long as you can. Take a break and repeat. Although this sounds like a simple procedure that couldn't possibly work, think again. Every bit of positive energy that you send to someone helps them.

Friendly Spell

Don't have any friends or need a change of pace? Try the Friendly Spell.

Moon Phase: New or full
Day: Sunday, Wednesday, or Friday
Planet: Sun, Mercury, or Venus
Supplies: Brown sugar; 1 teaspoon dirt; a brown candle (votive size would be best for this spell); a small fire-resistant bowl; a needle or a pin; 1 lemon

Check your yes/no stone to be sure that you should do the spell at this time. Cast your magick circle, call the quarters, and do your altar devotion. Place your supplies on the center of the altar. Cleanse, consecrate, and empower them in the name of friendship.

Place the brown sugar and dirt in the bowl. Hold your hands over the bowl and say:

> Element of Earth, I call your magick into my circle, and into this bowl.
> This sugar and dirt represent the fertile earth,
> a place from which new friendships for me can grow.

Scratch your name, some hearts, and the words "new friendships" on the candle. Hold the candle tightly in your hands, close your eyes, and say:

> Element of Fire, work my will by my desire.
> Bring me new friends that will treat me well.
> Fiery bird, send out my word, bring back some honest, loving friends.

Place the candle upright in the bowl of brown sugar and dirt. Pack the brown sugar around the candle so it won't fall down. Make sure the candle sits evenly in the brown sugar and dirt. Hold the lemon in your hand and say:

> Lemons, bring honest friends my way, protect my feelings every day.

Cut the lemon and squeeze the juice onto the brown sugar and dirt around the candle in as even a circle as you can.

Light the candle. Hold your hands over the bowl (don't burn your hands) and say:

> I search the universe for friends
> Strong, and true to the very end.
> I look in field and fairy glen
> And where the dragons once have been.
> I search for truth and honesty
> I look for love and loyalty
> I touch the pulse of energy
> I manifest a friend for me.
> As I will, so mote it be!
> With harm to none.

May this spell not reverse, or place upon me any curse,
and may all astrological correspondences be correct for this working.
So mote it be!

Let the candle burn while you visualize yourself surrounded by loving, honest, and loyal friends. Open your eyes. Snuff out the candle. Thank Spirit for helping you. Close your quarters. Release the circle.

For the next seven days, light the candle each night and repeat the verse and visualization. If you do not have new, true friends in thirty days, repeat the spell.

Doodle Bug Love Spell

The doodle bug love spell is designed just for you to help you raise your self-esteem.

Moon Phase:	New to full
Day:	Sunday, Monday, or Friday
Planet:	Sun, Moon, or Venus
Supplies:	An art drawing pad; a selection of colored pencils or markers

Sit in a quiet place. Outside would be delightful, if you can, or sit in your room. You may like to burn some of your favorite incense and put happy music in the tape deck or CD player. Everybody has their own love doodle bug, and no doodle bug looks alike. The only way you will know what your doodle bug looks like is if you design it yourself. Experiment with your markers or pens, designing your doodle bug. Doodle bugs are never mean, and they are always pleasant and full of love. If you like, you can have lots of variations of your doodle bug. You might like to design your doodle bug with some magickal symbols I taught you earlier in this book, or you may wish to make up some of your own.

Now, write on the shells (or bodies) of the doodle bugs what you feel you need most: love, compassion, healing, et cetera. Put your hands over each doodle bug and say:

Doodle bug, Doodle bug,
Buzz and glow
Doodle bug, Doodle bug
Let the *(say the name of what you want)* grow.

Once you've designed your doodle bug, you can use it for most things, including carrying messages or sending loving or healing energy to a friend or family member in need.

⁺ₓ⁺ Posies and Honey Parent Love Spell ⁺ₓ⁺

Okay. You've really done it this time. Your father isn't speaking to you and your mother only mumbles in your general direction. You know you've done something wrong, and are truly sorry. Now it's time to do some damage control.

Moon Phase: Full

Day: Sunday or Friday

Planet: Sun or Venus

Supplies: A clean, empty medium-size soda bottle with resealable cap; honey; small flowers and herbs of love, such as clover, a rose bud, and a daisy; a pinch of basil; your favorite perfume; a piece of paper with your name on it

Check your yes/no stones to see if you should do this spell at this time. Cast your circle and call your quarters. Do your altar devotion. Cleanse, consecrate, and empower your supplies in the name of love.

Hold the flowers in your hands and say:

> **Petals soft, and fragrance pure**
> **Love of family will endure.**

Put the flowers in the bottle as gently as possible. Hold the basil in your hand and say:

> **Herb of friendship**
> **Herb of love**
> **Power of sympathy**
> **Purity of dove.**
> **Bring the energy**
> **Of Spirit above.**

Put the basil into the bottle. Pick up the perfume and say:

> **Scent of mine**
> **Love times nine.**

Add nine drops of the perfume to the contents of the bottle. Pick up the piece of paper with your name written on it and say:

> This my name in my hand of write.
> I mix, I stir, I make things right.
> I bring the change, with loving light.

Pour the honey into the bottle until the honey covers the flowers. Say:

> Liquid gold, fluid of love, gift of herbal gold
> Meld together the energies of this bottle.

Put the piece of paper with your name on it in the bottle. Seal the bottle. Hold the bottle in your hands and chant "I bring the change, with loving light" repeatedly, as long as possible. When you have finished, take the bottle to each of the four quarters and ask for the blessings of the elements on the bottle. Stand in the center of your circle and say:

> With harm to none.
> May all astrological correspondences be correct
> for this working, and may this spell not reverse
> or place upon me any curse.
> So mote it be!
> The change has begun!

Close your quarters and release the circle. Take the bottle, shake it three times, then set the bottle in your room somewhere. Shake the bottle three times every day until the change you have requested happens, then bury the bottle in your backyard.

Magnolia Beauty Spell

If you would like to be more beautiful, inside and out, try this little beauty spell.

Moon Phase: Full

Day: Sunday, Monday, or Friday

Planet: Sun, Moon, or Venus

Supplies: All your makeup, beauty supplies, body cleaning products (such as soap, shampoo, and deodorant), and jewelry; holy water; an empty mister (the bottle kind that you can buy at the drug store for about 89 cents); a hand mirror

On the night of the full moon, do this spell by a window that will allow you to reflect the rays of the full moon onto your things. If this isn't possible, put your things into a box and take them outside. Do the ritual outside or, after you do the ritual inside, let the items sit outside under the moon for at least half an hour.

Set everything on an altar. Cast your magick circle, call your quarters, and do your altar devotion. Cleanse, consecrate, and empower all of your things in the name of love and beauty. Call on the energies of Venus or Aphrodite to help you in creating a beautiful, new you.

Pour the holy water into the mister. Hold the mister in your hands and say:

> Element of Water
> Blessed and empowered by Spirit
> Awaken the beauty within me.

> Element of Water
> Moving, flowing, transforming.
> Loving Venus, Beautiful Aphrodite
> Touch this water
> Bring your essence of love and beauty
> Into my body.

Lightly mist each item sitting on your altar, each time saying:

> The power of beauty in me, around me, on me.
> The power of love in me, around me, on me.

Take the hand mirror and shine the rays of the full moon on the objects while saying:

> Moon, moon, mother moon
> Brightest star and Witch's broom
> Sweep out negativity
> Fill my soul with your beauty.
> Constellations and comets too
> Loving words and sonnets new
> Full moon energy, shine and grow
> On my life please, blessings bestow.
> Round and round
> Up and down

Circle near

Enter here!

May the blessings of the Mother be upon me

Now, and in my days to come.

So mote it be!

When you have finished, walk to each quarter and ask for the blessings of beauty and love upon you. Thank Spirit. Close the quarters, release the circle, and put all your things away. Do this spell once a month or when you replenish most of your beauty and body cleaning supplies.

✦ Your Cold Heart Spell ✦

I don't know about you, but I've met people who just don't want me to get ahead—no way, no how. In your life, this could be a teacher, a counselor, a friend, the parent of a friend, or even a relative. This spell is designed to remove the emotional walls they've put up against you, and allow them to see the truth. Sometimes, these people act on gossip they've heard and not on what they perceive for themselves. Although adults sometimes have a tough time believing their friends or family would purposefully deceive them, teens seem to have a real problem with this issue. Hundreds of times, various peers of both my daughters have tried to turn sister against sister with gossip and lies. Each girl had a hard time discovering that their peers only wanted to cause trouble for their entertainment. This spell, then, can do double duty for you, if necessary.

Moon Phase: Any time

Day: Saturday would be best, Tuesday is okay, also Friday

Planets: Saturn, Mars, or Venus

Supplies: A cube of ice; a dish; a piece of paper on which you write the other person's name with a black pen or marker; if you have a picture, you could use that, too

Check your divination tool to be sure this is the right time to do the spell. Put the picture (if you have one) and the person's name on the plate. Place the ice cube on top of the picture (or the paper). Chant the following:

I melt your cold, cold heart with angel fire
The truth you'll see, and not the mire.
As this ice melts, the truth will appear,
Pushing away all that you fear.
If gossip lies at the root of this
This little spell shall not miss
And then I shall expose the liar.
Angel fire, rise higher and higher.

Chant the last line as long as possible, the more the better. When you have finished, let the ice melt to warm water. Flush the water down the toilet, saying:

I flush the negativity away, and bring myself a brighter day!

Keep the picture in case you must repeat the spell. When you have the results you want, throw the picture away.

Magick Yule Seed Charm

Here's the perfect gift to give to friends and relatives, which won't empty your wallet. A charm wand is made by taking a small, glass vial and filling it with herbs and seeds. Country Witches believed that if any evil entered the house it would be forced to count all the seeds by dark, leaving no time to cause trouble among the family members of the house. Test tubes with stoppers work great. Vials from the flower store work well too. Fill the tube with seeds and small herbs of your choice (check the correspondence lists I gave you in the last chapter) and decorate with ribbons and glitter. Tie next to the door most used in the house, on your Yule (Christmas) tree, on wreaths hung on the door or in the house, as an extra decoration on a gift package, or as a party favor on New Year's Eve.

*⋆*6*⋆*

Healing

Surround me—Enfold me,
Heal me— Hold me.[1]

"*⋆*Gruttafoo" was the term used by my relatives to mean the healing of others by a Pennsylvania Dutch Pow-Wow doctor with
words, motions, and marks placed on the body and throughout
the home to ward off the evil of sickness. With this belief went a
profound faith in deity, signs, symbols, and homespun formulas,
better known to our generation as spellcasting. My people, in their
time, were considered ultra-religious, hard working, thrifty, and
concerned about the welfare of others often above themselves.
"Hexerie," to my people, meant to bless and perform acts of good
faith. Before the invasion of Christianity into my family history,
we practiced German Braucherei, or WitchCraft, and we excelled
in the healing arts.

Of all the realms where the Witches have made the greatest
strides in their exceptional abilities, the path of healer and the healing arts claims the largest success, perhaps because we practice this
art more than all the others. We've been trying for a long time to
get the medical community to catch up with us but old habits die
hard, and we're still pushing to have our alternative methods rec-
ognized. As I write this book, I understand that a major conference
recently took place in Boston, Massachusetts, where some of the
greatest surgeons of our time met popular religious figures to

learn more about the role of faith and prayer in the health and healing of the human.

Witches work with herbs, oils, hypnosis, and hands-on healing (to name just a few techniques) along with normal spellcasting procedures. We also do counseling to help our friends and family raise their self-esteem and overcome the emotional problems they may experience.

Did you know that every time you touch someone you send healing energy to them? Yes, you do. When a mother rocks her sick child, she is instinctively transferring her energy to the child. If she is aware of this energy transference, she can focus that energy to help her child get well faster. When you hug a friend who is crying, you transfer healing energy to them in their time of need. The simplest forms of expression through loving gestures pack more magick than you would believe.

None of the healing spells in this book require you to take anything internally. There's lots of information on medicinal herbs at bookstores today, should you wish to go that route. If this type of healing technique interests you, save your money and plan a trip to a book superstore where you can find material to study. Check in your local library for books on alternative healing. You may also try visiting your local herb merchant. They will have all sorts of information there for you to study. Let's go over the Witches' rules for healing.

Witches' Rules for Healing

1. The root of all healing is love and your desire to use that love to make someone (or your pet) well is more important than any incantation or spellcasting procedure.

2. You should always ask an individual's permission before you work magick for them. In healing magick, you may work through Spirit to help someone heal if you haven't asked their permission. This means that you ask Spirit for assistance first, before you work the magick, by saying: *"Spirit, please assist in this healing for (person's name). If they are to receive this healing energy, then guide my thoughts and words to them. If they are not to receive this healing energy, please give the energy to someone else who is in need. You know best."*

3. You can always pray for someone, with or without their permission.

---

1. Written by Breid FoxSong, British Tradition Witch with over twenty years' experience, from western New York.

4. Never use magick alone in the realms of healing. If you are ill, please see a doctor and follow the doctor's instructions. Always seek a second opinion from a physician in another town (not in the same town) if the diagnosis is drastic. If a friend is in mental trouble, urge them to seek counseling. Don't be afraid, or ashamed, to use any of the hotlines available to you (check your yellow pages, for example).

One afternoon my younger daughter got off the bus and wandered into the house with a frown big enough to swallow the whole school plastered across her face. When I asked her what was wrong, she said nothing. This, I must tell you, is my daughter in typical form. She holds things in for a long while, and then, right before she pops her earrings out of her head from all the mental pressure, she will break down and tell me what's bothering her. On this day, I had to wait until after dinner for her to blow.

"I have a big problem, and I don't know what to do," she began. I was sitting at the computer, working on a book (what else?). She was seated cross-legged in front of the television.

"What might that problem be?" I asked, not fully into the conversation yet. I still had one eye on the blinking cursor, wondering whether or not the sentence I'd just written made any sense at all.

"There's this girl at school," she said quietly, "and I think she's really in trouble. I don't know what to do about it."

I turned from the computer and sat back in my chair. "What sort of trouble are we talking about?" (I'm a Virgo, therefore, I must have all the details.)

My daughter played with her hair for a moment, then said, "She's hurting herself. She showed me on the bus today, and then in the bathroom at school. She's proud of it! I thought it was sick! She laughed and showed me where all she'd cut herself. I know she's in trouble, but if I tell someone, then I'm going to be the bad guy. I don't want to squeal, then she'll be mad at me."

I rocked in my chair a bit, digesting what I'd heard. Finally, I said, "If she doesn't want anyone to know, why did she tell you?"

My daughter rubbed her forehead with her fingers. "I don't know, but I wish she hadn't told me. What do you think I should do?"

Ah, I thought, the parental opening. "When people do bad things to themselves, they aren't thinking clearly. The fact that she told you means that she's crying out for help, though she doesn't consciously know she's doing it. Tell me, has she told anyone else?"

Another moment of hair twirling. "Yes, two of my other friends."

"What do they think?"

"That she's sick and needs help, but they don't know what to do either."

"It sounds to me like she wants people to know she's hurting herself. That means she wants some help," I said. "Do you want me to call the school tomorrow and talk to the guidance counselor?" (Oh, no! The dreaded Mom-will-go-to-the-school curse!)

My daughter picked at a pretzel crumb on the floor before speaking. "No, I think I'll go down. Maybe my friends will go with me."

"And if they don't?"

She sighed and held her chin up. "Then I'll just go by myself."

"If you need me to back you up, I will. You just let me know, okay?"

"Okay."

My daughter and her friends did go to the school counselor the next day. As a result, the young girl got the help she needed. Yes, she was mad at them for a day or two, but in a little while she expressed her gratitude to the girls for trying to help her. Whether you are young or old, these situations occur. Lots of times we're not responsible, but somehow we find ourselves in the middle. Spirit puts people where they are most needed, whether they know it or not. It was not the job of the girls to "fix" the problem, but to help their friend find the help she needed. Many times we must wrestle with what is the right thing to do as opposed to the easiest thing we can do. Often, the right thing is a much harder road but worth it, in the end.

The friend who hurt herself tried to make my daughter and her friends enablers. An enabler is someone who knows that a friend or loved one has a problem (like drug abuse, alcoholism, or mental abuse), sympathizes with the person, but does nothing to help them. In reality, you are saying that it is okay that they mess themselves up. It isn't okay. An enabler sits by and watches everything go down the drain. This happens because the enabler may experience fear, or because they don't want to get involved, or because they think that the cure is far more painful than the problem. Sometimes the enabler gets dragged down with the person who created the mess. My daughter stepped out of the enabler role when she sought help. You can too.

5. The last rule for healing magick is: Don't give up. Keep working. My family has an old adage: "You didn't get sick in a day—you're not going to get well in a day." Healing magick is a repetitive process until the sick person gets well. Although I've had many personal successes large and small, in the realms of healing magick, two stand out firmly in my mind: When Jane Stall had a tumor, and then Jane Stall did not (with no surgery and no drugs), and when Patrick Albert had AIDS, and then Patrick Albert tested clear (several times). In both cases, my covenmates and I worked very hard for these two people. I'd like to think we had some sort of effect, if nothing short of our shared loving energy sent to these two people. On the other end of the spectrum, don't feel you are responsible if someone passes away. If grandma or grandpa is sick, and you have been working all sorts of healing magick for them, and they go to the other side anyway, you may feel that you didn't do enough, or didn't do your healing magick right. No. Spirit takes us when it is our time. Perhaps your magick made their passing easier in ways you will never know—but never, ever think you did the work wrong, or not enough, or at the wrong time.

Healing

Healing Correspondences

Witches have lots of magickal correspondences for healing. Let's look at these energies that work in sympathy before we go about casting spells.

To banish an illness from someone, Witches might work on the dark of the moon, or they may begin on the full moon and work right through to the new moon. To heal someone from illness or injury, they would work from the new moon to the full moon. Check your almanac to find the full, new, or dark moon dates.

The planet most associated with healing is the sun (success), though you can use the energies of Saturn to banish illness or Mars to attack illness.

The colors of healing are green (general healing), blue (spiritual healing), purple (psychic healing), lavender (healing others), dark green (regeneration), yellow (success in healing), gold (sun energy in healing), or white (healing with Spirit). We use black to banish an illness from an individual or animal. When working healing magick, there is a rule that some Witches employ: When using the black candle, burn also a larger white candle for purity of mind, soul, and body.

Fruits and vegetables of healing are apples, beans, blackberries, chili peppers, cucumbers, garlic, lemons, limes, olives, onions, plantains, and potatoes.

Herbs and plants of healing are allspice, angelica, barley, bay, carnation, cedar, cinnamon, eucalyptus, fennel, gardenia, ginseng, ivy, mint, nettle, oak, peppermint, persimmon, pine, rose, rosemary, spearmint, thistle, thyme, violet, willow, and wintergreen.

We can use the four elements in our healing magick: Air for carrying sickness away and bringing healing energy to the patient; Fire to consume the illness and provide purification of body, mind, and spirit; Water to cleanse the body, mind, and soul and to transform negative energy into positive energy; Earth to stabilize a patient's condition, provide new cell growth, and build a barrier between the sick person and negative energy.

Symbols of healing include the caduceus (you know, those entwined snakes on the posters in your doctor's office); a red cross (used to attack disease); images of the sun, flowers; green and white beads; pictures of favorite saints; dolphins; and angels. I'm sure you could think of some universal symbols I've forgotten to mention.

Healing Sew Spell

Even if you aren't a whiz with a needle and thread, this spell sends healing energy to someone who is ill.

Moon Phase: New to full

Day: Sunday

Planet: Sun, Moon, Venus

Supplies: A piece of 7-inch by 7-inch white cloth; a small embroidery hoop; a pencil; green embroidery thread; a needle; ½ teaspoon rosemary (love and healing); ½ teaspoon nutmeg (health); ½ teaspoon crushed walnuts (health and wishes); a picture of the person (if you don't have a picture, write his or her name on a small piece of paper); a green or white ribbon

Cleanse, consecrate, and empower all supplies in the name of healing. You may wish to ask the First Mother, Ana, to help you in this spell. Sit in a quiet place to begin your work. Take your pencil and lightly write or print the sick person's name in the center of the white cloth. Attach the embroidery hoop around the name. Follow your outline with your green thread. With each stitch, say the following:

> Holy Ana, Mother Divine
> Bring healing energy
> To this friend of mine.

When you finish, tie the end and cut the thread. Remove the embroidery hoop. Turn the white cloth inside out (so the back is facing you). Put the person's picture in the center of the cloth. Hold the rosemary in your hand and say:

> Gentle rosemary,
> you are the power
> you are the change
> make *(person's name)* well again.

Sprinkle the rosemary over the picture. Hold the nutmeg in your hand and say:

> Gentle nutmeg,
> you are the power
> you are the change
> make *(the person's name)* well again.

Sprinkle the nutmeg on the picture. Hold the crushed walnuts in your hand and say:

> From mighty tree in magick dell
> Walnuts, make my friend be well.

Sprinkle the walnuts on the picture. Take up the four corners of the cloth so that you make a pouch. Twist the edges loosely together, then tie the ribbon around the twist with a bow and a double knot.

Hold the medicine bag or charm bag in your hands and say:

> Each stitch in time
> Each little rhyme
> brings the power closer.

Repeat this section of the spell as often as possible while visualizing your friend (or relative) getting better and better. Hold the visualization and chant as long as you can. When you have finished, thank Ana and give the medicine bag to your friend or relative. If, for some reason, you cannot give the bag to them, put the bag in a safe place until they get well. If you kept the bag, wait until your friend has recovered, open the bag, hold your hands over the bag and thank the energies for helping to make your friend well. Imagine the magick within the bag slipping back to the earth. Witches call this **de-magicking** an item. Let the air take the herbs and the ground walnuts to the earth. Burn or throw away the ribbon. Cleanse and consecrate the picture and the bag. You may need to use them another time for healing. If you had your friend's name on a piece of paper, burn the paper. Again, thank Ana for her assistance. If you become ill, you can make a bag like this for yourself.

de-magicking v. The process of returning magickal energies back to the earth.

Soap Sympathy Spell

Magick works best if you can have several things that are "in sympathy" with the person for whom you are working. Sympathy items can be jewelry that belongs to your friend or relative, a lock of hair, a piece of clothing, fingernail clippings, a half-used lipstick tube, a button from clothing they own, their signature on a piece of paper, their photograph (which we've used in other spells), et cetera. Try to keep the items small. If you begin to stack your altar with your mother's shoes, her purse, her winter coat and other assorted items, she's going to wonder if you have a major problem.

Moon Phase: Dark or full (this spell banishes illness, which is why I've chosen the dark of the moon rather than the new moon)

Day: Saturday

Planet: Saturn

Supplies: A few things in sympathy with the person: A small bar of soap; a pen; a medium-size bowl of water; a new wooden spoon; 2 pictures of the person or 2 pieces of paper with the sick person's name on the paper; an African violet plant; a dark green or black candle; a bright green candle (use if you have permission to burn candles—omit if you can't have them)

Cast your circle, call your quarters, and do your altar devotion. Cleanse, consecrate, and empower all the items on your altar for banishment of negativity and illness. Carve the sick person's name into the soap with the pen (use a pen that you can throw away). Carve the following on the black candle: *Banish illness from (person's name)*. Carve the following on the bright green candle: *Heal (the person's name)*.

Put the person's picture under the black candle. Light the black candle. Ask Spirit to drive out the illness from your friend or relative. Allow the candle to burn as you work on the next part of the spell.

Surround the bowl of water with the things that belong to the sick person. Anything disposable (like hair, nail clippings, et cetera) goes into the bowl of water. Place the soap in the bowl of water and begin to stir the water with the wooden spoon in a counterclockwise (widdershins) direction. I suggest you learn the following charm, which you can use for many medical ailments in many situations, from cancer to the flu. The charm is to be said three times, three times daily.

> Out of the blood, and into the marrow,
> Out of the marrow, and into the bone,
> Out of the bone, and onto the skin.
> Off the skin and into the hair,
> Out of the hair and into the sea,
> Out of the sea and onto dry land—
> As surely as God made woman and man!
> So mote it be!

Continue stirring, repeating the word "out" for as long as you can. Visualize the disease leaving the person's body and going into the ground. Put the other picture under the green candle. Light the green candle, saying:

> The air, the fire, the water, the health
> Return, return, return, return!

As both candles burn, walk to each quarter, clockwise (deosil) beginning at the North, and ask for the banishment of illness and healing energy for your friend or relative. Return to the center of the circle and thank Spirit for helping you.

Pick up the African violet and ask the plant to speed the healing of your friend or relative and to provide protection for him or her. Add the usual:

With harm to none.
May this spell not reverse
or place upon me any curse.
May all astrological correspondences
be correct for this working.
So mote it be!

Close the quarters and release the circle. Let the soap continue to disintegrate in the water. Put out the candles. Light them again each night for five to seven minutes until the sick person completely recovers. Leave the sympathy items around the bowl, if you can, until the person gets better. Give the plant to your relative or friend with appropriate instructions on how to care for the flower.

Excellent Egg Spell

Folk magick all over the world, from every century and culture, has employed eggs in healing spells. The old way involved using an unfertilized egg from a black hen. These days, unless you live on a farm, you have no idea whether or not the egg in the foam container at the grocery store came from a purple hen, let alone a black one. With modernization we learn to accommodate—use a jumbo brown egg. If you can't get a brown egg, a white egg will do.

Moon Phase: Dark or full (we will banish)

Day: Saturday

Planet: Saturn

Supplies: A black marker; 1 egg; the person, or a picture of the person (if you do not have a person, draw a stick picture on a piece of paper and write the person's name on top)

Hold the egg gently in your hand, and write the following with the black marker on the egg: *Banish illness from (person's name).*

In sacred space, cleanse, consecrate and empower the egg. If you can, carefully rub the egg over the person's body, envisioning the illness entering the egg and leaving the person. If you don't have the three-dimensional person, then rub the egg over the picture and say:

> *(The person's name)*
> Within, without
> Up and down
> I banish the illness
> All around.

When you have finished, throw the egg in a living body of water, asking the element of water to take the illness away from your friend or relative.

Stuffed Animal Sweet Dream Spell

When children are sick or depressed, we want to make them feel better. You might try this spell for that favorite little person. (This is also a great birthday or Yule gift for a child, or make one for yourself!)

Moon Phase:	New or full
Day:	Sunday, Monday, Wednesday, or Friday
Planet:	Sun, Moon, Mercury, or Venus
Supplies:	A new stuffed animal (my daughter used a horse, named after the Goddess Epona); 1 purple candle; 1 teaspoon lavender (protection, sleep, sweet dreams); 1 teaspoon marigold flower (protection and dreams); 1 teaspoon rose petals (love); 3 each slender purple and white ribbons; a needle and thread; seam ripper; a small bowl; holy water

Use your yes/no divination stones to ensure this is the right spell for the person you have in mind. Cast your magick circle, call your quarters, and do your altar devotion. Cleanse, consecrate, and empower all supplies for sweet dreams. Put the three different flowers in the bowl and mix with your fingers. Repeat the words "Sweet Dreams" until you have mixed the dried petals well. Add one small drop of holy water to the mixture. Find a seam in the animal where, if you re-sew the seam, the repair won't show. Open this seam one inch with a seam ripper. Pour the petals into the animal. Sew the seam tightly shut and say with each stitch:

Sweet Dreams and Love.

Sprinkle the animal with holy water.

Hold the purple candle in your hands. Close your eyes and say:

As this candle burns, the magick begins.
Across the plains of dreamtime,
pleasant thoughts the angels send.

Light the candle and place the candle on your altar.

Take the stuffed animal to each quarter, beginning with the North, and ask that the elements attach sweet dreams to the stuffed animal. When finished, go to the center. Call Spirit and your guardian angel, making the same request.

Sit on the floor and hold the stuffed animal. Close your eyes and rock back and forth, saying the words "Sweet Dreams" repeatedly, until you wish to stop. The more times you say the words, the better. Thank Spirit and your guardian angel. Close the quarters. Release the circle. Allow the candle to continue burning. Give the stuffed animal to the child and say that the animal's name is "Sweet Dreams."

Rock 'n' Roll Healing Spell

Use this simple spell to move illness away from a person.

Moon Phase: Full to new

Day: Tuesday or Saturday

Planet: Mars or Saturn

Supplies: One basket of pebbles half the size of the palm of your hand or smaller (not too small, or you will not be able to write on them—try to find at least 21 rocks or pebbles); a boom box; your favorite music; a black marker

In sacred space, cleanse, consecrate, and empower your supplies in the name of healing for the person. Ask the angels of healing to help you banish the illness from your friend or relative. Write the words *Banish illness from (the person's name)* on each rock.

Take your boom box and your basket of rocks outside to the top of a hill where you will not be disturbed. Turn on the music. Think of your friend or relative and roll the rocks down the hill, one at a time. As you roll the rocks, imagine the illness leaving your friend or relative.

Snow Person Healing Spell

Make a mini-snow person that represents your friend or relative. Make twenty-one snow balls. As you make each snowball, think of your friend and of banishing the illness from him or her. Set the snowballs around the snow person to form a nice circle. Chant the following:

Surround her, enfold her, heal her, hold her. or
Surround him, enfold him, heal him, hold him.[2]

Walk around the snowballs in a counterclockwise (widdershins) direction as you chant. Clap if you think no one is watching. When you feel you are finished, hold your hands toward the snow person and say:

Winter winds on a winter day
Winter sun melt her troubles away.
Wheel revolve, death to birth
Air to fire, water to earth!
May this spell not reverse, or place upon me any curse.
May all astrological correspondences be correct for this working.
So mote it be!

The Rosary Spell

For those of you who live in a Catholic household, here's a different way to use your rosary. For those of you who do not have a rosary, you can make a string of beads (or even a string of macaroni) to use. Some of my friends use shoestrings or thin strips of rawhide,stringing the beads with a knot in between each bead. String at least thirty-three beads.

Moon Phase: Any time
Day: Any day
Planet: Sun, Moon, Mercury, or Venus

In sacred space, cleanse, consecrate, and empower the rosary or the beads and string. If you plan to make your healing rosary, then do this in sacred space and

---

2. Ibid.

ask for the blessings of each quarter. When you are ready to use the string of beads (or rosary), sit quietly and hold your string of beads. Think of the person who is ill. You may set a picture up in front of you to help you. Close your eyes, slowly turn the first bead, and say:

Angels of healing, bring healing energy to *(person's name).*

Continue saying the same thing as you turn each bead on the string or rosary. When you finish with the last bead, say:

Holy Spirit, bless and keep *(the person's name)* **from illness or harm.**
Help them to heal quickly. So mote it be!

Angel Healing Spell

You will need a picture, a pin, or a statue of an angel for this spell. You will give the angel you choose as a gift to the sick person to help them heal faster. The angel should stay with them, even in the hospital room.

Moon Phase: Any phase

Day: Any day

Planet: Sun, Moon, Mercury, or Venus

In sacred space, call the angels of healing and your guardian angel. Cleanse, consecrate, and empower the gift angel in the name of healing. Respectfully ask the angels of healing and your guardian angel to help the sick person. Tell them that you will be giving this gift to the person, and ask for their blessings and healing energy on the person and the angel.

Give the gift to the sick person, and tell them to keep the angel with them at all times.

The Takin' Off Spell

This is an old Pennsylvania Dutch healing spell designed to take anything off of you that shouldn't be there, whether we're talking about negative energy or an illness that has manifested.

Moon Phase: Any time

Day: Any day

Planet: Sun, Moon, Mars, or Saturn

Supplies: A ball of red yarn; a lighter; a fire-proof bowl

Have the sick person stand in front of you. Take the free end of the red yarn and place the yarn at the top of the person's head. Have them hold the yarn for you while you measure all the way down to their heel with the yarn. Hold your finger at the spot on the yarn that matched their heel. Have them sit down and take off their shoe. Add the measurement of their foot onto the yarn that you are holding. This means that the yarn will measure their height plus one foot measurement. Cut the yarn at the end of the measurement.

Hold the yarn in your hand and say:

> **I remove, I banish, I take off any sickness or negativity**
> **on** *(the person's name).*
> **So mote it be!**

Burn the yarn in the bowl and say:

> **Fire coil and fire roil, dragon's tail and cauldron boil!**
> **Remove the negativity from** *(the person's name),* **now!**
> **So mote it be!**

Be careful, don't burn your fingers. If you are not allowed to use fire, then throw the yarn in a living body of water, or bury the yarn off of your property.

Aura Cleansing Spell

This spell works much like the one above, although you will be scraping the aura this time, rather than lifting negativity from the aura of the person.

Moon Phase: Any time

Day: Any day

Planet: Sun, Saturn

Supplies: A spool of black thread; a lighter; a fire-proof bowl

Wrap the free end of the thread around your hand several times. Let approximately seventeen inches unravel from the spool. Cut the thread off of the spool. Wrap the free end several times around your other hand. Draw the string tight (not too tight) between your two hands. Have the sick person sit in a chair. Stand behind them. Lift the string up and over their head, and then back to you three times. Now move to your right so that you are standing beside them. Repeat the procedures. Stand in front of them and do the same thing. Stand on the other side and scrape the aura around their head again. Another way to do this is to have the sick person lie down on a blanket or bed while you move the string up and down their body (about three inches away from them) envisioning that you are removing negativity from the body. When finished, burn the string or throw the string in a living body of water. You can also bury the string off of your property.

The Potato Spell #1

Folk spells have incorporated the use of a potato as a sympathetic image for several centuries.

Moon Phase: Full or new (to promote healing)

Day: Sunday, Monday, or Friday

Planet: Sun, Moon, Venus

Supplies: A potato; a green marker; holy water; ¼ teaspoon marjoram; 1 dried oak leaf; ¼ teaspoon nutmeg; the contents of a mint tea bag; 1 crushed peppermint; a lock of hair from the sick person; a small mixing bowl or mortar and pestle

In sacred space, cleanse, consecrate, and empower all supplies in the name of healing. Mix the marjoram, crushed oak leaf, nutmeg, the contents of the tea bag, the lock of hair, and the crushed peppermint in a bowl. Say:

> **Now is the time, now is the hour,**
> **Spirit is magick, Spirit is power.**

Keep repeating this charm until you have mixed the contents of the bowl.

With the green marker, draw two eyes, a nose, and a mouth on the surface of the potato. Hold the vegetable in your hand and say:

> **I forge the astral link between** (*sick person's name*)
> **and this vegetable for the purpose of healing.**
> **So mote it be!**

Close your eyes and visualize the sick person. Open your eyes and see that image on the surface of the potato.

Put the potato in the mixing bowl. Sprinkle some of the mixture over the potato. Add three drops of holy water. Say:

Guardian angel, please bring healing and happiness to *(the person's name)*.

Hold your hands over the bowl. Repeat the same charm over and over again, visualizing your friend getting better and better. Do this for as long as you can. When finished, thank your guardian angel for helping. Keep the potato in the bowl until the person gets well. After the person has recovered, de-magick the contents of the bowl, including the potato. Give the herbs to the winds and the potato to the earth.

The Potato Spell #2

This potato spell concentrates on banishing illness from a person.

Moon Phase: Dark or full

Day: Saturday

Planet: Saturn

Supplies: A potato; a knife; holy water; black thread

Hold the potato in your hand and ask the vegetable to take the illness of your friend. Sprinkle holy water and a little salt on the potato. Cut the potato in half. Hold one half of the potato over the afflicted area (such as a wart, burn, rash, et cetera). Imagine the affliction seeping into the potato. Put the potato back together and hold it shut. Wind the black thread around the potato so that it will not come apart. Take the potato outside and bury it off of your property. Say:

> As you rot, so my friend will get better.
> The affliction leaves him/her now and he/she can safely heal!

Owie-Fix Spell

Try this little spell for those bothersome cuts or scrapes, or even acne! Hold your hand over the afflicted area and say:

> Owie-fix, owie-fix
> You're the fairy that I pick.
> Bring the healing
> Come right quick!

Keep repeating this spell until the pain goes away. Be sure to seek appropriate medical treatment.

Healing Waterfall Shower Spell

I use this spell every morning, whether I'm sick or not. The visualization helps to banish any negativity from your body and keeps your spirits up when you don't feel well. While in the shower, visualize yourself standing under a waterfall. Ask the spirits of water to cleanse, consecrate, and empower your body, mind, and spirit in the name of healing. I also ask Epona, the horse goddess of sweet water, to add her blessings. As the water runs down your body, visualize the negativity swirling off of you and down the drain. When you towel dry, ask the spirits of air to cleanse, consecrate, and empower your body, mind, and spirit in the name of healing as well.

I Love Fluffy Spell

Over time, our pets become part of our family. We sometimes think of them as people with fur (or scales for you amphibian lovers) rather than pure animal. When your pet gets sick, you want to do everything you can for him or her. Pets respond extremely well to magickal applications. If you work a lot of magick, many pets will prefer to sit in the magick circle with you. Cats like to sleep on altars and shrines, while dogs prefer to sleep on you (or as near as they can get to you). Pets also respond well to hands-on healing. When my dog, Joey, gets sick (which isn't often, thank the Goddess) I inscribe his name on a green candle and ask the Lady to heal him. Then I work on him three times a day, with hands-on healing energy (after the trip to the vet, of course).

If your pet is the holding kind, or can sit on your lap, gently run your hands up and down the body, visualizing healing energy going into your pet. If, for some reason, you cannot put your hands on the pet, then hold your hands as close as you can to the animal. If your pet is at the animal hospital, then hold a picture of the animal in your hands. The first five minutes of any hands-on healing activity will be the most powerful. You can make up a chant to go along with the movement of your hands, or you can hum, or whisper loving words to your pet. Do this at least three times a day, more if your pet is very sick.

·*7·*

Prosperity and Abundance

Gold and Silver
Coins galore,
All are coming
To my door.[1]

·*Love, healing, and money magick all deal with the individual's state of mind. In money magick, if you think yourself poor, you will be poor. This is the same in love and healing magick but, for some reason, many people just can't believe that how they think manifests into hard financial dollars and cents. It took me a long time to learn this myself.

I've also discovered that the group mind of your family and close friends relates to your health and financial success. If one member of the family is a hypochondriac, then you can bet many family members have a habit of thinking up diseases for themselves, even if they don't vocalize their fears. If one person suffers from abuse, the whole family suffers. Nothing—no pain, no sorrow, no happiness, no joy—comes to any one person alone. Your financial status works the same way. If your parents always worry about money and talk constantly of "being poor," then you will think that way too. Consequently, your family will draw negative energy into the family finances. Repeated statements of "how poor you are" provide a nasty cauldron of failure, rather than success. When I was a kid, my father always told me "A Baker (that was my last name) never has any money." I heard that statement so often, I believed it. I struggled through many years of this kind of negative thinking and very tough financial times, especially when my kids were little.

Although all magickal applications rely on your belief of a positive future, I've found that money magick requires that you let go of all negative inhibitions (thoughts and feelings) you may have had about money in the past. You need to open your arms and accept the abundance of wealth. This is, indeed, a choice.

Many people, for whatever reason, have a subconscious mantra that convinces them they do not deserve wealth and abundance. I'm not quite sure where this idea comes from. I know I had the idea for years. The "poor boy" mentality could come from our parents (as I talked about earlier), our neighborhood, friends, where we work or hang out, church (giving is better than receiving)—who knows? Maybe a little bit of all these things. It's incredibly difficult (especially for older people) to offer their empty basket up to the universe and pull that basket back toward themselves filled with the abundance they seek.

Finally, money magick, especially when you look for large-ticket items or need a great influx of cash, depends on your personal goal programming. Many people don't want to take the time to plan. They simply want abundance, NOW, and aren't willing to exercise a little patience. Let's take a moment and go over the rules for money magick.

Witch Rules for Money Magick

1. Prosperity is a state of mind as much as prosperity manifests into material items. You don't have to be a millionaire to experience prosperity. Choose wisely what sort of prosperous environment will make you happy.

2. Never work prosperity magick that involves taking an item or energy from another person. Don't plan where the money will come from. It isn't right to magick Mom, Dad, Grandma, or your guardian to give money to you. Don't use someone's generous nature against them.

3. Be sure that what you are working for is exactly what you want.

4. Always use your divination tool, several times if necessary, to ensure you are making the right decisions and have chosen the correct magickal application.

5. As with healing magick, money magick is directly related to your emotions. If you allow yourself to get depressed over your finances (or the finances of

1. Bried FoxSong.

Mom, Dad, or your guardian), you've let defeat sniff at your doorstep. Keep a positive outlook as much as possible. Don't be poverty bait.

6. Do not share your magickal money operations with others. You can tell someone that you are praying for them for healing, and they will accept that, but the moment you tell Grandpa that you cast a spell so that he will get the money he needs for the mortgage, you open yourself up to persecution and a whole lot of negativity that will bust your spell to pieces. Grandpa will tell Grandma, who will think you are sweet but stupid, and then tell her friends at bingo or the church bazaar and everyone will get a laugh out of your good intentions. The information will filter back to mom or dad, who will think you took this magick thing too far. Telling your friends may not be a good idea either, because there is always one wet rag in the pack who's just itching to find something to bring you down. Often this person has very low self-esteem and delights in picking away like a vulture at your magickal armor. Don't let this happen.

Prosperity

Prosperity Correspondences

As with love and healing magick, prosperity magick has correspondences too. How about we review those items and energies that will work in sympathy with your prosperity magick?

To start a new project, find a job, or fill your personal piggy bank, you can work over the full moon or begin on the new moon and work through the full moon. You can banish poverty on the dark of the moon, or begin on the full moon and work to get rid of poverty through the new moon.

The planet most associated with prosperity magick is Jupiter, though the sun (success) carries excellent energies for money magick too. We use Saturn to banish poverty.

The colors of money can get a bit tricky, so be careful and experiment. We associate green with the fertility of the land and the color of American money. Money in other countries isn't green, so if you live in another country, you may wish to try a color that most matches your monetary exchange. Silver and gold are good universal money colors too. White, for some reason, works very well in money magick for me. Orange appears to function as a good color for money gained through work or career. You can use red to set the fire under someone who owes you money.

Fruits, vegetables, and foods of prosperity are alfalfa; almond; banana; blackberries; buckwheat; cashews; grain; green pepper; grapes; maple syrup; nutmeg; oats; onions; oranges; peas; pecans; pineapples; pomegranates; rice; sesame seeds; tea; tomatoes; and wheat.

Herbs and other plants of prosperity are allspice; basil; cedar; cinnamon; clove; comfrey; dill; fern; flax; ginger; goldenrod; honeysuckle; jasmine; marjoram; mint; moss; myrtle; oak; patchouly; pine; poplar; poppy; seaweed; snapdragon; and tulips.

We can use the four elements in prosperity magick as well: Earth to stabilize our finances, help us build our bank accounts, and help us in burying our poverty; Air to bring opportunity and abundance to us, and to push poverty away from us; Fire to get our creative juices flowing, to help us find passion in our work, and to burn poverty from our lives; Water to carry poverty away from us, pull prosperity and abundance to us, and cleanse us of negative energies that promote poverty.

Witches use some of the following symbols for prosperity magick: The dollar sign ($); a silver dollar; stars; the pentacle; a gold bow; silver and gold beads; a picture of wheat; a treasure chest; gem stones; a piggy bank; a bracelet made of coins; a metal disk; Monopoly money; sequins; glitter; a four leaf clover; or a circle.

Now that we have all these neat and nifty ideas for prosperity, let's see what kind of magick we can whip up! Remember, you can add any of the ideas above to the spells I've given you below.

Angel Shopping Spell

Never go shopping alone—always take your guardian angel with you. Before you leave the house, whether you plan an all-out clothes buying spree or have only a single item in mind, ask your guardian angel to help you find deals for your money. Guardian angels like to grocery shop, too—don't forget to take them along for a stroll down the bread aisle. If you think angels don't care about how you spend your money, think again. I bought a new, gorgeous prom dress for my daughter's friend for ten dollars with the help of my guardian angel.

Goddess Bowl Spell

Witches make money bowls in all shapes and sizes.

Moon Phase:	New to full
Day:	Sunday or Thursday
Planet:	Sun or Jupiter
Supplies:	Box of ready-made terra cotta clay or some other air-drying (non-firing) clay or the Fimo or Sculptie plastic clays; a piece of paper; a pencil

Cast your circle, call the quarters, and do your altar devotion. Cleanse, consecrate, and empower your supplies. If you are familiar with clay work, you may have tools to use that I've not listed under the supply section. You'll want to bless these items too. Take your time and design your Goddess bowl on the piece of paper. Mine begins with a small bowl that merges into the upper torso and head of the Goddess. You may have another design in mind.

Once you've settled on how you want your bowl to look, begin working with the clay, saying:

I bend, I shape,
I manifest prosperity in my life.

Keep chanting as you work. When you've completed your Goddess bowl, set the bowl in the center of the altar. Cleanse, consecrate, and bless the bowl in the name of prosperity. Ask the Lord and Lady to instill their power into the bowl. Take the bowl to each quarter and ask for the blessings of each quarter. If the bowl is too flexible to carry, leave the bowl on the altar and walk to each quarter, asking for the blessings. Leave the bowl on the center of the altar to dry. Thank Spirit. Close the quarters. Release the circle.

When the bowl has dried, write your prosperity request on a small piece of paper. Put the paper in the bowl. You can add herbs if you like. Ask the Lady to grant your request. You can do this in ritual, or in sacred space—it doesn't matter. Leave the paper in the bowl until your request has been granted. Burn the paper to release the magick or bury the paper in the ground.

Star Money Spell

You can use the star spell for almost any type of magick, though I've found, for me, it works best for money magick. Here, you will be making a talisman (an object worn or carried to attract a specific influence, such as love, luck, money, or health).

Moon Phase:	New to full
Day:	Sunday or Thursday
Planet:	Sun or Jupiter
Supplies:	A piece of green construction paper; 1 piece of white paper or tracing paper the same size as the green construction paper; glue; green glitter; ⅛ teaspoon dried mint; a few pine needles; 3 cedar chips; a green marker; a pencil; scissors; 1 green ribbon, 17 inches long

Cast your magick circle, call the quarters, and do the altar devotion. Cleanse, consecrate, and empower all tools. Draw a big, five-pointed star on the white paper—it's okay if you mess up, because the white paper will be your stencil. When you feel satisfied with the big white star, cut the star out of the white paper. Use the white star to trace a star on the green paper. Cut out the green star. With the green marker, write in the center of the green star exactly what you want: A job; $40 to go to the amusement park; $100 for groceries; et cetera. Hold your hands over the mint, pine needles, and cedar chips, and say:

Gifts of the Earth, bring (*state your desire*) to me.

Place a thin layer of glue on the center of the star. Before the glue dries, paste on the dried mint, the pine needles, and the cedar chips. Hold the green glitter in your hand and say:

Creature of Air, bring the winds of prosperity into my life.

Sprinkle the star with green glitter. Carefully, fold the top point of the star down so that it covers the center. Say:

I seal the magick.

Glue down the right arm of the star in the same manner. Now, the right leg of the star. Next, the left leg of the star. Last, the left arm of the star. Hold your hands over the folded and glued star and say:

> I empower thee, green star, to bring prosperity to me,
> specifically *(name your request)*. Prosperity, come to me.

Tie the green ribbon around the star. Close your eyes and say the last line repeatedly. Visualize yourself receiving what you asked for. When you lose the visualization, open your eyes and place the star back on the altar. Say:

> With harm to none.
> May this spell not reverse, or place upon me any curse.
> May all astrological correspondences be correct for this working.
> So mote it be!

Thank Spirit. Close the quarters. Release the circle. Allow the star to dry. Once the star has dried, take the star with you everywhere you go until your desire has manifested. When you receive what you wished for, de-magick the star and burn the talisman. If you can't burn the talisman, bury it on your property.

Money Maker Shaker Spell

The Money Maker Shaker Spell helps you to whomp up quick money.

Moon Phase:	New to full
Day:	Sunday or Thursday
Planet:	Sun or Jupiter
Supplies:	An empty can of Pringles potato chips with lid; 2 large sheets of green construction paper; a green marker; a handful of silver change; glue; scissors

Create sacred space. Cleanse, consecrate, and empower all supplies in the name of prosperity. Cut the green construction paper to fit the outside of the chip can. Glue in place. Allow to dry. Decorate the tube any way you like. Put symbols on the tube that represent money and prosperity to you.

In ritual, call on Rosemerta, Goddess of Abundance. Ask for her aid in making your shaker tube a magickal tool to bring forth prosperity. Place the silver coins in the tube. Glue or tape the lid in place so that your money won't roll out when you shake the tube. Sit quietly and shake the tube softly. Repeatedly chant:

Money come, on the run

When you finish, repeat our standard line:

With harm to none.
May this spell not reverse, or place upon me any curse.
May all astrological correspondences be correct for this working.
So mote it be!

Don't forget to thank Spirit, close the quarters, and release the circle. Put your money maker shaker in a safe place. The shaker isn't a toy.

Hot Wheels Spell

Time to get a new car, or maybe your first car? Here's a great spell for you to try.

Moon Phase:	New to full
Day:	Sunday or Thursday
Planet:	Sun or Jupiter
Supplies:	A toy car; a piece of white paper; a green pen; a green ribbon 17 inches long or a green rubber band

List all the things you want the car to have and what you want the car to look like. Be as specific as possible with your list.

In sacred space, draw a circle around your list. Put the car in the center of the paper. Fold the paper gently around the toy car and then tie with a green ribbon or wrap with a green rubber band. Hold the car in your hand and say:

Holy Mother, bring to me,
a car that's perfect just for me.

Close your eyes and visualize the car as you wish that car to be. See yourself (or your parents) happily driving the car. Keep the car and paper with you until your wish manifests. If you do not get the car within thirty days, reinforce the spell with the same chant in sacred space. Do every thirty days until you can get the car.

Rich Image Spell

The word "rich" means different things to different people. Some people think that lots of money makes you rich, where others feel that living in harmony shows what "rich" truly might be. Take a picture of yourself and glue the picture onto a big piece of paper. Around your picture draw the things that you think already make you rich, and things or qualities that you would like to have that you feel will put you in the "rich" category. Ask your guardian angel to help you manifest those things you truly need.

Magick Money Bag Spell

The purpose of the money bag is to keep free-flowing cash at hand. Once made, keep the money bag in your purse or pocket.

Moon Phase: New to full

Day: Sunday or Thursday

Planet: Sun or Jupiter

Supplies: A piece of red or green felt, five inches square; red thread; a needle; 3 almonds; 3 cashews; 3 pecans; ⅛ teaspoon cinnamon; 1 green votive candle; 1 orange votive candle

In sacred space, cleanse, consecrate, and empower your supplies for prosperity. Fold the felt in half and hand sew three sides closed. With each stitch, say:

As I sew, prosperity grows.

Set the bag in the center of your altar. Hold the nine nuts in your hands and say:

From the tree of prosperity, I ask that money come to me.

Close your eyes and imagine the nuts pulling money toward you. Place the nuts in the bag. Empower the cinnamon in the same manner and sprinkle on top of the nuts in the bag. Sew the bag closed, repeating the sewing rhyme. Hold the green candle in your hand and say:

Holy fire, work my will by my desire.
I cast a spell for prosperity.
Money, money come to me.

Light the green candle. Hold the orange candle in your hand and repeat the rhyme. Put the money bag in between the green and orange candles. Hold your hands over the money bag and repeat as often as you can:

I cast a spell for prosperity.
Money, money come to me!

End with our standard line:

With harm to none.
May this spell not reverse, or place upon me any curse.
May all astrological correspondences be correct for this working.
So mote it be!

Let the bag sit between the candles until both candles burn out. Carry the money bag in your pocket or purse. Re-enchant the bag about every three months.

Turn Back Poverty Spell

I've shown you some spells to work on the full moon and from new to full, but what about money workings from full to the dark of the moon? Normally, the waning and dark of the moon represent banishing times. With this easy spell, we'll concentrate on banishing poverty.

Moon Phase: Dark or waning

Day: Saturday

Planet: Saturn

Supplies: A cheap roll of toilet paper; a black pen

In sacred space, cleanse, consecrate, and empower supplies to banish poverty. On seven sheets of toilet paper, write the following: *I banish poverty*. Take the seven sheets into the bathroom and flush them down the toilet, repeating seven times:

I banish poverty.

Do this every day from the full moon through the dark of the moon.

Bean Jar Spell

This simple spell helps you to find wealth.

Moon Phase:	New to full
Day:	Begin on Sunday or Thursday
Planet:	Sun or Jupiter
Supplies:	A clean jar with re-closeable lid; 1 bag dried beans; a green marker; a small bowl

In sacred space, cleanse, consecrate, and empower all the supplies for prosperity. Select 100 beans from the bag. On each bean, draw a green pentacle. As you draw the pentacles, say:

I activate thee, symbol of wealth.

Put one bean in the clean jar. Hold your hands over the jar and say:

Each day my wealth grows.
Bean on bean.
Money on money.
Wealth on wealth.

Close the lid of the jar and say:

So mote it be!

Every day put a bean from the dish into the jar—one bean only. Say the same charm. When you have used the last bean, transfer all the beans back to the bowl. Empower the beans and begin again.

✦✦ Jiffy Job Spell ✦✦

When you're ready to go for that first job, try this spell. If you have a specific job in mind, use your yes/no divination stones first to decide if the job you're looking at would be right for you.

Moon Phase: New to full

Day: Sunday, Wednesday, Thursday

Planet: Sun, Mercury, Venus

Supplies: A piece of white paper; a small, empty matchbox; grated orange peel; a few grains of rice; cinnamon; a small bowl

In sacred space, write on the paper everything you are looking for in a job, including money you want, the type of environment, the hours, the kind of people you want to work with, et cetera. Be as specific as possible. Fold the paper as small as you can. Hold the paper in your hand and ask your guardian angel to help you find the right job for you. Put the paper in the matchbox. Mix the orange peel, rice, and cinnamon in the bowl. Hold your hands over the bowl and say:

Element of Earth, fruits of your bounty,
please bring me a job that's just right for me.

Add the contents of the bowl to the matchbox. Close the matchbox and hold the box in your hands. Close your eyes and say:

Sun and stars, moon and comment,
bring me the best employment.

Repeat as often as you can, visualizing yourself happy in a new job. Take the matchbox outside and place in the sunlight for an hour. Ask the sun to empower your job box with success. Carry the box with you until you receive the job you want. After your first day on the job, de-magick the box. Burn the paper. Scatter the herbs to the winds. Keep the box.

Penny Power Spell

To keep prosperity in the home, take a roll of pennies and, in sacred space, cleanse, consecrate, and empower them to prosperity. Ask the angels to bless the pennies. Put a penny in each quarter of every room in the house. As long as the pennies stay in place, wealth will be drawn into the home.

Abundant Food Spell

To ensure there's always enough food in the house, try this Pennsylvania Dutch folk spell.

Moon Phase: New to full

Day: Sunday

Planet: Sun

Supplies: A small bowl; ¼ cup uncooked rice; a large safety pin; dried apple peels; salt; brown sugar; cinnamon

In sacred space, mix all ingredients together in a small bowl. Hold the open safety pin in your hands and say:

There is always more than enough food in this house.

Put the pin in the bowl. Hold the bowl in your hands and say:

I call abundance forth from the universe.
May the contents of the bowl act as a magnet for food aplenty.
So mote it be.

Close your eyes and envision the bowl filled with white light. When you finish, put the bowl in the kitchen. Renew every three months.

Money Tree Spell

Whenever you receive money from anyone (even a check or money order), place the money in the center of a table, face side up. Hold your hands over the money with your two index fingers and two thumbs touching, making a hole you can see the money through. Concentrate on the money. See the money turning into a money tree. Let your visualization become like a fast-action camera that shows the money tree blossoming repeatedly. The blossoms are bills in large denominations. When you lose the visualization, put the money away.

Yule Prosperity Ornament

You will need a nice piece of ginger root from the grocery store, glue, silver and gold glitter, and green and white ribbons. Decorate the ginger root with the glitter and ribbons. Empower to bring prosperity into your home all year through. At midnight on December 24, hang the ornament as high as you can on your Christmas tree, saying:

> Ginger, Ginger, glitter and spice
> Earth and air, fire and ice
> Gold and Silver, coins galore
> Bring prosperity to my door!

Quick Money Tips

1. When you can, sprinkle cinnamon on your money to help your wealth increase.

2. Never just hand money to someone. Fold the money in half so that the face does not show. Hand the folded end to the person. If you hand the open end to someone, your riches will escape.

3. Rub your hands with mint and a little cinnamon before a major shopping day and envision that whatever you spend comes back to you threefold.

4. Sprinkle a little dried mint and cinnamon in the bottom of your purse or wallet.

5. Every day drop a penny in a jelly jar and say, "My life is filled with abundance, and all my needs are met."

6. Think twice before you run up the phone bill. Is that long distance call really necessary?

·*·*8·*·*

Psychic Power and Wisdom

··Although psychic power and wisdom don't fall within the broad range of topics I've previously given, I didn't feel comfortable lumping them in the "other" category. All humans carry psychic tendencies. You can develop psychic power, just like wisdom, over time and experience. I can't think of any tried and true rules for this type of magick other than patience to improve your skills. You're not going to become a psychic hotline overnight.

Most situations in life do fall under our standard categories of love, health, prosperity, and protection. I added psychic power and wisdom as an additional category for those of you who seek this type of magickal work. Every once in a while you'll come up with something that just doesn't seem to fit snugly into these five categories. What to do? Use your intuition, the best tool available to you. Go through the tables and correspondences I gave you in the other chapters and this one, and see what you can come up with to do a specialized ritual or spell for a specific occasion that does not fall neatly within the categories already provided.

Correspondences of Psychic Power and Wisdom

Several planets lend their energies toward psychic power and wisdom, most notably the moon. Mercury, with its wisdom from Spirit and Ancestors, comes in a close second. Venus, with her aspects of divine love and wisdom from the heart, comes in third.

The colors corresponding to psychic power and wisdom are silver (pure psychic power); dark purple (calling in ancestral wisdom); indigo blue (to reveal secrets, whether we want information from the here and now, the future, or the past); gold (to attract wisdom); and white (wisdom of the Spirit).

Fruits and vegetables of psychic power are celery and onions.

Fruits and vegetables of wisdom include peaches.

Herbs and other plants of psychic power are bay, cinnamon, crocus, grass, honeysuckle, jasmine, lilac, marigold, mimosa, peppermint, rose, rosemary, thyme, and yarrow.

Herbs and other plants of wisdom are iris, sage, and sunflower.

As in the other magickal applications, we can use elemental correspondences to help us in our rituals and other operations: Earth for wise council; Air to bring us wisdom and psychic power; Fire to fill us with brilliant ideas; and Water to transform our thoughts into wisdom and psychic visions.

Symbols of wisdom might be a little more difficult to conjure. Try birds in flight; a crown; a scepter; an owl; a turtle; a book; a dove, a key, a scroll; or a feather. Symbols of psychic power—that's a hard one. Let's see—the moon; a divination tool; bells; angels; saints (two good ones to fall back on); a raven; a cat; a cauldron; a mirror—what can you come up with?

Although our list of correspondences for these two topics isn't as long as some of the others, I'm sure there's enough here to get you started in the right direction and to help you make substitutions in the spells below, should you find changes necessary.

⋆ Psychic Journal Spell *⋆*

Increasing your psychic power comes with practice. You can't wave a magick wand and, ta-da, you're psychic. Certain items do enhance your practice of psychic power.

Moon Phase: Full

Day: Monday

Planet: Moon

Supplies: Create your own psychic journal; decorate the cover

Begin your psychic journal on the full moon. In sacred space, cleanse, consecrate, and empower your book. Write a book blessing on the first page. From this point on, write down all your intuitions, hunches, or ideas. Don't worry if you get things wrong. The mind works in mysterious ways. The longer you practice listening to your inner self, the more psychic you will become. Each person "feels" different when they get a psychic impression. Some people have a "dead calm" feeling in the pit of their stomach. Others feel a fluttering sensation around their neck or shoulders. Some people feel hot, others cold. You have to watch your body to determine what your psychic signal is. Everyone has a psychic signal, you just have to learn to be quiet and listen for it.

⋆ Psychic Meditation Spell *⋆*

Moon Phase: Full

Day: Monday

Planet: Moon

Supplies: Blue or violet candle; silver glitter; jasmine incense

In sacred space, cleanse, consecrate, and empower your supplies. Hold the candle in your hand, close your eyes, and say:

> I set to fire the inner light,
> so that I may see with second sight.
> So mote it be.

Light the candle. Hold the glitter in your hand and say:

> I empower you to shine the way,
> the future I will see today.

Sprinkle the glitter in a circle around the base of the candle. Hold the incense in your hand and say:

> Spirits of air, come to me.
> Bring me psychic energy.

Light the incense.

Sit quietly and gaze at the candle flame. After a while, pictures might come to mind, or a feeling of "knowing" on a particular issue. Write your impressions down in your psychic journal.

Owl Wisdom

Through the ages, the owl has carried the symbolism of Wisdom. Find a picture or statue of an owl. When you have a question, ask owl energy for help.

> Sacred owl, bring wisdom to me.
> Help me make the right decisions.
> Assist me in planning my future.
> Walk with me on my spiritual path.
> Show me the way.

⋅⁺*q*⁺*⋅*

Protection

⁺⁺*A*lthough fear can play a small role in your desire to work health, love, or prosperity magick, I find that fear carries an extra wallop in our rituals for protection. Let's face it, we probably wouldn't be working protection magick if we weren't afraid of something or someone. I find it a sad state of affairs that we're forced to work protection magick at all but, until the world decides that crime and hatred are passé and that love and harmony are the "in" thing, we've got to deal with protecting ourselves, our homes, our friends, and our families.

Young people often feel that because they don't have bodily strength and years of wisdom behind them, they have no weapons of protection at their disposal. Wrong. You've got three very important assets: common sense, our American system of justice, and WitchCraft. I'm not saying your life will slip safely through the pounding seas of injustice if you practice the Craft, but then again . . . you never know.

The Rules of Protection Magick

Let's talk about the rules of protection magick. There are a few more than under our other topics, so bear with me, please.

1. Always do everything possible to protect yourself in the "real" world. This means that a smart teen Witch exercises common sense above all else. Don't go walking, alone, in the dark—anywhere. Don't go to the bad section of town with your friends just because your favorite band plays there (wait until they get famous and buy the CD). Don't drive drunk, or get in a car where you think the driver is on drugs or drinking. For three consecutive years in my little town, kids killed themselves and their friends in broad daylight on the highway because they were drinking after school. These were supposedly the "good kids": the preps, the college-bound sweethearts, and cream of the graduating class. Don't take drugs. We need your brain functioning properly to save the planet, or maybe you will discover a cure for cancer, help disadvantaged kids through art and dance, or help protect our streets from the evil brain-dead of the world who did (or do) take drugs. You think I jest? You do have a choice.

   Don't leave yourself open for attack in any way. Your mouth does not have to become a violent foghorn. Don't morph your car into a fighter plane. When around large crowds of people, don't consume anything that you haven't purchased yourself. Don't hang around gangs or people who you know involve themselves in criminal activity. Even if you are an innocent bystander, your mother or guardian will have heart failure if you call from jail for bail. It's not pleasant to mess with your parents' minds. They're already half insane with trying to be good adults, let alone jump into mind-numbing hell because you wanted to talk to Sally or Gerald and just happened to be there when the cops swooped in from justice central and herded you all away. If only Gerald hadn't put his roach in the ashtray . . . please, spare me. If you think you are safe from the big, bad world—think again. A few years ago, in my hometown of less than 1,800, a sixteen-year-old girl started to walk home from her job at Hardee's. They found her mutilated body in the woods a week later. Oh yes, they caught the murderer, with the help of the television show *America's Most Wanted*, but a lot of good that did her after she was dead. Don't you be wide-eyed, clueless, and not breathing. Bad things do happen to good people, especially those who aren't thinking.

2. If you have a problem where you feel the need for protection then, for goodness' sake, talk to someone! Physical and mental abuse runs rampant in teen years. Sometimes this abuse stems from the home but there's lots of abuse happening in teen relationships, too. I know; remember, I have three teens, and they tell me EVERYTHING (well, almost everything). **If you are suffering from mental or physical abuse, you've got to tell a responsible adult right away.** Do not allow yourself to fall into what's called Victim Patterning, where you choose abusive relationships, partner after partner, for the rest of your life. You think I jest? Think again. Most cases of domestic abuse come from learned behavior, either by direct contact in the family environment or through one's boyfriend or girl-friend in the teen years. You will carry this with you like a rotten sack of smelly potatoes for the REST OF YOUR LIFE if you don't do something about it NOW!

    Why am I so adamant about this topic? Because I've known women who have died from abuse. I was once an abused spouse myself. Two years of that crap and I got the heck out of Dodge. Did it leave scars? Yes indeedee. Physical and mental ones.

    If you are a parent reading this book, and think this will never happen to your child, think again. Last weekend my daughter was getting ready for the prom. Her friend, let's call her Sylvia, came over to help her get ready. You know, the girl-thang. Falynn was all ready, prancing around like a nervous hen, waiting for the fellow to come pick her up and yapping at me because I wanted to videotape them together when he got there.

    Out of the blue, as Falynn ran back and forth in the dining room, Sylvia said, "Well, I'm glad I got rid of Tom."

    Falynn stopped mid-prance and whirled around, her satin skirt twirling in the process, sweeping over the dog's head at my feet. He didn't particularly care for that. "I'll say. Just look what he did to her arm!"

    Sylvia shoved her sweater up to reveal a nasty bruise. Naturally, my mother fangs sprung from my mouth and my fingernails grew an involuntary inch. "He did that to you? Who is this boy? Where does he live? This is an outrage!"

    Falynn rolled her eyes. "Calm down, mother. It's over. She dumped him. Good thing too!"

    My gaze swung to Sylvia, my eyes narrowing to the famous mother-piercing sabers of destruction. "Did you tell your mother?"

Sylvia swallowed, looked at Falynn, then back at me. "No."

"Why not?"

"Because it's over, I got rid of him. It'll never happen again."

Falynn snapped the skirt back over the dog's head. He grumbled and moved an inch. "Yeah, she broke up with him once, but he told her he would never hit her again. She went back and . . . ."

"He hit me again," mumbled Sylvia.

I clapped my hand over my forehead in perfect mother-melodramatics. "The oldest con in the book. Don't you ever fall for that again, Sylvia!"

She smiled sheepishly. "Yeah . . . well. I've got a new boyfriend now."

"You should tell your mother," I said authoritatively. "You don't understand. Think of the next girl this boy dates. What's going to happen to her? Do you realize that he could, and probably will, go too far one of these days and seriously hurt someone—or worse, kill them? Abuse is no game, Sylvia. You must tell your parents. They have a right to know."

Falynn's date arrived and, of course, this event stopped the flow of sensible conversation. A few days later Falynn and I went to the post office together. "How's Sylvia?" I asked.

"Oh, that's what I forgot to tell you!" Falynn always says that, so my teen gossip hotline is often several days behind the in-school one. "Sylvia told her parents about Tom."

"Really? What prompted her to do that?" I asked in amazement.

"Why, you did. You know, mom, that often we kids don't want to listen to our own parents, but we'll listen to someone else's. That's what happened here. Looks like you got through to her."

I don't know what Sylvia's parents will do. I hope they take the issue as far as it can go, for Sylvia's sake, and for the sake of that unknown girlfriend whose future path might unfortunately collide with his. If you have encountered such a situation, or have a drug or alcohol problem, please seek help. Even if you think you can't talk to your parents, I'm sure there is a teacher at school, the parent of a friend, or a teen hotline. If an adult tells you that this type of abuse is acceptable (I've known clergy to do this) then know that the person you spoke to is as sick as the abuser—in fact, they're probably an abuser themselves! Beware of that person and find one with brains in their head. No one ever "asks" to suffer abuse, or "deserves" to be abused. Don't you forget that!

Okay, now that we got that topic out of the way, let's go on to a few others.

3. Never target the innocent. Every Witch learns how to send back negativity. We don't create evil intentions but, if someone sends evil our way, we can promptly send that evil back. We don't always know who the culprit might be, so it's better not to mention a name when repelling negativity. Just ask Spirit to protect you and send the negative energy back to where it belongs—in the lap of the originator.

4. Don't wait for a situation to flatten you like your favorite CD (trust me, you won't play as well), or zap yourself on the bug light of life before you do something about the problem, either mundanely or magickally. Protection magick really should be preventive magick. You work protection magick now so you don't have to dig yourself out of a massive hole later. Consider protection magick like the screen on your front door in the summertime—a woven veil of magick to help keep those negative mosquitoes away.

5. Do not entangle yourself in the sordid soap operas of other people and then stand there with an astonished look on your face when you get attacked from behind by the girl who was your best friend yesterday but is Attila the Hun today. Stay away from gossip, escalating emotional time-bombs, and other people-generated nonsense. The spoken word can carry great magickal power. Use your words responsibly.

6. If you do something morally, ethically, or criminally wrong, don't expect to use protection magick to save yourself. The universe will right the wrong, no matter how many rituals you do or how much magick you throw at the problem. You can never duck the responsibility of your own actions, not even in the Craft.

7. Never put anything in writing that you don't want the world to read. Is this a magickal rule? Nope. My father told me that rule when I was eleven. He was right.

8. Finally, last rule—a big one. If you've gotten yourself into a nasty scrape, don't expect to wave your little fingers to make the bad thing go away. Sometimes, in order for things to be set right, they have to get worse. No kidding. This is especially true in abuse cases, where the victim refuses to find mundane help (like calling the authorities) but works magick in hopes that everything will get better. Magick balances. Magick will not sugar-coat a problem. More than likely the abuse situation will escalate,

forcing the person to bring in the authorities (which he or she should have done in the first place). I've seen this happen repeatedly.

I knew a mother once who was one of the best at preventive magick. Day after day, year after year, the family chugged along smoothly. Oh, there were the bumps and upsets every family experiences, but nothing really bad. Every few months or so, this Witch mother would work major protection magick for her children. Then three of her children entered the (gasp) teenage years. Life would never be the same. One summer morning, right before school got out for the year, the Witch-mother did the normal major protection ritual for her children. That afternoon, her world tilted more than she ever thought possible. One of her children got suspended from school for carrying a vial of pot. One of her kids got smacked around on the bus. One of her kids failed their driving test. What happened? Did her protection magick not work? Did she fail? Was her world ending? Did someone work bad mo-jo on her? Was she really a bad mother?

No. Actually, her protection magick worked quite well. Remember, magick balances. The first child agreed to carry the drugs in their book bag for some new friends—kids older than them. If the first child hadn't been caught, what might have happened down the road? Yes, things were bad for a while. Her child had succumbed to peer pressure and made the wrong choice; however, this gave the mother the opportunity to give the child the further protection they needed. Now the mother could work with her child and help the child make better choices in the future. The kid on the bus? Three boys had been bullying several children on the bus all year. No one said anything. When they picked on the Witch's kid, they made a grave error. The fact that she'd just done a protection ritual made the whole situation a lot worse. By the next day, those three were suspended from school and their parents were forced to drive them to school for the following year, keeping them from hurting anyone else on the bus. The one who failed the driver's test? I guess this kid wasn't competent enough to drive safely, and needed more practice. Perhaps by failing, they missed involvement in a fatal accident. Who's to say?

Okay, okay, I've twisted your brain enough. Now you know why they call me Mama Silver.

Protection Correspondences

Let's get down to business, shall we? Witches use protection magick mostly for preventive reasons, though on occasion we do work protection magick for a situation that just won't resolve itself in the normal manner. Keep in mind that protection magick BALANCES things. If you've been nasty to someone, and they retaliate, and then you work magick to fix the problem, don't expect to not pay for what you've done.

Let's check out those items in sympathy with protective energies:

Several planetary correspondences work well in protection magick: Sun (for success); the moon (protection for women and children); Mars (when we have to turn negativity back quickly); Mercury (when our words must be accurate or we need the truth about something); Venus (when we wish to flood a situation with love rather than negative energies); and Saturn (when we banish a difficulty or wish to push something negative away from us).

The colors of protection are white (purity of Spirit); black (to banish); blue-black (for healing and protection); dark purple (for calling our ancestors to help); indigo blue (astral protection, truth, and defense); blue and royal blue (power and protection); light blue (protecting your home, apartment, or trailer); dark brown (protecting a friendship); brown (peace in the home); and off-white (peace of mind).

The fruits and vegetables of protection are barley; beans; blueberries; blackberries; coconut; garlic; gourds; limes; lettuce; leeks; olives; onions; peppers; plums; radishes; raspberries; red peppers (justice); rhubarb; rice; tomatoes; turnips; yellow peppers.

The herbs and plants of protection are African violets; aloe; angelica; ash; bamboo; basil; bay; birch; broom; cactus; carnations; cedar; celandine; cinnamon; clove; clover; cotton; dill; dogwood; fern; frankincense; geranium; ginseng; grass; heather; holly; honeysuckle; hyacinth; ivy; lavender; lilac; lily; lotus; marigold; mimosa; mint; mistletoe; mustard; myrrh; nettle; Norfolk pine; oak; parsley; periwinkle; pine; plantain; rose; rosemary; sage; sandalwood; snapdragon; Spanish moss; thistle; tulip; Venus flytrap; violet; wax plant; and willow.

The four elements can play a very successful part in our protection magick: Earth to stabilize our foundations and hide our treasures; Air to push negative people or situations away from us, and to bring protective energy toward us; Fire to blind our enemies with its brilliance and heat (too hot to touch) or burn away negative energies that seek to overcome us; Water to transform a bad situation into a good one, to help us learn the lessons attached to each difficulty, and to carry love into stormy territory.

Symbols of protection can be the circle; the pentacle; the broom; angels; saints; stones or a circle of stones; wolves (any predatory animal); a shield; or a blanket. Do not choose weapons, like a gun, spear, ax, et cetera, for your symbol of protection, as these items draw violence rather than deter violence.

We've got lots of items here to work some protection magick. Remember, if a spell calls for an ingredient you don't have, you have your correspondences listed above so that you can make substitutions.

The Bully Frog Banish Spell

No one likes a bully, yet there always seems to be at least one hopping around in our midst. Most bullies are all croak and no punch, but occasionally they get too big for their pond and try to make our lives miserable. Here's a spell to banish the bully frog splashing around in your pond.

Moon Phase: Dark or full

Day: Saturday

Planet: Saturn

Supplies: A plastic frog; a piece of paper with the bully's name on it; a rubber band; a box that the frog will fit into

Check your yes/no stones to make sure this spell is okay to do. Cast your magick circle, call the quarters, and do your altar devotion. Cleanse and consecrate all supplies in the name of banishment. Hold the frog in your hands and say:

I link this frog to *(bully's name)*.

Close your eyes and see the bully in your mind. Now open your eyes and superimpose the bully's face over that of the frog. Funny, isn't it? Take the piece of paper with the person's name on it and rubberband the paper to the frog. Put the frog in the box and close the lid. Say:

(Person's name), I forever banish you from my life.
With harm to none.
May this spell not reverse or place upon me any curse.
May all astrological correspondences be correct for this working.
So mote it be!

Bury the box outside as you repeat:

Away, away, I banish thee, away!

Tie His/Her Tongue Spell

Gossip can manifest as one of the most hurtful forms of energy, especially in the teen years. A little bit of gossip can turn into a big, horrid rumor without any help from the person who started the gossip in the first place. Sometimes you just have to do damage control.

Moon Phase: Dark or full

Day: Saturday

Planet: Saturn

Supplies: A piece of red felt; black embroidery thread; a black marker; an empty jelly jar with lid; scissors

Check your yes/no stones to be sure you should do this spell. In sacred space, cleanse, consecrate, and empower all items for protection. Make a big tongue out of the felt. Cut out the tongue. Write the person who spread the rumors and gossip about you on the tongue with the black marker. If you don't know who the culprit might be, then write: *Whoever is spreading gossip.* Take the embroidery thread and sew along your lines of writing. With each stitch, say:

> I tie your tongue, you nasty one,
> so you can harm no more.

When you've finished, cut the thread and say:

> I push your evil away from me.
> Whatever you sent to me, goes back to thee.

Tie the tongue into a big knot and say:

> Guardian angel, please protect me from this person's gossip.
> Send back their negative energy.

Put the tongue in the jar, seal the jar, and say:

> I confine your evil to yourself.
> May Spirit help you deal with your own low self-esteem.

Keep the jar in a safe place. If the person ever bothers you again, open the jar and do the spell a second time.

The rule with any type of banishing is not to do a banishing in anger. You must not send negative energy from yourself. The idea is to turn the energy they have sent you on themselves. Sometimes, we should wait until we cool down to do our magick so that our work will carry the most effect without our anger as a crutch.

A derivation of this spell is the **Zipper Lipper Spell**. Do in the same manner, except use a zipper with the person's name written on the top side in a black marker. Be sure to zip the zipper shut or the spell won't work.

My Castle Spells

Ever heard the old saying "My home is my castle?" Here are some protective ideas to keep your home safe and secure.

- Each night, go to every window and door. Make the sign of the pentacle over the window or door, and say:

    Spirit, protect this place from all evil,
    and may the angels guard this home and all within.

    Check to make sure your doors and windows are securely locked.

- Hang a broom empowered for protection on your bedroom door or the front door of the house.

- Keep a sliced onion on the kitchen window sill (onions repel negativity). When the onion sprouts, replace the old onion with a new one.

- Sprinkle all doors and windows with holy water once a month.

- Grow plants and herbs associated with protection in the windowsill or in well-lit places around the house. Talk to the plants often, and keep good care of them. Ask them to help protect your home.

- Place statues of angels in your room for protection.

Frost Giant Spell

Of all the spells used by my children, I think this one gets the most workouts in my home. The spell is easy and anyone can do it without much effort, whether you are eight or eighty-two. Whether you want to stop gossip, cool an argument, stop harassment, or banish a problem, the Frost Giants are *always* willing to help you.

Moon Phase: Any time

Day: Any day

Planet: Saturn or Pluto

Supplies: A piece of paper; a pen; a baggie; your freezer

Write the name of the person who is bothering you on a piece of paper. Put a vertical line on the paper (this is the rune Isa). Fold the paper into a small square and put the paper in the baggie. Seal the baggie. Open the freezer door, and say:

Chill out!

Throw the paper in the freezer and shut the door. Say:

Frost Giants, please sit on *(say the person's name)*
so they won't bother me anymore.

One warning: we've found that if you take the baggies out of the freezer, they'll start again. Best to keep them in there for a while. This spell never hurts anyone.

The Fire Giant Spell

This spell is opposite the Frost Giant spell and is used to get someone to tell the truth, or to heat up a situation that has stagnated and you need to get things moving. This spell works especially well when you *must have* the truth. **Warning:** You must have a good, moral reason for needing the truth of the situation. This spell won't work if you plan to use the truth to hurt someone.

Moon Phase: Any time

Day: Any day

Planet: Mars

Supplies: A very, very small piece of paper; a pen; a microwave

Write the person's name on the piece of paper from whom you need the truth. If you don't know the person's name, then just put "the truth." Fold the paper into a very, very tiny square. Put the paper in the microwave (you cannot do this in the oven or the toaster—you will cause a fire). Close the door. Set the timer for seven seconds. Before you push the start button, say:

> **Fire Giants, please send me the truth on** *(name the situation)*
> **as quickly as circumstances allow!**

Push the start button. Nuke the paper every day until you get your answer. Then burn the paper.

Pucker Up You Sucker Spell

You've told someone a secret, and now you think they're going to run at the mouth. Although you should have used your better judgment, now you're worried that the world will know that you still sleep with your stuffed lambie. To prevent someone from telling the intimate details of your life, try this spell; however, if you have done something legally or morally wrong, this spell won't work.

Moon Phase: Any time

Day: Any day

Planet: Sun

Supplies: One lemon lollipop (lemon because it makes you pucker and is good for ridding negativity and general banishing)

Check your yes/no stones to be sure you should do this spell. Hold the lollipop in your hands and say:

My secret will be safe with you;
keep my secret tried and true.

Give the lollipop to the person to whom you told your secret. If you think they won't eat the lollipop, put the pop in a glass of warm water and leave it there until the pop dissolves.

Just Say No Spell

Any kind of illegal drug damages your mind and your body. Here's a spell to help yourself "Just Say No" to illegal drugs and alcohol.

Moon Phase: Any time

Day: Any day

Planet: Saturn

Supplies: A picture of yourself; salt

In sacred space, cleanse, consecrate, and empower your supplies for purity and protection. Place your picture in the center of your altar. Surround your picture with an unbroken circle of salt. Chant:

Goddess loves me this I know
For the Spirit tells me so
Little ones to Her belong
Addicts are weak, but I am strong.

Keep the salt and picture in place for as long as you think you need it.

Power Animal Patrol

Pick your favorite animal. In a quiet place, close your eyes and talk to your power animal in your mind. It's okay if they answer back. Ask your power animal to protect your house. I have four panthers that patrol my yard. The only rule here is not to forget them. You have to talk to them every day and thank them for watching over your house.

Dynamite Diana Spell

The Goddess Diana (daughter of Aradia, Queen of the Witches) is well known among magickal people for her protection of children. Also called Diana the Huntress, she will watch over you and protect you from harm. This is one of the few spells that calls for a statue or a picture of the Goddess as you perceive her. The black stones are to turn back negativity, not to hurt anyone.

Moon Phase:	Full
Day:	Saturday or Tuesday
Planet:	Saturn or Mars
Supplies:	Black paint; white paint; 6 stones, smaller than the palm of your hand; your picture; holy water; a picture or statue of the Goddess as you perceive her to be; a piece of white paper

In sacred space, paint five stones black and one stone white. As you paint, repeat the word "protection." Allow to dry. Paint the rune Algiz in black in the white stone (ᛉ). Paint the same rune in white on the five black stones. Allow to dry.

Cast your magick circle, call the quarters, and do your altar devotion. Cleanse, consecrate, and empower the six stones and your picture for protection. Draw a pentacle in holy water on the back of your picture. Place your picture under the picture or statue of the Goddess.

Draw a large pentacle on the paper. Arrange the five black stones in a star pattern: one on top, one on each side, and one stone on each of the lower points. Put the white stone in the middle. Hold your hands over the stones and say:

> Gracious Diana
> Lady of the Moon
> Daughter of Aradia
> I call you this night *(day)*
> to help me, I pray.
> Bless me with your protection
> your love, and your guidance.
> Keep all harm from me
> and let me walk in the circle
> of your light.
> So mote it be!

Close your eyes and envision yourself surrounded by white light. This white light will stay with you wherever you go. Keep the white stone with you for your protection. Thank Spirit. Close the quarters. Release the circle. Leave the black stones where they lie.

Elf Locker Spell

To keep people from breaking into your locker, try this spell.

Moon Phase: Full or dark

Day: Saturday

Planet: Saturn

Supplies: Holy water; a locker mirror; black pepper; milk; honey

At home, empower the mirror for protection. Put the holy water in a mister. At school, hang the mirror, asking the locker elves (yes, there are elves in school) to protect your locker. Spray inside your locker with the holy water (spray lightly to avoid ruining your books and papers). Sprinkle the pepper at the bottom of the locker to keep thieves away.

> **Dancing elves and fairy glen**
> **Weave the magick out and in.**
> **Twilight dell and forest deep**
> **Keep my things from every thief.**

Slam your locker and say:

> **So mote it be!**

At home, set the milk and honey outside to nourish the fairies. Renew every three months.

Sibling Sugar Spell

This handy-dandy spell sweetens everyone's disposition and is another Pennsylvania Dutch magickal idea to keep the house running smoothly. Simply write your name and your sibling's name on a piece of paper. Roll up the paper, and stick the paper in the bottom of the sugar bowl.

Interlock Internet Spell

To keep those pesky people from bothering you on the Internet, simply chant the following:

Mercury and Cyber Space
Stamp your feet and start the chase.
Boogies of the 'Net be gone
Beware my magick CD Rom.
I cleanse, I clear, I scare away
Don't come back another day!

Don't forget to use your ignore button.

Sky-Spirits Law and Order Spell

Sometimes you need the system to help you. If you have called the police or are involved in some sort of court battle, here's a spell to help your case. Justice might be blind but the universe isn't. If you've done something wrong, this spell will not help you. In Runic lore, the sky-spirits are angels of justice, and therefore no one can pervert them.

Moon Phase: New or full

Day: Tuesday

Planet: Mars

Supplies: A red bell pepper; sunflower seeds; rosemary; cloves; garlic;
a small red piece of paper; a red or black ribbon;
a black marker

Check your yes/no stones to decide if you should do this working. Cast your magick circle, call the quarters, and do your altar devotion. Cleanse and consecrate all supplies. On the piece of paper with the black marker draw the Tyr symbol (↑). Underneath the symbol, write your name. Cut the red bell pepper in half. Clean out the seeds. Place your paper in one half of the pepper. Place the sunflower seeds, rosemary, and garlic on top of the paper. Put the pepper back together and tie with the red ribbon.

Hold the pepper in your hands and say:

> Ye hallowed powers and spirits of the rune Tyr,
> My words echo forth from the heights of the Heavens
> To the depths of the Underworld.
> Resounding through the planes of the astral realms
> To the roots and green boughs of the World Tree.
>
> Bearing forth my spell from the night of becoming
> Into the daytime of being.
> For this my will (state the purpose of the spell)
> So mote it be!
>
> I call the Sky-Spirits
> Great Spirits of the Rune Tyr
> Go forth
> Go forth
> That the wheel of fate be turned
> According to my wish and will.
>
> As I say
> It shall be done.
> With harm to none.
> May this spell not reverse
> Or place upon me any curse.
> And may all astrological correspondences be correct for this working.
> So mote it be![1]

Thank the sky-spirits for helping you. Close the quarters. Release the circle. Bury the pepper on your property.

---

1. The original version of this spell appears in the book *The Rune Mysteries* by Nigel Jackson and Silver RavenWolf (Llewellyn, 1996; pp. 180–181).

Ancestor Water Protection Spell

I use this spell at home and when traveling. Simply take a clean glass and fill it half full with water (spring water if you can get that kind). Hold the water in your hands, close your eyes, and ask Spirit to cleanse, consecrate, and bless the water. Ask your ancestors (you can list them by name or you can simply say "Ancestors") to protect you and your home (or the place you are staying). Change the water every day, following the same steps as above.

Magick Mirror Spell

The magick mirror is the quickest way to send back negative energy. In ritual, cleanse, consecrate, and empower the mirror for protection. Hang the mirror opposite your bedroom door.

Chameleon Spell

The invisibility spell takes practice and falls into the realms of meditation and mental magick. Memorize the poem, then practice making the edges of yourself fuzzy while chanting the poem. No, you won't disappear in front of someone's eyes. If a person isn't thinking about you, then you can move well without being seen, sort of like a chameleon that blends in with its surroundings.

> Dragon fog and chameleon sight
> I command the shrouded sea.
> I blend the mist, I mix the light
> Refract, around, behind me.

This spell will not work to hide criminal activities, as dragons don't care for people who do things wrong and won't even flare a nostril to help you.

✦✦10✦✦

Fun Spells

✦✦I've added these last spells just for fun. Enjoy!

✦✦The Crabby Teacher Spell✦✦

Sometimes, no matter how hard we try, there's a teacher who seems to have it in for us. Everything we do wrong, he or she magnifies to grand proportions; and if we do anything right, that teacher either ignores us or yells at us anyway. Here, we'll use the power of the sea to turn that tide of discontent into a gentle wave of kindness.

Moon Phase:	Full or dark
Day:	Friday
Planet:	Venus
Supplies:	7 seashells; an aqua candle; a small box of sand; brown sugar; a dinner plate; a piece of paper with your teacher's handwriting on it

Check your yes/no divination tool to make sure this spell is okay to do. Cast your magick circle, call the quarters, and do the altar devotion. Cleanse, consecrate, and empower all tools for kindness. Put the paper with the teacher's signature on the plate. Pour the sand over the top. Even out the sand. Arrange the seashells in the sand in the shape of a circle. Hold the aqua candle in your hand and say:

Goddess of the sea
With hair of foam and spray
Change *(person's name)* idea of me
Bring me kindness every day.

Place the aqua candle securely in the sand. Light the candle. Hold your hands over the plate (be careful not to burn your hands) and say:

Goddess Oceana
Who reflects the rising of the sun
And the golden rays when day is done
Whose ebb and flow follows the moon.
Your power changes the land
Carves inlets in the sand.
Bring change for me
Bring change.

Chant the last two lines as long as possible. Visualize the teacher being pleasant to you (of course, you will be nice back). See that teacher smiling, talking politely, helping you with your work, and giving you praise. When you have finished, thank Oceana for helping you. Close the quarters. Release the circle. Let the candle burn until nothing is left. Leave the seashells intact until the teacher changes his or her attitude. If in thirty days no change occurs, repeat the spell.

The Exam Spell

There's no excuse for not studying, and this spell won't help you if you haven't put in the work to deserve a good grade; however, to keep your confidence high and the pre-test jitters low, try the following.

The night before the exam, study in ten-minute bursts. Studies have shown that we retain only ten minutes' worth of studying on any subject in a single setting. Therefore, take breaks. Walk around the room. Go brush your teeth. Whatever. Check over those last-minute areas of the subject you feel unsure about. Cleanse, consecrate, and empower the pencil you will use for the exam in the morning for success. Don't forget to take the pencil with you!

Empower a white candle for confidence and clear thinking. Burn the candle while you study. Before you fall asleep, ask the black swans of dreamtime to help you sort out the information you learned so that you will be clear-headed for the exam. Don't go to bed too late, get plenty of rest, and eat a good breakfast in the morning. Empower and drink a cup of spearmint tea before you leave for school (scientists say that spearmint actually helps you think and retain information).

Sacred Walk Spell

One of the most rewarding spells a Witch can cast consists of a walk outdoors, seeking the gifts that nature has to share. Whether you live near the beach, a forest, or in the city, you can always find the special things that nature has to share. Spend the day. Plan a picnic. Sit quietly and listen to the secrets whispering in the wind. Hug a tree. Talk to the flowers. You'll be surprised at what you learn.

When you're worried about something, or need to think a problem through, the sacred walk spell may help. I've also done prosperity walks, where I take a trip to the woods and think about bringing abundance into my life. I collect all sorts of gifts from nature, then go back and make a talisman out of what I've found. Sacred walk treasures also make great gifts for your friends.

Beach Baby Sun Spell

At the beach and no sun? Try this quickie. You will need a bottle of suntan lotion and a pair of sunglasses. Draw a circle in the sand with your finger. Put a dot of suntan lotion at the center of the circle. Set your sunglasses in the circle up above the dot of lotion. Say:

> **Sun and sand**
> **Skies of blue**
> **Beach Baby Weather**
> **The whole day through!**

Close your eyes and visualize blue skies and lots of warm sun. Repeat the spell until you lose the visualization. I've seen this spell work in five minutes, or take up to an hour, depending on weather conditions.

✦✦ The Gentle Rain Spell ✦✦

Several years ago, South Central Pennsylvania suffered through a nasty summer of drought. It got so bad that a local businessman put up a big sign that said "Make it rain, and I'll pay you $1,000." The first time I drove by the sign, I laughed. The old adage "desperate times call for desperate measures" ran through my mind. My kids saw the sign too. Immediately they said, "Mom! You can make it rain. Why don't you go see that guy?" I told them magick doesn't work like that. If I walked up to that man and said I could make it rain in twenty-four hours, and then failed, I would be the laughing stock of the town. Magick often won't happen on demand, especially if you agree to do it for a fee. Still, my kids wouldn't let the matter rest. Finally, I broke down and agreed to try to make it rain, though I refused to go see the man with the sign. If it rained, then that was my gift. If it didn't, well, then . . . it just wasn't supposed to happen.

Remember I told you that the best magick is that which you make yourself? Well, I whipped up this little spell.

Supplies: Cotton balls; a handful of rice; a small, empty Sanka jar (or any jar); blue construction paper; pencil; glue; blue glitter; 3 small silver bells; a 17-inch piece of blue yarn

In sacred space, cleanse, consecrate, and empower all supplies for life-giving, gentle rain. Be specific. Place the rice in the jar. Close the lid tightly. Cut the construction paper to fit the flat portions of the outside of the jar. Glue in place. Decorate the blue paper with rain drops. Put blue glitter on the raindrops. Glue wisps of cotton near the bottom of the jar. Allow to dry. Tie the three bells in the center of the blue yarn, one inch apart. Wrap the blue yarn around the jar, underneath the lid. Tie securely. Cut off excess yarn. You now have an instrument I call the Thunder Bumper.

All musical instruments, from the most expensive violin to the trash can drum, have a signature pattern—a special voice. The pattern or song you play on that instrument most often becomes the signature pattern, or the special voice of the instrument. Sometimes the voice emerges in complicated rhythms, where in other cases the voice lilts in a simple, gentle pattern. Your Thunder Bumper will have a special voice, too. Play with the instrument for a while and this voice will come to you.

Go outside and sit on a hill or a place where you have a good view of the sky. Close your eyes and begin visualizing gentle rain. Begin shaking your rainmaker in the special pattern you discovered. Keep up the visualization as long as you can. You might like to add the following chant to your visualization:

> Gentle rain
> Drops of water
> Send your gifts
> To the thirsty ground.

If it doesn't rain in twenty-four hours, go outside and repeat the spell.

Bad Bus Driver Four Element Spell

Does your bus driver drive like a maniac? Is he or she sullen, grumpy, and mean? Does he or she belong in the cast of a horror movie, rather then zipping you through the streets to the halls of learning? Then try this spell to get a new bus driver.

Moon Phase: Any time

Day: Sunday or Wednesday

Supplies: A small square of paper; a black marker

In sacred space, cleanse, consecrate, and empower all supplies. In the center of the paper write the following: *Please bring us a bus driver who will drive safely and treat us well.* Stand facing the North. Bend one corner of the paper and say:

> Element of the North, please bring us a stable, kind bus driver.

Turn to the East, bend another corner of the paper down, and say:

> Element of the East, please bring us an intelligent bus driver
> with good driving skills.

Turn to the South, turn another corner of the paper down, and say:

> Element of the South, please bring us a bus driver
> who will never get lost.

Turn to the West, fold down the last corner of the paper, and say:

> Element of Water, please bring us a kind and caring bus driver
> who won't let the bullies on the bus have their own way.

Fold the paper in half, stand in the center of the four quarters, and say:

Spirit, please bring us a good bus driver
who will be kind, stable, and experienced in driving.

Fold the paper up into a tiny little square. Hold the paper in your hand and visualize everyone on the bus smiling, being happy, et cetera. Leave the little piece of paper in the bus.

Little Bo Peep Spell to Find Lost Objects

Objects can be returned to you if they have not been destroyed and they want to come back. Objects carry energy too, even if they don't "think" in the way we do.

On a piece of paper, write a description of the object you have lost. Hold the open paper on the palm of your hand. Say the words "Little Bo Peep" three times, then crumple the paper in your hand, as if you've just caught a fairy—which you just did! Keep the paper closed in your hand . Search for the object you have lost. Don't let the fairy out until you find the object.

(And you thought fairy tales were just kiddie stories!)

Sometimes the energy of the object would be better off somewhere else. If this happens, the object will not return to you. If you can't find what you lost within a week, be sure to let the fairy go.

Un-Ground Me Spell

My daughter Falynn cooked this one up. Spin a Frisbee counter-clockwise on your finger and say:

Let me loose,
Let me out,
Swing around and turn about.
Sentence lifted.
Spirit gifted.
Grounding over without a doubt!

Keep repeating the spell until the Frisbee drops. One warning: If you haven't learned your lesson, within a very short time you'll find yourself in deeper trouble than you were in the first place.

✦ Jump Start Balloon Spell ✦

If you need a goal to manifest quickly or an issue to move along at a fast pace, try this spell. Get a balloon (choose the color to match the goal or situation). Close your eyes and think of an image that relates to your goal or situation. Keep the image in your mind as you blow up the balloon. Blow the balloon as big as you can, then hold the end tightly shut. Say:

> Sacred air and holy breath
> I move along another step.
> And when I let the air be free
> What I wish will truly be.

Pop the balloon. Keep the pieces of the balloon until your goal manifests.

✦ Peace and Quiet Spell ✦

Do you need some time just to relax and feel in harmony with the universe? My daughter Falynn whipped up this spell for me when things appeared particularly rough in my life. The spell worked wonderfully.

Choose fragrant flowers from your garden or from a floral shop. If you pick the flowers yourself, don't forget to ask the plant's permission before you take the flower away. Cut the stems of the flowers off underneath the blossom. Fill a bowl with spring water. Float the flowers in the bowl. Hold your hands over the flowers and empower them for tranquillity. Light your favorite incense and ask the Lady to bring peace and harmony into your life. Keep the flowers near your work area, on your desk, or in your room until they slowly fade away, or you can dry them and use the petals in any love, harmony, or peace spells.

✦ Rainbow Curfew Spell ✦

My oldest daughter, Angelique, thought this one up. Let's say you have a general curfew on school nights of 9:30 P.M., and on weekends you must be home by 11:00 P.M. An event comes up and you need an extra hour or two, or perhaps prom night looms ahead and your parents feel that 11:00 P.M. is sufficient but everyone will be going to a local restaurant afterwards and you want to go, too.

Angelique designed this spell to give you that extra time. She has one warning, though: you should be home on time, and you'd better be where you said you would be, when you said you would be there, with whom you said you would be there with. If not, the spell will backfire.

You need a plain piece of paper, colored pencils, and the time (reasonable) you think your curfew should be. Draw a big rainbow on the paper and color the rainbow any way you like. On each band of the rainbow, write the time you want your curfew to be, along with where you want to go. Close your eyes, hold your hands over the paper, and say:

> Rainbow in the heavens
> Time without time
> Seconds, minutes, hours
> Suspend within this rhyme.
> Rainbow in the heavens
> Time without time
> Extend my curfew limit
> I'll not step out of line.
> Rainbow in the heavens
> Time without time
> Keep me safe and happy
> Tell my parents I'll be fine.
> Rainbow in the heavens
> Time without time
> Magick grows, expands, and moves
> Time without time.

Angie also informs me that this spell works well when you need more time to think about a problem and make a wise decision.

Tree Curriculum Spell

Once you hit high school, everyone seems to yap at you about your curriculum. How, when you have just reached the age of fourteen, will you know what's right to choose for your career? Most of the time, you don't. Lots of people go to college for one thing and wind up doing something else entirely by the age of thirty-five. I'm one of those people. I never dreamed, at age fourteen or even age twenty-one, that I'd be writing books, let alone be successful enough at it to support four children. I had many clues along the way that I didn't pay attention to. Spirit tried to tell me over and over again, but I wouldn't listen. Finally, I had to lose a good job in a nasty, hurtful way to turn my hand at what I should have been doing for years. Adults often say, "Live and learn." Boy, I've got that one down.

My best advice on your career is: Do what you want to do—what makes you happy. Choose something that sparks your interest, deep inside. Don't allow anyone to force you into a decision that you will regret later—pick what *you* like. Some guidance counselors at school are good and others aren't so good. For example, the counselor at my daughter Falynn's high school told her not to look into an art career because "she wouldn't make any money doing that" (geeze, shades of my own mother on that one). Falynn came home deeply distressed. Art flows from her fingers. If that's what she wants to do, then that's what she should choose. Sometimes we have talents in many areas. You might like to draw but you also have a fascination for criminal investigation. Why not major in one subject and minor in another? Most of all, don't be so hasty in your decision. Schools have a habit of telling you that if you "don't take this, this, and that, then you won't be able to get into college." Oh, please. The first two years of any college are a repeat of stuff you learned in high school. That's how they make their money off of you. Colleges are a business, just like any other business. They are selling a service. You, or your parents, are buying. Don't let anyone fool you. If you didn't take something in high school, don't have heart failure—you can get what you need in your college curriculum.

To help you decide what career belongs to you, you might like to try this spell. Get a big poster board. Draw a large tree on the board with lots of branches. The trunk of the tree will be you. The branches of the tree represent all that interests you. Write down everything—from colors you like, to sports, to careers you're interested in. Let this tree be you! You don't have to write everything down at one sitting. Fill in the tree over time. Each time you finish working on the tree, say:

> Sturdy oaks from acorns grow
> Holy Spirit let me know.
> Roots run deep and flowering leaves
> I create what I will be.
> Fire and air, water and earth
> I design, I give birth.
> This tree is me, and I the tree
> Let angels guide what I will be.

Over time, your interests will change. That's okay. Keep adding new branches. You may want to cut leaves out of construction paper and add those to your poster. Each leaf could represent a talent or a desire. **You** are the magick.

Magick Bulletin Board Spell

If you have many things that you would like to accomplish, you may like to try the magick bulletin board spell.

Supplies: A bulletin board; construction paper; scissors; markers; thumbtacks

Separate your bulletin board into sections. For example, the left corner could be for items of prosperity, the right corner for healing, the lower left corner for protection, and the lower right corner for love. The center would be for things that don't fit in the four categories. Cut the construction paper into lots of shapes. Let your imagination wander as far as you'd like. You could have red and pink hearts for love, or maybe an angel shape. How about green snakes for healing, or even a green heart? Rectangles (books) for education and studies; a blue triangle for dreams or psychic work; a cloud for rain magick, or a sun for that pleasant day you need when you go to Hershey Park or camping.

Before you add the shape to the bulletin board, hold the shape in your hand, close your eyes and visualize what you need. As you pin the shape to the board, say:

Shapes and paper
Wishes and dreams
I bend
I change
move
and arrange.
I mold
I spin
whirl
and win.
Shapes and paper
Wishes and dreams
I weave the magick
With silver moonbeams.

When your dreams manifest, take the shape down. Burn the paper if your parents permit you to do so. If you can't use the element of Fire, bury the paper in your backyard and use the element of Earth.

I've provided over seventy spell ideas for you to do in the last several chapters. To learn and grow at your own pace, take these ideas and begin to create your own spells, charms, chants, and minor magick. I *know* you can do it!

Where to Go From Here

*⁺**O**kay, so you've been doing ritual and working magick for some time now, and you're itching to share with someone. Perhaps you've been talking to your parents from the beginning, perhaps not. Although I've talked a little bit about speaking to others about your work, let's cover a few of these subjects again.

Talking to Your Parents

This might present difficulties for you. Some parents just won't get past their fear and listen. I've had lots of letters from teens who tell me that their parents refuse to even carry a logical conversation on the subject. My response usually sounds something like this:

I sympathize with you, but since they aren't behaving in an adult manner, you've got three choices: Step up to the podium and start a personal PR campaign, practice in secret, or pack up your Witch goodies and wait until you're older. The smartest move, in my mind, would be curtain number one—introduce the subject slowly, and ask them to make correlations for you between their religion and the one you're interested in. Hey, maybe they're Jewish and you want to be Catholic. It can happen.

Of course, there is the sneak attack. Start studying ALL the major religions of the world, past and present. Actually, this idea carries a great deal of credibility and you might find enjoyment in understanding how the human creates his or her idea of God through the ages. This may help you in your own search of what is, and is not, right for you.

Then we've got the double sneak attack—working only with angels. Angels, angels everywhere and Mom or Dad won't even care. Sure, because *everyone* likes angels. Here again, this idea isn't a bad one at all, because angels transcend all religions and, in actuality, create bridges between religions. Angelology contains lots of information on religions past and present. Not a bad topic to delve into, if I do say so myself. In fact, I wrote a whole book about angels that parents usually like. I say "usually" because you've always got that oddball in there that will lose their false teeth even over angels.

It's best not to drop the "I'm a Witch, Mom" bomb under any circumstances. Some parents laugh at their teens when the subject of magick and the Craft comes up, hoping that if they find humor in the idea, you'll lose interest. These parents know better than to overreact. Yep, some parents are very slick indeed. I've used this tactic myself. A few parents get foolishly hysterical. These people irritate me. Sorry. Others say, "Okay, talk to me about it. Let me see what you are reading." Ah, a planned course of action. Brilliant parental move. They're sure to win points with this one.

Like I said—start slow. Talk about God. What would it be like, Mom, if God was REALLY a woman? Her eyebrows ought to shoot up on that one. What do you think about the scientific evidence that everything on this planet is made of energy? Ohhh, good opening for Dad. That's the one I used all those years ago. Did you know that gorillas perform funeral rites? Who do they pray to if they aren't Christian? (Fact, I kid you not.) Did you know that all religion was either matrifocal or hedonistic (duo-divinity) before the arrival of Judaism, and that even the early Jews had a female divinity? (I heard it on The Learning Channel.) Did you know that the early Christians believed in reincarnation? (Yes, indeed they did.) Here's one that will really get them rolling; if you're lucky, it will at least get them thinking. In the Bible, it says that Cain slew Abel, then left his parents, Adam and Eve, and went to the Land of Nod. There, he married a girl of another tribe. If Adam and Eve were the first humans, who or what did Cain marry? An antelope? A cheetah? He had children, so I guess he picked a woman. She couldn't have been Adam and Eve's daughter, stolen from the Garden of Eden Hospital, because we'd all be insane by now. Genetics have taught us a great deal in the last hundred years, particularly the fact that you can't inter-marry. After a few generations, the genes will break down and produce sickly or insane children. Finally, the piece de résistance—did you know that Mary Magdalene was not a temple prostitute? That the word "Magdalene" is a title of leadership, not the woman's last name? And that the Mary Magdalene of Bible fame ran a temple to the Goddess, designed to educate the rich girls of Jerusalem? True, true . . . all true. AND, the reason the men hated her was because she believed in the Goddess, and they wanted to get rid of the Goddess. Eventually, these men told the people that women had no souls and were no better than property, like a chicken or a mule. Sad but true just the same.

It is facts like these that you will discover if you seriously research the religions of the world. Try Barbara Walker's two books titled *Woman's Encyclopedia of Myths and Secrets* and *Woman's Dictionary of Symbols and Sacred Objects*. What a major eye-opener, let me tell you!

Back to Mom, Dad, or your guardian. Be easy on them. They're only worried about your welfare. Try to get them to read this book or others you'll find listed in the Suggested Reading List at the back of this book. I'm sure if you give them a chance, and at least meet them halfway, they will try very hard to understand why you're interested in the Craft.

If they still don't budge, pray.

The Mother will hear you.

Talking to Your Friends

A nasty thing happens to teens when they talk to their friends about the Craft—they lose a lot of them. Here's where you separate the true friends from those who have no clue. This happens to adults too. Once you start moving to a higher level of consciousness, it is natural that those people who aren't on your wavelength will drift away. Some will go quietly and others will raise a big stink in the process. A few will try to "save your soul." Those are the real winners, but they mean well. They don't understand that you are embracing God, not walking away from God; and, more often than not, their jaws flap so fast that their ears close. Big people can be like that too, trust me. You may cultivate a new set of friends rather quickly, or you may be a loner for a while. That's a chance you're going to have to take if you speak out.

If you tell your friends you are a Witch just to be different, I feel sorry for you. You belong in the clueless line. Please go back to the religion from which you came because you don't understand what Wicca is all about.

If you use the name Witch to frighten your friends, beware! The Craft doesn't stand for fear or terrorizing others, and the law of return will boot you right in the backpack. A girl at my daughter's school actually tried to frighten someone she didn't like by telling the girl she cast a spell to make all of her hair fall out. How absurd. What this little vixen didn't count on, in her vapid mind, was that my daughter was MY daughter. First, Angie did damage control by assuring the terrorized child that such a thing would never happen to her, and then they launched a laughter campaign. Immature, granted, but it worked. Every time the girl opened her mouth to threaten her victim, the girls around her would begin to hum the Witch's song from *The Wizard of Oz*, laced with peals of laughter. She finally got the point and shut up.

Okay, back to talking with your friends. Be careful. Don't share if you don't have to. You open yourself wide up for a compendium of human-imposed stupidity that just isn't necessary at your age. If you find a few kids who think the way you do and aren't into frightening people, and are looking for positive change in their lives, that's great. Consider yourself lucky. Other than that, remember the Witches' Pyramid: To Know, To Dare, To Will, and To Be Silent.

Talking to Other People

This, in itself, can be dangerous territory for you, so step lightly, please. Because of the vast amount of misinformation given to the public over the centuries, and the insistence of some religious orders of our times who think it is their sworn duty to hurt Witches and lie about WitchCraft, you could get yourself, and your parents, into a serious pickle. You will meet adults who are Crafters, but they might not tell you for sure, because they don't want to lose their jobs or suffer persecution. This isn't really a problem in the big cities, but a lot of small-minded communities still exist in America. Until they reach enlightenment (and they will, in time), be careful to whom you spout off.

Discrimination

In the beginning of the book we talked a little about discrimination. If you "come out of the broom closet" you will experience discrimination. Once you've experienced discrimination, and get over the shock of such monstrous behavior, you'll never discriminate against anyone ever again. Discrimination slams you with a major wake-up call—I can tell you this from firsthand experience, and so can my children. Discrimination comes in insidious forms. I lost a high-paying job several years ago because I made the mistake of telling one of the girls in the office about my interest in the Craft. I could never prove I was fired because I was a Witch, but I lost my job just the same. We suffered several years of financial hardship until I came to terms with my faith and grew to understand the meaning of true spirituality. Now, when I do go for the occasional part-time job, I tell them my faith first. I figure if they're going to fire me, I'll save them the trouble. I've had two excellent jobs with this approach and met many good people on my journey. When Angelique was in middle school, a kid slammed her into a locker and screamed the word "Witch!" at her. I promptly called his mother. When Falynn was in middle school, a girl down the street got a gang of kids together and attacked her on the next to last day of school. This girl also told everyone in town that we had a bloody goat's head in our dining room. Of course, lots of kids, and dumb adults, believed her. I had to go into the school on that one because the parents told me that "kids have to work these things out among themselves"—right.

On tour, I take a bodyguard, sometimes two, with me wherever I go. Why? Because not all people are pleasant or sane. If discrimination has taught me anything, it has taught me to walk with wisdom and protection.

What do adult Witches do about discrimination? Sometimes they fight, and sometimes they walk away. Many pick their battles wisely, if they must fight at all. We do have several organizations now operating within the community, including WADL (Witches Anti-Discrimination Lobby); WARD (Witches Against Religions Discrimination); WPLA (Witches League of Public Awareness); and several others. These organizations seek to inform the public of the ways of Wicca and protect Witches from harassment and discrimination in many forms, with chapters and branches in all fifty states.

There will come a time when Witches won't have to worry about any of these things. This time is moving quickly within our grasp. The more people educated on the beliefs of the modern Witch, the faster we will become part of the norm, rather than the odd duck in the lot. Witches do not normally try to convert others to their faith, so this step into the open has been difficult for them. They don't seek to swell their numbers with fancy talk and promises of saving your soul. All they really want centers on respect and the confidence that they can practice their belief in safety. Wisdom and education are our weapons.

networking

Networking for individuals between the ages of thirteen and eighteen in the Craft community isn't easy. Most metaphysical and Craft-oriented stores will not allow you to attend classes or sell you materials without the permission of your parents. Several newsletters, magazines and journals exist for adult Witches and a sporadic few for younger Witches. If you contact any Wiccan/Pagan organization or publishing company, you must submit a stamped legal sized self-addressed envelope to get an answer from them. Most kids (and some big people too) send their letter off without the stamped envelope and then wonder why they don't get a reply. Most of these organizations consist of volunteer help and don't have the resources to answer unsolicited mail.

As a teen, your best bet for networking is through the Internet. Most major services, including AOL, Prodigy, and CompuServe, have Wiccan/Pagan Chat areas. Several have chat rooms for teens. Surf the Internet with your search engine, using the keywords *Wiccan, WitchCraft,* or *Pagan.* Not all sites are valid. Some are bogus. You're going to have to use your better judgment. If the site contains anything dark, strange, or gross, don't go there again. This isn't what Wicca is all about. If the site tells you that WitchCraft and Satanism are the same—beware. Someone has launched a misinformation campaign to scare you. On the Internet, don't ever give your address or your password to anyone. Don't send your picture to anyone either. Not everyone on the Internet is who they say they are. Criminals and insane people lurk there, just like they slither everywhere else.

My Internet site is http:\\www.silverravenwolf.com. I hope you stop by and visit!

Where to Go From Here

If you like what you've read in this book, and feel ready to continue your training, then you might like to go on to my New Generation WitchCraft Series. There are two books, each moving to a more advanced level of study:

To Ride A Silver Broomstick: New Generation WitchCraft. This book represents a complete Wicca 101 guideline, allowing you to become an active participant in the world of WitchCraft. The book delves into the following categories: Getting Acquainted with the Religion; Magickal Jargon; Religion vs. Science; Your Special Days of Celebration; Gods, Goddesses and Human Balance; Choosing Your

Magickal Name; Mental Programming; Visualization; Dreaming; Sacred Space; Stocking Your Magickal Cabinet; Cleansing, Consecration, and Charging; Magickal Record Keeping; Designing and Performing Rituals; Webweaving; Networking; Workshops; Festivals; Divination; Drawing Down the Moon; Color, Candle, and Sympathetic Magick; Gems; Herbs; Healing; Telepathy; Psychometry; Mind Power; Astral Projection; Power Animals; Reincarnation; and other topics, all for the solitary Witch.

To Stir A Magick Cauldron: A Solitary Witch's Guide to Casting and Conjuring. This book covers Spiritual Balance; Personal Acts of Joy; Tools; Grounding; Daily Devotions; Blessing the Land; The Salute of the Cauldron; The Eternal Flame House Shrine; Laughter and Magick; Focus; Triggers; The Sacred Symbol Salute; The Lunar and Solar Draws; The Lord and Lady Salute; Choosing a Patron Deity; Summoning, Stirring, and Calling; Elements vs. Elementals; The Watchtowers; The Airts; The Angels; Totems; Ancient Ones; Ten Ways to Raise Power; Invoking Divinity; Trance Work; Rituals; Lineage; Degrees; and several circle casting techniques.

Also look for the third installment, *To Light A Sacred Flame: WitchCraft for the New Millennium,* coming soon in 1999.

Another excellent book for ages sixteen and older is Scott Cunningham's *Solitary Wicca* (Llewellyn). This is a positive, practical introduction to the religion of Wicca, designed so that any interested person can learn to practice the religion alone. This book presents the theory and practice of Wicca, including the Standing Stones Book of Shadows and rituals for Esbats and Sabbats. Cunningham also created an excellent book to give to your parents: *The Truth About Witchcraft Today* (Llewellyn).

If practicing the Craft still makes you nervous, you may wish to explore another of my books, *Angels: Companions in Magick.* Moms, dads, and kids alike love all the practical magickal projects, information, and legend found within.

Writing to Me

Although I love to receive letters from you, there are some things we ought to get straight before you pick up your pen and compose a letter to me.

1. I am not a certified counselor. If you have a problem, please don't write to me about it. It isn't that I don't want to help you but, in fairness, I may not be qualified to do so. Instead, talk to your parents or a reliable adult. Seek help from a teacher or clergy. If you are sick, see a qualified physician.

2. If you want more spells and advanced material, you can get this information from my New Generation series that I mentioned previously, or any of the other fine books I've listed in the Suggested Reading List. I no longer have this material at home.

3. If you are looking for contacts you will find them in my New Generation series, where I have listed several newsletters and organizations that you can write to. Remember to enclose your stamped, self-addressed, legal sized envelope with your request when you write to these newsletters or organizations. You cannot reach them by writing to me.

4. Please do write to me and let me know if this book has helped you, and if you enjoyed the material. Don't forget to enclose the stamped legal sized self-addressed envelope for my reply. Because I receive so many letters, my staff goes through them first. If the envelope isn't there, I'll never see your letter. Allow six months for me to answer you—yes, I get that much mail! (Hint: It also helps if you keep your letter to one page.) I also won't answer letters that talk about Satanism or black magick. I have no interest in those subjects. You can write to me at the address on page ii of this book.

You and the Craft

This is it. We're all done. I hope you've found answers to many questions you had about WitchCraft. There are lots of seekers out there, just like you. Never feel that you are alone.

Never stop dreaming.

Never give up.

And always remember . . . you are the magick and the magick is love.

With love,

⁺⋆*Silver RavenWolf

June 21, 1997

Suggested Reading List

For the Seeker

Ancient Ways by Pauline and Dan Campanelli (Llewellyn)

Animal Speak by Ted Andrews (Llewellyn)

Animal Magick by D. J. Conway (Llewellyn)

Celtic Devotional: Daily Prayers and Blessings by Caitlin Matthews (Harmony Books)

Charms, Spells and Formulas by Ray Malbrough (Llewellyn)

Cunningham's Encyclopedia of Magickal Herbs by Scott Cunningham (Llewellyn)

Earth Magic by Marion Weinstein (Phoenix)

Flying Without A Broom by D. J. Conway (Llewellyn)

Holy Book of Women's Mysteries by Z. Budapest (Harper & Collier)

Illusions by Richard Bach

Jude's Herbal Home Remedies by Jude C. Williams, MH (Llewellyn)

Living Wicca by Scott Cunningham (Llewellyn)

Magical Hearth by Janet Thompson (Weiser)

Magickal, Mythical, Mystical Beasts by D. J. Conway (Llewellyn)

Maiden, Mother, Crone by D. J. Conway (Llewellyn)

Original WitchCraft—Charms, Chants and Herbal Magicks by Silver RavenWolf (Llewellyn)

Practical Color Magick by Raymond Buckland (Llewellyn)

Reading the Tarot by Leo Louis Martello (Avery)

Pagan Rites of Passage by Pauline and Dan Campanelli (Llewellyn)

The Sabbats by Edain McCoy (Llewellyn)

The Spiral Dance by Starhawk (Harper & Row)

The Wheel of the Year by Pauline and Dan Campanelli (Llewellyn)

The Complete Book of Magical Names by Phoenix McFarland (Llewellyn)

The Rebirth of WitchCraft by Doreen Valiente (Phoenix)

The Truth About WitchCraft Today by Scott Cunningham (Llewellyn)

To Ride A Silver Broomstick: New Generation Witchcraft by Silver RavenWolf (Llewellyn)

True Magick by Amber K. (Llewellyn)

Wicca: A Guide for the Solitary Practitioner by Scott Cunningham (Llewellyn)

Just for Solitaries

A Witch Alone by Marian Green (Aquarian)

Living Wicca by Scott Cunningham (Llewellyn)

Of Witches by Janet Thompson (Weiser)

To Stir A Magick Cauldron by Silver RavenWolf (Llewellyn)

To Ride A Silver Broomstick by Silver RavenWolf (Llewellyn)

Wicca: A Guide for the Solitary Practitioner by Scott Cunningham (Llewellyn)

Just for Families

The Family Wicca Book by Ashleen O'Gaea (Llewellyn)

The Pagan Family by Ceisiwr Serith (Llewellyn)

WiccaCraft for Families by Margie McArthur (Phoenix)

Just for Angel Lovers

A Book of Angels by Sophy Burnham (Walker & Company)

Angels: Companions in Magick by Silver RavenWolf (Llewellyn)

Carmina Gadelica Hymns and Incantations by Alexander Carmichael (Floris Books)

Angel Power by Janice Connell (Ballantine Books)

In Search of Angels by David Connolly (Perigree)

Ask Your Angels by Alma Daniel (Ballantine Books)

A Dictionary of Angels by Gustav Davidson (Free Press)

A Woman Clothed With the Sun by John Delaney (Image / Doubleday)

Touched by Angels by Eileen Elias Freeman (Warner Books)

Angelic Healing by Eileen Elias Freeman (Warner Books)

Your Guardian Angels by Linda Georgian (Fireside)

Angels: An Endangered Species by Malcolm Godwin (Simon & Schuster)

Angels: The Mysterious Messengers by Rex Hauck (Ballantine)

Commune with the Angels by Jane M. Howard (A.R.E. Press)

The Angels Within Us by John Randolph Price (Fawcett Columbine)

Angels Beside You by James Pruitt (Avon)

The Complete Angel by James Pruitt (Avon)

Know Your Angels by John Ronner (Mamre Press)

Do You Have A Guardian Angel? by John Ronner (Mamre Press)
Creating With Angels by Terry Lynn Taylor (H. J. Kramer, Inc.)
Guardians of Hope by Terry Lynn Taylor (H. J. Kramer, Inc.)
Messengers of Light by Terry Lynn Taylor (H. J. Kramer, Inc.)

Other Books of Pagan/Wiccan Interest

The Twelve Steps by a Pagan Twelve-Stepper (available from OALM, Box 6677, Madison, WI 53716)

national Hotlines

The following numbers were collected by a Pennsylvania sheriff (a friend of mine) in case you ever need them. Don't be shy. If you need help, please call. If you have to do a report in school on any of the issues listed below, the people at these numbers will be happy to supply you information.

Alcohol and Drug Abuse

Al-Anon & Alateen	1-800-356-9996
National Clearinghouse for Alcohol & Drug Information	1-800-SAY-NOTO
National Cocaine Hotline	1-800-262-2463
Alcohol & Drug Dependency Hopeline	1-800-622-2255
National Institute on Drug Abuse Hotline	1-800-622-HELP
Mothers Against Drunk Driving	1-800-438-MADD

Abuse

Bureau of Indian Affairs Child Abuse Hotline	1-800-633-5133
Boys Town	1-800-448-3000
Child Help USA	1-800-422-4453
National Respite Locaters Service	1-800-773-5433
National Domestic Violence Hotline	1-800-799-7233
National Clearinghouse of Child Abuse and Neglect	1-800-394-3366
National Resource Center on Domestic Violence	1-800-553-2508
Rape, Abuse & Incest National Network	1-800-656-4673
Resource Center on Domestic Violence, Child Protection and Custody	1-800-527-3223

Runaway Hotlines

Covenant House Nineline	1-800-999-9999
National Runaway Switchboard	1-800-621-4000

national Child Welfare

Child Find of America	1-800-I-AM-LOST
Child Quest International Sighting Line	1-800-248-8020
National Referral Network for Kids in Crisis	1-800-KID-SAVE

Health & AIDS/HIV

AIDS Helpline	1-800-548-4659
Ask A Nurse Connection	1-800-535-1111
National AIDS Hotline	1-800-342-AIDS
STD National Hotline	1-800-227-8922

Index

H

I

T